A PROFILE OF MODERN GREECE

A PROFILE OF MODERN GREECE IN SEARCH OF IDENTITY

YORGOS A. KOURVETARIS

and

BETTY A. DOBRATZ

CLARENDON PRESS · OXFORD

1987

Oxford University Press, Walton Street, Oxford OX2 6DP
Oxford New York Toronto
Delhi Bombay Calcutta Madras Karachi
Petaling Jaya Singapore Hong Kong Tokyo
Nairobi Dar es Salaam Cape Town
Melbourne Auckland

and associated companies in
Beirut Berlin Ibadan Nicosia

Oxford is a trade mark of Oxford University Press

Published in the United States
by Oxford University Press, New York

British Library Cataloguing in Publication Data
Kourvetaris, Yorgos A.
A profile of modern Greece: in search of identity.
1. Greece
I. Title II. Dobratz, Betty A.
949.5'076 DF717
ISBN 0–19–827551–X

Library of Congress Cataloging in Publication Data
Kourvetaris, George A.
A profile of modern Greece.
Bibliography: p.
Includes index.
1. Greece. I. Dobratz, Betty A. II. Title.
DF717.K68 1987 949.5 87–15404
ISBN 0–19–827551–X

Typeset by Cambrian Typesetters, Frimley, Surrey
Printed and bound in
Great Britain by Biddles Ltd,
Guildford and King's Lynn

In memory of my beloved parents Andreas and Sophia Kourvetaris and my sister Panagoula whom time will never overshadow. This book is also dedicated to my family—Toula, Sophia, Andreas, and Nikos in search of their own identity as Greek-Americans.

Yorgos

To my parents Arthur and Helen Dobratz with love and appreciation.

Betty

Eleftheria Betty

PREFACE

THIS short book provides a general survey of Greece's continuity and change. We make an effort to be informative and analytical about Greece, the country which has been described as the cradle of Western civilization. While people may know of the Greece 'that was', this book tries to blend the past with the present and inform the reader about the Greece 'that is'. Our theme is the search for identity, which while a universal phenomenon of people everywhere, is more central to the Greeks than to many other nationalities. In spite of its rich historical past, Greece did not become a nation-state until the nineteenth century and only then after a 400-year period of Ottoman domination and with the help of several foreign powers. An integral part of the search is the quest to answer the question 'What does it mean to be Greek?'

In trying to shed light on this difficult issue, the book contains chapters on the land and people, modern Greek history, government and politics, economy, international relations, and society and culture (language, education, family, religion, music, theatre and folklore, and literature). More specifically we discuss the struggle for national independence and nationhood and the political and social forces that shaped the present institutions. The recent political and social developments, particularly those following the 1974 restoration of democracy, are emphasized.

Greece is Europe's furthermost south-eastern frontier with Asia to the east and Africa to the south. It is a peninsula of sharp contrasts with landscapes ever changing between sea and shores, valleys and mountains, islands and harbours. Greece's geography has tremendously influenced the character of its people, their way of life and culture, and their relationships with other nations. Despite numerous civil wars, conflicts, and invasions, Greece has struggled to maintain its culture and ethnic identity. Being at the crossroads of three continents, Greece has been affected by the convergence of three major civilizations—those of classical antiquity, Christianized Byzantium, and the Ottoman Empire in the eastern Mediterranean. Since its inception as a modern state in the first quarter of the nineteenth century, Greece has been searching for national identity and independence.

While the geography and location of Greece are certainly important, so is its level of socio-economic development. Economically, Greece occupies a mid position between developed and undeveloped countries. The more powerful nations of Europe and the US have influenced its political and social institutions, indeed its modern history.

The work on this book was approximately equally divided. In a joint effort of elucidation and scholarship, it is always difficult to determine exactly who did what. The finished product involved a long process of discussion, exchange of ideas, and cross-fertilization which spanned many hours, days, and indeed years of a working relationship. We have worked together on many joint projects and have benefited from each other's scholarship and professional experience. For substantive comments on various chapters of the book we wish to acknowlege Panos Bardis, Constantinos Danopoulos, Nicholas Gianaris, John Kozyris, Scott McNall, Nicos Mouzelis, and Speros Vryonis Jr.

We wish to thank Lana Pennington of Morehead State University and Tamara Pfantz of Iowa State University for collecting material on Greece and the following organizations for providing material relevant to this book: Bank of Greece, Centre of Planning and Economic Research, Embassy of Greece (in the US), Hellenic Industrial Development Bank SA, Institute of European Studies and Research, Institute for Political Studies, Ministry of Culture and Sciences, Ministry of National Economy, Ministry of National Education and Religion, Ministry to the Prime Minister's Office—Secretariat General of Press and Information, National Bank of Greece SA, National Centre of Social Research, National Investment Bank for Industrial Development, National Statistical Service of Greece, and the political parties of New Democracy and the Panhellenic Socialist Movement. We also want to extend our thanks to Kay Chapman and Sarah Brennan, secretaries of the Sociology Department, Northern Illinois University, and to Denise Baldwin, Deb Novak, Melinda Wallrichs, and Jean Sheeley, Sociology Department secretaries of Iowa State University; and to those working in the Liberal Arts & Sciences word processing at Northern Illinois University: Karen Blaser, Susan Amaloo, Amber Oldham, Crystal Swanson, Cheryl Fuller, Denise Owens, and

Michelle Starr. We would like to express our appreciation to our copy editors Carol Gosselink and Kathy Wright. Last but not least, we are grateful to an anonymous reviewer of the manuscript for helpful comments, and Henry Hardy, Nina Curtis, and John Veale, of the Oxford University Press for providing editorial assistance.

Yorgos A. Kourvetaris

Betty A. Dobratz

CONTENTS

MAP AND TABLES

MAPS AND TABLES

I

PEOPLE, IDENTITY, AND LAND*

GREECE, a small peninsular country in south-eastern Europe with a rugged and mountainous terrain, has an illustrious past which has provided a legacy for Western civilization. Ideas from some of Greece's greatest philosophers, thinkers, poets, and artists shaped Western institutions. Rich in classical, Byzantine, and modern treasures, and in archaeological sites supplemented with unmatched natural beauty and all the trimmings of modern life, Greece provides both leisure and learning for the casual visitor or the scholar.

Greece has always been called the birthplace of democracy, but it has also seen many tyrannies which have played a major role in both its past and present. This contrast attests to the unpredictability of human nature and has constantly reminded Greeks that life can be as rough as their rocky terrain, and at the same time enriching and exciting.

Their land has been at the crossroads of many cultures and ways of life. The visible monuments of a glorious Hellenic past along with the Byzantine and the modern coexist in Greece, making the Greek homeland as much a state of mind as a place on the map. Despite the harshness of nature, the turmoil, the natural calamities, and the wars, Greeks have a zest for life and perpetual restlessness. The Dionysian and Apollonian aspects of life blend together within the individual and the culture. The sounds and smells of the open market-place, the emphasis on light, the sun, and sea are ever present, and all represent a continuity in time and a celebration of life and death as depicted in the motion picture 'Zorba the Greek'.

Greece can be considered a European, Balkan, and Mediterranean country whose early civilization laid the foundation for the Western world. Since Greece's official independence as a nation-state in the 1820s, it has struggled to become part of the more industrialized West, but at the same time it has striven to maintain its cultural

* Yorgos A. Kourvetaris is the author of this chapter.

uniqueness. Greece is part of the Balkan region of Europe and shares cultural and historical experiences with its neighbours, originating in their common religion of Eastern Orthodoxy and their domination by the Roman, Byzantine, and Ottoman Empires. Various peoples in this region have struggled to maintain their ethnic identities while pursuing national independence from Ottoman rule. At the same time Greece is part of the Mediterranean basin. With the Mediterranean Sea before them, Greeks have been a seafaring people since the dawn of history; because of poor terrain, the sea provided an outlet for commercial activities and colonization, and Greeks historically came into contact with many peoples and cultures in the Eastern Mediterranean and Aegean.

There has probably been a tendency in the West to idealize Greece's heritage from classical times and to view modern Greece as a direct descendant from the Golden Age. Such a viewpoint exaggerates the impact of classical Greece on modern Greece and understates the impact of Mediterranean and Balkan influence on modern Greek identity. Common cultural and historical experiences have shaped the identities of the peoples residing in Europe, the Balkans, and the Mediterranean, and modern Greek identity in particular has been affected by wars, foreign domination, geographical facts, religion, and other historical, economic, and political forces.

Lambiri-Dimaki (1983), summarizing the structural features of Greek society, outlines five major patterns or themes which affect the life-styles and opportunities available to Greek people and distinguish Greece from most Western European nations. (1) There is a limited number of statuses partly because Greece is an ethnically and religiously homogeneous society, and also because Greek society has no indigenous aristocracy which makes the social class structure less rigid. Furthermore, Greece has fewer occupational categories owing to its lack of technological development. (2) Achievement rather than ascriptive orientation of statuses is stressed. However, seniority (gerontocracy—rule by the old) rather than neaniocracy has been traditionally more common than in other more technologically advanced European societies. (3) The dual stratification system between agrarian and urban sectors, especially until the 1960s, resulted in a system of inequality. (4) The existence of a large, poor agricultural class, an industrial proletariat, and an expanding small entrepreneurial class had a negative impact on the status of women. (5) The more rewarding positions are held by the males in the upper segments of Greek society which have been maintained by a conservative and clientelistic polity that has dominated the political life of Greece for the forty years before the rise to power of the socialists.

IDENTITY AND NATIONHOOD

There is a sense of community and identity that binds Greeks together, especially in times of crisis, and the forces that contribute to the unity are common religion, popular culture, language, and passion for political discourse. The population of Greece is homogeneous with Greeks making up 95 per cent of it; among the other groups are Turks, Albanians, Jews, Romanians, Bulgarians, and gypsies. Almost all the people (98 per cent) belong to the Greek Orthodox Church although there are some adherents of the Moslem faith, Protestantism, Judaism, and Roman and Greek Catholicism.

Before and after Greek independence there was a debate over whether Greece should take its sense of identity from the West or from the East. Those who advocated a Western identity called themselves Hellenizers. The Hellenizers embraced a worldly approach to life, similar to that of the secular humanists of the West, and, like their Western counterparts, they tried to recapture and revive classical models of Greece. The Westernizers had a cosmopolitan viewpoint and considered Greece the cradle of Western civilization. They were eager to accept Western institutions such as a bureaucratic state and monarchy, they believed in the rational ability of the human individual, and they were optimistic about man's human nature and perfectibility. Adherents of Byzantine Eastern tradition, on the other hand, stressed the other-worldliness of life and were sceptical of introducing Western institutions and applying such notions as individualism and secular humanism to Greek identity. The Byzantine tradition emphasized communal life, *koinovion*, which valued family and primary group relations; community and group life were viewed as more important than the individual. Those who favoured the Eastern approach were more local in their orientation and believed the emerging Greek identity should be drawn primarily from Eastern Byzantine and Ottoman traditions. This issue of what constitutes Greek identity remains unresolved even today. The Hellenizers stressed nationality or Greekness as the basis of identity while those who adhered to Eastern tradition stressed the Greek Orthodox religion. Thus the emergence of the modern Greek state can be traced to the interplay between the major forces of Hellenism as embodied in the classical ideals of ancient Greece and Byzantine Orthodoxy, the eastern branch of Christianity. The newly independent nation-state came out of long authoritarian Ottoman rule with shallow roots in Western type political institutions.

Elements of Identity

Tsaousis (1983), in a comprehensive article on ethnic identity throughout Greek history, speaks of a horizontal or synchronic/modern identity and a vertical or diachronic identity. The diachronic vertical type gives a sense of continuity in time and unity in space. Tsaousis identifies two dimensions of Greek identity, one dynamic and aggressive in which the Greeks themselves define their identity, and one passive or defensive in which others define it. He traces three main phases that gave impetus to modern Greek identity. The first period was the pre-revolutionary period which awakened Greek nationalism. Much of the initiative for Greek independence actually came from abroad including the *Filiki Etairea* (Company of Friends—Secret Society) of Greek entrepreneurs in Odessa, Russia, the ballads of Rigas Feraios, and the writings of classicist Adamantios Korais as well as other intellectuals. The second period was the revolutionary which involved the actual struggle for independence (1821–1827) when the Greek fighters themselves and the philhellenes who aided them struggled to escape Ottoman dominance. The third period is the post-revolutionary (1830s–1923) which focused on the building of the emerging nation, the nature of its institutions, and the extension of the boundaries of the original Greek nation-state. During these periods Hellenism was defined by one's Greekness (nationality) and not vice versa. Greek identity was maintained even in areas that were not part of the official Greek state, and there was a unity of purpose despite the conflicts between the *autochthones* (native born) and the *heterochthones* (born abroad) Greeks.

The inception of Greece as a new nation-state resulted in the convergence of cultural and political/national identities. This convergence had a built-in contradiction to it. On one hand, Greece, as a new political/national entity, sought to identify with the West, and on the other, it tried to maintain its uniqueness and independence as a cultural entity. This antithesis led to notions of tradition vs. modernity or even Greekness vs. Europeanness. From 1923 to 1974 a different phase of identity emerged, a divergence between nationality (political) and ethnicity (cultural). For example, the Greeks of the diaspora politically are citizens of the country they reside in, but culturally they have some affinity with Greek customs (ethnicity).

McNeill (1978) identifies several elements of Greek tradition—Greek language (an unbroken literary tradition since the days of Homer), Orthodox Christianity (a traditional doctrine which is in conflict with the young and with social change), Hellenism—Greekness (an asymmetry existing between Hellenism of Greece proper and that of the Greeks in the diaspora) and the heroic image. Language and religion have been sustaining factors of Greek identity, central to the national image of Greeks abroad as well as to those in Greece proper. Orthodox Christianity, however, is not uniform between the Greeks of Greece proper and the Greeks of the diaspora. For the first generation Greeks abroad, Orthodoxy and Greekness are both integral parts of their identity, but this is not the case for subsequent generations. For the younger generations Greekness is defined primarily in terms of their religion and the Dionysian aspects of the Greek ethnic subculture, and less in terms of their nationality and Greekness.

The heroic image is embodied in military virtues, *leventis*, *pallikar*, and *philotimo* (Kourvetaris, 1971a). The concept of *pallikar*, for example, part of Greek legend carried over from the Byzantine frontier days to the present, portrays the heroic image of a person who fights for a cause or an ideal such as liberty or social justice. One's incentive to fight does not derive from material gain but from an inner compulsion and moral imperative that transcends the self. The concept of *leventis*, related to the heroic image, encompasses the moral quality of a magnanimous and brave man, and it is desirable for those who lead people in war and peace. *Leventia* is a product of culture and character training and includes both moral and existential qualities such as self-reliance, pride, self-sacrifice, honour, and inner direction.

Philotimo, also considered an important element of Greek

identity literally means one who loves honour and embodies the notions of dignity, self-esteem, equality, individualism, and sentimentality. Ideally every Greek must possess it to be a Greek. According to Lee (1953: 80–4) the greater the intensity of Greek *philotimo* the greater the degree of one's Greekness. A person who possesses this quality is conscientious in work and wants to be distinguished because *philotimo* provides the mainspring and exhorts the person toward self-enhancement and self-realization. It is an emotional rather than rational quality, associated particularly with rural values; by implication, people with lots of *philotimo* are viewed as naïve or folkish while those who do not possess it are viewed as lacking in self-consciousness, an inward sensibility.

Campbell (1983) examines some of the other salient traditional values which are also related to Greek identity. The notion of *timi* is 'a subjective awareness of integrity and independence, of not being touched or humiliated before others through particular kinds of failure'. It is related to a number of other concepts which express qualities or states of mind such as manliness, self-regard, shame, envy, cleverness, cunning, greed, respect, and self-interest. Especially in Greek rural society, the family, the village, and the nation emphasize the moral identity of the individual within the group, and any insult to one group member is an insult to all the members. This notion of *timi* becomes more essential as a dimension of group identity as manifested in the community, the church, the army, the nation, or the family. Other subjective cultural values among Greeks include *mesa*, or political connections; *parea*, or the informal gathering of the local folks; *philos*/*philia* meaning friend or friendship; and the notion of *seira*, or rank. As far as rank is concerned, Greeks perceive only the highest and the lowest as polar opposites and do not quite accept gradations (Campbell, 1983).

Boulay (1974) speaks of change from traditional and symbolic thinking to more modern and secular thinking, and to a way of life in tune with the natural rhythms of the physical world. To the Greek villager mankind is an extension of the concept of the Christian Orthodox world; the idea of humanity is Christendom from which non-Christians are excluded. For the most part a villager has a local identity, an awareness of common fate. *Patrida* or the fatherland, the land of one's ancestors, is inseparable from the concept of loyalty to the family and distrust of outsiders.

McNall (1974) believes that Greece needs more universalistic rather than particularistic values to be modernized. Along the same theme, Campbell (1976) and McNall (1976) argue that regionalism is functionally related to local interests and political patronage and one of the barriers to modernization and development in Greece. This particularistic world view has a bearing on Greek identity, for a Greek thinks primarily in localistic terms which impinge on the development of a more encompassing national identity. This is in part due to geographical as well as to socio-historical, political, and cultural factors. Regionalism is a general feature of Mediterranean societies caused by traditionalism, individualism, extremism, and static conformism (Campbell, 1976). Although Greece is gradually changing, it is still trying to maintain traditional values while modernizing its structures. Modernity and tradition are not necessarily antithetical to each other, as is shown by the example of Japan which successfully combines the two.

Koty (1958: 331) summarizes the contradictions of modern Greek national character in these words: 'the spirit of democracy along with stubborn conservatism'; 'extreme individualism' along with 'cooperativeness and touching hospitality', 'skepticism and criticism' are paired with 'religious credulity and superstition'; 'patience and stoic endurance along with excitability, grumbling and discontent'. And he continues:

> Inquisitiveness and the passion for learning are often marred by intolerance and distrust of free inquiry; haughtiness is often coupled with servile subordination. One observes on the one hand warm patriotism which makes any sacrifice seem easy, and on the other, flagrant disobedience of the laws of the country. Trickiness and thirst for profit are often relieved by boundless generosity; cordiality, kindness, and expressions of sympathy for others may go together with total disregard of human rights—especially of social inferiors—verging at times on unpardonable indifference. Outbursts of enthusiasm, which may lead to daring exploits, are followed by spells of gloom, dejection, and despair; great sensitiveness to abstract justice on the one hand, and an incurable dependence on favoritism, on the other; meticulous cleanliness, and complete indifference to the most elementary principles of hygiene.

These contradictions give us one perspective of the Greek identity. The Greeks have the ability to change with circumstances, but at the same time they remain sceptical of change and faithful to their main cultural traditions, seeming to possess an inexhaustible reservoir of faith and hope which propel them to strive, to achieve, to fall and—like the mythological Sisyphos—to rise again, and finally to master their social milieu and transform it (Kourvetaris, 1971b).

Triandis, Vassiliou, and Nassiakou (1968) have suggested that the most central distinguishing features of Greek national identity are extreme competitiveness, both at the individual level and between in-groups and out-groups, and anti-authoritarianism (against authority figures of the out-group). While Greeks are inclined to follow directions from authority figures from the in-group, or to co-operate, this is not the case when these directions come from authority figures who are members of the out-group, primarily because of a basic mistrust and suspiciousness of outsiders.

LANDSCAPE

In addition to cultural, historical, and political elements, geography and topography are important factors that shape Greek identity. The physiography of Greece consists of two basic elements: the crystalline topography of the eastern and north-eastern regions and the folded sedimentary mountains and basins of the western and southern parts of the country (Diem, 1979). Greece's irregular and colourful landscape with its steep mountains, hills, valleys, basins, islands, and coastline of 15,021 km, or 9,334 miles, never bores travellers.

The Greek landscape and topography are conspicuous for their beauty, complexity, and diversity. Their first element is the sea, ever-present with its clusters of beautiful islands, inlets, and shores; often even very remote places in Greece are only fifty miles or so from the sea. The second element, the mountains, form interlaced networks with the valleys and basins, and are the most characteristic feature of Greece forming almost 70 per cent of the land area of the country. The Pindos range forms the bulk of mountains and used to have abundant timber resources which now are limited owing to forest fires, the German occupation during World War II, and the Civil War. There are about twenty-eight mountains which exceed 2,000 m.; Olympus (2,917), Smolikas (2,637), Voras (2,524), and Grammos (2,520) are the tallest. Because the mountainous terrain is not conducive to cultivation and making a living is therefore difficult, the population of mountain communes has dramatically declined in the last forty years or so. The third element of the topography is the lowlands with their fertile soil. The principal flatlands are the plains of Boeotia, Thessaly, central and eastern Macedonia and Thrace, and the Amalias and Argolis plains (in Peloponnesos). The rest of the arable land is in the foothills where the soil is suited for the growing of tobacco, wines, olives, fruit, and cotton. All three elements—sea, mountains, and lowlands—give Greece its particular physiognomy and Greek identity, even though the lack of natural resources limits the potential for economic development.

The quality of the light is one of Greece's greatest treasures. The interplay of light and landscape is remarkable: the olive, lemon, and orange trees, the numerous coastal communities and islands against the background of ancient shrines and monuments all add to the landscape of Greece. And the blue Aegean waters and sky contrast vividly with that landscape.

As the map shows, Greece is bounded on three sides by the sea—on the east by the Aegean, on the west by the Ionian, and on the south by the Mediterranean. Moisture-bearing winds from across these seas embrace the Greek peninsula. Only in the north does Greece have a land frontier which totals 1,170 km. (727 miles).

Greece is divided into three broad physical regions: the mainland, the Peloponnesos, and the islands. The Greek census subdivides the nation into ten main geographic regions: greater Athens, the rest of central Greece and Euboea, Peloponnesos, the Ionian Islands, Epirus, Thessaly, Macedonia, Thrace, the Aegean Islands, and Crete. Table 1.1 provides the urban, semi-urban, and rural population and area for the various regions of Greece. Each region consists of several administrative units or departments called *nomoi* which number fifty-two in all. Each *nomos* (department) is further subdivided into smaller administrative units called *eparchies* (counties). Table 1.2 shows the population of the departments. The mainland is everything except the islands and Peloponnesos. With the exception of Greater Athens, the rest of central Greece and Euboea, and some islands, most of the mainland gained its independence at the end of the nineteenth or beginning of the twentieth century.

The southern part of Greece called Peloponnesos is also known as *Moréas*, taking its name from the mulberry tree which was used to feed the silkworms in early times. It was the first region to gain

YUGOSLAVIA
BULGARIA
Serres
THRACE
Kavala
Alexandroupolis
Edessa
MACEDONIA
ALBANIA
Florina
Thessaloniki
THASOS
Kozani
SAMOTHRAKI
LEMNOS
TURKEY
Ioannina
Larisa
EPIRUS
THESSALY
Volos
AEGEAN SEA
KERKYRA
SPORADES
LESBOS
Lamia
Agrinio
SKYROS
CENTRAL GREECE
EUBOEA
IONIAN SEA
ITHACA
CHIOS
Patra
Athens
KEPHALLENIA
SAMOS
Pyrgos
Tripolis
ZAKYNTHOS
PELOPONNESOS
CYCLADES
Kalamata
Sparta
KYTHERA
RHODES
N
W
E
S
CRETE
Iraklion
MEDITERRANEAN SEA

TABLE 1.1 *Urban, Semi-Urban, and Rural Population and Area of Greece, by Geographic Region (Census, 1981)*

Geographic Region	Population and Area								
	Total	Sq. Km.	Urban		Semi-Urban		Rural		Total
			No.	%	No.	%	No.	%	
Greece	9,740,417	131,957	5,659,141	58.1	1,125,547	11.6	2,955,729	30.2	100
Greater Athens	3,027,331	427	3,027,331		—		—		
Rest of Central Greece and Euboea	1,099,841	24,391	324,961	29.5	340,730	31.0	434,150	39.5	100
Peloponnesos	1,012,528	21,379	350,709	34.6	131,344	13.0	530,475	52.4	100
Ionian Islands	182,651	2,307	36,901	20.2	26,629	14.6	119,121	65.2	100
Epirus	324,541	9,203	78,457	24.2	29,379	9.0	216,705	66.8	100
Thessaly	695,654	14,037	293,643	42.2	101,731	14.6	300,280	43.2	100
Macedonia	2,121,953	34,177	1,095,044	51.6	300,995	14.2	725,914	34.2	100
Thrace	345,220	8,578	121,910	35.3	51,183	14.8	172,127	49.9	100
Aegean Islands	428,533	9,122	139,061	32.5	84,059	19.6	205,413	47.9	100
Crete	502,165	8,336	191,124	38.1	59,497	11.8	251,544	50.1	100

Source: National Statistical Service of Greece (Yearbook), 1983: 17–21.

TABLE 1.2. *Urban, Semi-Urban, and Rural Population of Greece, by Geographic Region and Department*

Geographic Region and Department	Total
Greater Athens	3,027,331
Rest of Central Greece and Euboea	1,099,841
Aetolia and Akarnania	219,764
Attica	342,093
Boeotia	117,750
Euboea	188,410
Evritania	26,182
Phthiotis	161,995
Phocis	44,222
Peloponnesos	1,012,528
Argolis	93,020
Arcadia	107,932
Akhaia	275,193
Illia (Elis)	160,305
Korinthia	123,042
Lakonia	93,218
Messenia	159,818
Ionian Islands	182,651
Zante	30,014
Corfu	99,477
Cephalonia	31,297
Lefkas	21,863
Epirus	324,541
Arta	80,044
Thesprotia	41,278
Yanina	147,304
Preveza	55,915
Thessaly	695,654
Karditsa	124,930
Larisa	254,295
Magnisia	182,222
Trikala	134,207

Geographic Region and Department	Total
Macedonia	2,121,953
Grevena	36,421
Drama	94,772
Imathia	133,750
Salonica	871,580
Kavala	135,218
Kastoria	53,169
Kilkis	81,562
Kozani	147,051
Pella	132,386
Pieria	106,859
Serres	196,247
Florina	52,430
Khalkidiki	79,036
Aghion Oros	1,472
Thrace	345,220
Evros	148,486
Xanthi	88,777
Rodopi	107,957
Aegean Islands	428,533
Dodecanesos	145,071
Cyclades	88,458
Lesvos	104,620
Samos	40,519
Chios	49,865
Crete	502,165
Iraklion	243,622
Lasithi	70,053
Rethymni	62,634
Canea	125,856

Greece, TOTAL = 9,740,417

Source: National Statistical Service of Greece (*Yearbook*), 1984: 22.

its independence from Turkish rule in 1827. It has a hand-like shape which is attached to the rest of continental Greece through the Isthmus Canal, or Korinthos. Most of its population is rural (530,475 or 52.4 per cent) with its urban population making up 34.6 per cent of the total and its semi-urban 13.0 per cent. Except for the plains of Akhaia, Ilia, and parts of Argolis, most of the Peloponnesian terrain is mountainous and the soil is poor, which is why most of the early-twentieth-century transatlantic migration to the new world was from this region.

Peloponnesos is rich in natural beauty, classical archaeology, ancient, medieval, and modern history, and culture in general. Patra, its largest city and the fourth largest city in Greece, is famous for its role in the Greek Revolution of 1821 and is a seaport city linking western Peloponnesos with the Ionian Islands and Italy. It is also an administrative, educational, commercial, and tourist centre for western Peloponnesos. Olympia, also in western Peloponnesos, is the pan-hellenic sanctuary of the Olympic games of the ancient Greek world. In the central Peloponnesos is Tripolis, the capital of Arcadia, famous for its contribution to the cause of freedom from Turkish rule in 1821. Further south of Tripolis is the well-known and historical town of Sparta with the adjacent town of Mistra, the medieval seat of Byzantine princes, and its famous *Pantanassa*, a Byzantine church of the Virgin Mary.

North of Peloponnesos is the mainland of Greece which is subdivided into six main regions—Greater Athens, the rest of Central Greece and Euboea, Thessaly, Epirus, Macedonia, and Thrace. Greater Athens is the most populated area of Greece with roughly one third of the population. Also as the most vital administrative, political, commercial, cultural, and intellectual area of the country, it stands out in contrast to most of the rest of Greece. Athens is the capital of Greece and is an international tourist attraction with Piraeus its major seaport.

The rest of Central Greece and Euboea extend from the Aegean to the east to the Ionian Sea in the west and, along with Peloponnesos, was among the first regions to gain independence. It is an area of mountains and plains. Thessaly is north of Central Greece and borders Epirus to the west, the Aegean Sea to the east, and Macedonia to the north. It has some of the richest plains in Greece, and Volos, its major seaport, is gaining in international trade. Larisa is an administrative, military, and commercial centre also. Thessaly's population is relatively evenly divided between rural and urban groups with a total of 700,000. It gained its independence from the Turks in 1881.

Going north along the eastern coastline of Central Greece, one finds a landscape of immense variety. Thousands of years ago Central Greece was geographically one piece with the present island of Euboea. The change of scenery as one sails up the Gulf of Euboea is enchanting and includes along the way numerous fishing villages, small coastal towns, and tourist resort areas such as Kamena Vourla with its medicinal springs. A little further away from the charms of the sea are the towns of Thebes, Levadia, and Orchomenos, famous either in ancient times or during the Greek Revolution. Beyond these lie Thermopylae, no longer a narrow pass as in the days of Leonidas, the King of the Spartans.

Further north, along the eastern coastline of Thessaly in the thick woods and verdure of Mount Pilion, there are some of the most beautiful villages in the whole of Greece. Many foreign visitors and Greeks come to the Pilion region for their summer holidays or to buy property and spend their weekends there. Something similar is happening a little further north in the region of Aghia and Platamon where villages flourished in the eighteenth and nineteenth centuries. The most alluring area even further up is the valley of Tempi which is a short distance from Mount Olympus, believed to be the seat of the twelve gods and goddesses in Greek mythology.

Epirus, Macedonia, and Thrace all share their borders with foreign countries. The border with Albania to the west extends for 247 km. (153 miles); with Yugoslavia to the north 246 km. (153 miles); with Bulgaria, also northward, 474 km. (295 miles); and with European Turkey 203 km. (126 miles) to the east. These northern regions gained their independence from Turkey during the Balkan Wars of 1912–13 and Epirus is still known for its gallantry in the face of Turkish oppression. One famous example of this is the story of the women of Zaloggos who preferred death over enslavement under the Turks. They first threw their children over a cliff and then one by one danced to their own deaths by jumping off the cliff. The notorious Turkish Ali Pasha, known as the Lion of Epirus, tried to secede from the Ottoman Empire and establish his own fief. Epirus is the most rural area of Greece. Ioannina, its most important city, is linked by ferry-boat with the island of Corfu through the port city of Egoumenitsa. It is near the Albanian border, close to where the Greeks repelled the Italian invasion in World War II. Albania has a large Greek population, and there is still great tension in this region because many Greeks feel it should be part of northern Epirus.

Macedonia is the largest geographic region of Greece with the second largest population after Greater Athens with 2,121,953 people. It borders the socialist countries of Albania, Yugoslavia, and Bulgaria, and has endured some of the fiercest battles and ethnic rivalries in the entire Balkan peninsula. In the 1920s, in the aftermath of the Greek—Turkish war, there was a population exchange between the two countries, and many Greeks from Turkey settled in Macedonia and Thrace, the recently liberated Greek territories. The largest city in Macedonia and the second largest city of Greece, is Salonica (Thessaloniki) known as the country's co-capital. It has one of the best seaports in the Eastern Mediterranean. The Byzantine influence has been very strong in Macedonia as can be seen in the impressive Byzantine architecture of its churches and numerous monasteries and hermitages on Mount Athos in the Chalkidiki peninsula. Off the coast of Kavalla lies the island of Thasos, one of the greenest in the northern Aegean Sea. Even further east is Thrace with its famous port Alexandroupolis, and south of Alexandroupolis are the islands of Samothraki and Lemnos, where controversy has developed over its fortification and NATO exercises. Thrace borders with European Turkey and still has a large Turkish Moslem minority of about 150,000. It has very rich plains for agriculture and a population that is still about 50 per cent rural.

The Greek sovereign state includes the islands which are historically and culturally an integral part of its territory. Legendary Crete with its rugged and harsh landscapes is the site of the Minoan civilization. The Aegean and Ionian islands are grouped into clusters: eight Ionian Islands off the west coast of Greece; seventeen islands in a circle, the Cyclades in the south Aegean; nine islands in the north-eastern Aegean; thirteen referred to as the Dodecanese, the largest of which is Rhodes, in the south-eastern Aegean; the four North Sporades Islands; and the five Argolic-Saronic Islands. There are many more islands, but most of them are not populated.

Some of the islands are quite important for their tourist industry, although in reality, most islands are poorly developed economically.

A dozen or so are particularly popular and busy catering for Greek and foreign visitors during the summer tourist season, including Kerkyra (Corfu) in the Ionian Sea close to Italy, Rhodes in the south-eastern Aegean, Myconos in the Cyclades, and more recently Crete, which is by far the largest island of the Greek archipelago and the fifth largest island in the Mediterranean. The islands and the entire coastline of Greece blend harmoniously with the land and give Greece its unique physiognomy and physical attractiveness. Many people develop all kinds of romantic and poetic images about the islands, viewing them as peaceful settings protected from the rapid pace of life in the urban areas of the mainland. Taken together, the islands represent about 12 per cent of the total population.

The cultural and physical distinctiveness of the regions of Greece has encouraged diverse customs throughout the country. For example, each region has different types of dances, and within each region there are also sub-regional variations. The dancers dress in colourful costumes that represent their own local area. Yet all these variations do not detract from the overall Greek identity; rather there is an integration of the diverse parts.

POPULATION

The population of Greece during the War of Independence from 1821 to 1828 was less than 1 m. (938,765) and during that war Greece lost 2 per cent of its population. Despite the tremendous losses due to wars, mass migration, diseases, and natural disasters, Greece's population has increased tenfold since independence. Today Greece has an area of 131,990 square km. (50,962 sq. miles) and an ethnically homogeneous population of roughly 10 m. inhabitants with another 4 m. Greeks in the diaspora. In 1984, its population was 9,789,513 (males: 4,812,732 and females: 4,976,781). Between 1921 and 1940 there was an average of forty-seven inhabitants per square km. and between 1950 and 1981 an average of sixty-five inhabitants. In certain areas Greece is densely populated, with 60 per cent of the population concentrated in one-third of the land area, and over 50 per cent in communities of 2,000 or more (National Statistical Service of Greece, 1983). The most concentrated area of Greece is Greater Athens with a population of 3,027,331 or roughly one third of the total population of Greece and an average of 5,800 inhabitants per square km. The least concentrated areas are Aghion Oros (Mount Athos) in Chalkidiki (Macedonia) with six inhabitants per square km. and Epirus with thirty-six. The reasons behind Greece's pattern of density are natural, ethnic, and historical.

The 1920s were marked by an extremely important demographic change, namely the flood of Greek refugees from eastern Thrace, Asia Minor (Turkey), the Pontos, and certain other regions. This influx was the result of the population exchange and the uprooting of Greeks following the Asia Minor war in 1922. The urban areas of Macedonia, central Greece, and Thrace absorbed most of the Asia Minor refugees. According to the *Economic and Social Atlas of Greece* (Kayser and Thompson, 1964), Greece added approximately 1,200,000 persons to its population between 1920 and 1928, an increase of nearly a quarter.

Since the 1920s Greece has been steadily urbanized. While in 1920 its population was 61.9 per cent rural, by 1981 only half of that percentage remained rural, although the percentage of semi-urban population has not changed so much. At present 30.3 per cent of Greece's population is rural, and the rest is urban (58.1 per cent) and semi-urban (11.6 per cent) (National Statistical Service of Greece, 1984). A country of many small settlements, about half of Greece's 11,516 communities, or 49.3 per cent, are hamlets whose populations do not exceed 200 persons. These tiny communal settlements are self-contained and in many instances are organized along kinship lines. Following World War II and its aftermath the social structure and life of the people changed, bringing a depopulation of rural Greece. Most young people have migrated to the larger or smaller cities or left for overseas. Peloponnesos and western Sterea Hellas have experienced the heaviest emigration; on the other hand, central and western Macedonia and Attica are the two fastest-growing regions of Greece. Most of the population has been absorbed by Athens, Thessaloniki, and Patra. Some three-fifths of the population is concentrated in about one-third of the land area, and two-fifths of the population is accounted for by the Greater Athens and Thessaloniki areas. Urban congestion and pollution have become so serious, especially in the Greater Athens area, that the government has offered monetary inducements to those who want to return to their provincial and agricultural communities.

From 1928 to 1940 the population increased by 1.1 m. During

World War II and the Greek Civil War Greece lost approximately 500,000 to 600,000 people, or 6.8–8.2 per cent of its total population, with the northern regions of Greece, the islands, and the Peloponnesos experiencing the greatest losses. The Civil War involved the forced internal migration of approximately 700,000 persons, most of whom moved to Athens or Thessaloniki. In the decade 1951–61, the Greek population increased by approximately 1 per cent per year. In the last two decades, however, the overall population increase has declined to less than 1 per cent annually. A further decline of Greek population has taken place through emigration which has been considered a national haemorrhage.

INTERNAL AND EXTERNAL MIGRATION

Greece is considered a nation of diaspora. In 1974 Elie Dimitras reported that for every three Greeks in Greece there was one overseas. Throughout Greek history we find Greek migration and movement within and outside the Hellenic world. After the fall of Constantinople (1453) many Greeks including *logioi* (intellectuals) fled to the West and contributed to the Renaissance including the famous painter El Greco (Dominicos Theotocopoulos), a Cretan *émigré* to Toledo, Spain. More recently, the late Aristotle Onassis was a Greek refugee from Asia Minor, and Maria Callas, the late world-renowned soprano, was an American-born Greek who studied in the Athens Conservatory of Music during World War II.

Internal Migration

During the 1960s researchers examined different aspects of internal and external migration in various areas of Greece. A number of studies on internal migration and urbanization were carried out by French, American, and Greek social geographers, social/cultural anthropologists, social demographers, and urban sociologists. In most of these studies the authors discussed the rural exodus and the migration to urban centres, especially Athens and Thessaloniki, noting that during and after the Civil War a massive portion of the rural Greek population moved overseas or poured into the cities by the thousands from the provinces, villages, and small towns. The population of greater Athens, including Piraeus and surrounding municipalities and communities, increased by 118.8 per cent between 1951 and 1981. Athens grew to a large metropolis of 3,016,457 inhabitants in 1981 and accounted for almost 40 per cent of the total population of Greece. Most migrants moved in search of employment and a better life. Indeed, the major reason for the rural depopulation of Greece was the post-World War conservative governments' inability to improve the quality of life in the periphery and to decentralize the economic, cultural, medical, educational, and political institutions.

Internal and external migration often come down to the same issue: people leave in order to better themselves economically. Starting in the 1950s, however, some internal and a large number of external migrants had a different motive. They wanted to pursue higher education either as international students or professionals, and many of the early migrants had relatives in the cities or abroad. Greek life-styles, family and kinship networks, entrepreneurial activities, neighbourhood coffee-houses, groceries, bakeries, butchers' shops, and the like were replicated in big cities. The agrarian oligarchy declined, transferring their interests to commercial fields and politics in Athens and other big cities. After all, moving to the city meant more social mobility and better education for their children.

It has been estimated (Kayser and Thompson, 1964) that the unemployment among immigrants was not significantly different from that of the rest of the urban population. Immigrants were strongly represented in service-oriented occupations, especially those associated with tourism, small shops, and parasitic occupations (i.e. peddlars who sell their merchandise either on the street or from house to house vendors). Also during the 1950s and 1960s the building trade in Athens and Thessaloniki was booming, but recently it has become one of the most depressed areas of employment. A study of 400 randomly selected migrants to Athens and a control group of non-migrants, carried out by Tina Gioka for the National Centre of Social Research, found that migrants actually have higher occupational levels than non-migrants (Sandis, 1973). This is also consistent with Lambiri-Dimaki's (1976) finding that migrants' children more often participate in higher education than children from the urban working class. Many observers of Greek urban life have commented on the rather successful adaptation of the Greek immigrants to the city.

The people who left the village rarely returned to stay permanently. Those who went back were not able to adjust to city life, wanted to retire in the village, or were downwardly mobile. The Greek immigrants faced the same problems that internal migrants in other countries did, the most serious of these being congestion, pollution, housing shortage, unemployment, crime, family disorganization, disease, isolation, loneliness, and alienation. The post-World War II governments have not stopped the depopulation of rural Greece. Their failure to improve the quality of life and create jobs in rural Greece has forced people to seek better opportunities elsewhere. If they cannot find them in Greece proper, they go overseas. The government wants Greeks to return to their villages and as an incentive even pays those who want to resettle in the rural areas, but this may be too little, too late.

External Migration

Before the 1890s most external migration was limited to eastern Mediterranean and Balkan countries such as Egypt, Romania, Pontos, southern Russia, and Turkey. However, at the beginning of the twentieth century Greek migration shifted to the new world—to the US and Canada, and, beginning in the 1950s, to Australia.

After the 1973 oil embargo and the international economic crisis of western capitalism, there was massive unemployment in the US and Western Europe. West Germany, for example, paid migrants to return to their countries, and thousands of Greeks did return to Greece from Germany and other Western European countries. As of 1984 there were about 166,900 Greek guest-workers in Western Europe; most of them in West Germany (138,400) (Christian Science Monitor, 25 Jan. 1985). Since the mid-1970s, external migration from Greece has declined dramatically, and in 1984, more Greeks were repatriated than left the country. This reversal process is rather significant because Greece has always been a country of diaspora.

Vergopoulos (1975) argues that Greece changed decisively between the two wars because of two important events—the international economic crisis of 1929 and the Asia Minor débâcle of 1922 which resulted in the massive repatriation of Greek refugees. Both events according to Vergopoulos, contributed to the national development of the Greek economy. The author singles out three basic contributions made by the Asia Minor Greek refugees: they provided cheap, specialized labour power; they diversified the internal market by introducing new businesses; and they inspired agrarian reform (dividing up the *chifliks*). As a result, the working class and the Communist Party emerged in Greece. About 1,300,000 people came to Greece from Turkey, while, in exchange 400,000 Muslims and Bulgarians left Greece. Most of the Greek refugees settled in Macedonia, Thrace, Piraeus, and Greater Athens.

Something similar happened to the prosperous Greek communities of Egypt, considered the most important Greek settlements abroad outside of the United States. From the early stages of Greek migration to Egypt, Greeks formed capitalist and intellectual middleman entrepreneurial activities (Kourvetaris, 1987). However, the Greek merchants and bankers in Egypt were a tiny minority among the Greeks. According to Kalkas (1979) joint ventures between Greek and Jewish investors were frequent during the early twentieth century. A substantial number of the wealthy Egyptian Greeks gave donations to the Greek state. Then, owing to the rise of Nasserism and Pan-Arabism, most Greeks decided to leave Egypt and other Middle Eastern societies, although Egypt did not force Greeks to leave as Turkey did.

Today the largest Greek presence outside Greece proper is in North America (US and Canada) and Australia. Although Greek transatlantic external migration to these continents will be 100 years old, we sometimes refer to these immigrants as though they arrived yesterday. We can identify early and late Greek immigration periods, one from roughly the 1890s to the 1920s, and the other from the 1950s to mid-1970s. While there is no exact count of how many Greeks live in North America and Australia, a rough estimate might be between 3 m. and 3½ m., most of them in the US. Although we find a smattering of Greek communities in Latin America, Africa, and the Middle East, they are small, unlike the approximately 300,000 Greeks in Australia who make up the third largest immigrant group after the British and the Italians. Although the presence of Greeks in Australia can be traced back to World War II, the majority migrated there in the 1950s and 1960s. By the early 1980s the external migration to Australia had almost stopped.

During the first two decades of the twentieth century about 370,000 Greeks left for overseas, and about 352,000 (95 per cent) migrated to the US (Psomas, 1974), but a large number of them also returned to Greece during this period owing to adjustment problems and nostalgia for the old country. Between the 1920s and 1950s Greek transatlantic immigration subsided. The second largest external migration (both inter-European and transatlantic) occurred during the 1950s, 1960s, and the 1970s, when an estimated 1,022,000 Greeks left the country, with almost half going to West Germany and the rest to Australia, the US, and Canada in that order. A large number of these migrants were Greek students and Greek professionals in general although most Greek immigrants to Germany and other Western European countries were temporary guest-workers. In the mid-1970s, owing to the energy crisis, widespread unemployment, and economic recession, many Greek migrant workers began to return to Greece from Germany. Dimitras and Vlachos (1971) found that many Greek workers in West Germany felt exploited and faced tremendous problems of adjustment and family conflicts, especially concerning the education of their children. However, Western Europe, and especially Germany in the 1950s and 1960s, provided more employment than Greece's industrial sector.

Kourvetaris (1973) found that Greece is considered one of the countries with the highest rate of 'brain drain'. The international migration of scientists and professionals was a post World War II phenomenon and according to the US Department of Immigration and Naturalization Service, during the 1960s (1962–71) about 4,500 Greek professionals were admitted to the US, 4.4 per cent of the total of professionals admitted. Although the exact number of Greek scientists and other professionals who temporarily or permanently migrated to other countries is not known, it has been estimated that Greece lost about 1,000 a year in the decade of 1960s (Coutsoumaris, 1968—quoted in Kourvetaris, 1973). By the 1980s the 'brain drain' from Greece and Europe in general to the US had stopped.

There are both advantages and disadvantages in external migration. The most frequently mentioned advantages are economic and occupational, i.e. immigrant remittances to the families in Greece, relief from unemployment, and educational and occupational benefits especially for the children of immigrants. Migration tends to be a safety valve for the Greek state and society. In the 1950s Greece solved its employment problem through emigration; for the most ambitious and energetic Greeks who could not be absorbed into the economic system of the country, migration overseas was a way out. Among the disadvantages, the most frequently mentioned are adverse demographic consequences, i.e. the loss of manpower, including the 'brain drain' that slows the development of the country, and various socio-psychological costs including problems of adjustment, nostalgia, loss of ethnic identity, and physical separation. On balance, the costs might exceed the benefits for the nation and the individual. Migration is both a blessing and a curse.

Furthermore, it must be kept in mind that remittances from Greek immigrants overseas cannot continue to serve as a source of invisible revenue for Greece in the future owing to the fact that now Greeks are born overseas and are the children and grandchildren of Greek immigrants. As the older generations die out the younger generations of Greek extraction do not feel committed in the same way to the country of their forebears. As external migration declines, and it is doing so rapidly now, Greece has to learn to become more autarkic and less dependent on the remittances of Greek immigrants and other invisible sources of revenue. The search for national identity is not only a problem of Greece proper, but a perennial problem for all Greeks of the diaspora. Greeks who settled in other lands always have struggled to maintain their ethnic identity and the Greek language, religion, literature, family, folklore, and music helped in this effort. However, assimilation is taking its toll especially in Anglo-Saxonic societies where Greeks along with other European immigrants lose their ethnic identity much faster than the Greeks of Asia Minor and Egypt.

2

A LOOK AT GREEK HISTORY*

WHILE Greece has been considered part of the Western world, at the same time it shares certain historical and geographical characteristics with its Balkan and Mediterranean neighbours that make it different from much of Western Europe. With a split identity given to conflicts at both the national and individual levels, Greece's Eastern cultural characteristics have often been in conflict with Western institutional ones. Accordingly, the emphasis on tradition, mysticism, and emotionality, as well as the deep distrust of political authorities may be regarded as Eastern, but the desire for rational organization as seen in the models for Greece's constitutions and government have been Western (Diamandouros, 1983; Papacosma, 1983).

Greek history is considerably different from that of its Western European neighbours. The Balkan peninsula has often been a battleground of empires and cultures. Indeed it can be argued that the Balkans now, as in the Middle Ages, form the transitional zone between Europe (the West) and the Islamic East (Vryonis, 1967). While much of Western Europe was experiencing major socio-political transformations such as the Renaissance, Reformation, and the French Revolution, Greek culture was lying somewhat dormant within the declining Ottoman Empire. After Greece was liberated in the 1820s with the support of various Western nations, it tended to be in the Western sphere of influence but not as an equal political or economic partner. Thus, despite its current membership in the European Community, Greece has followed a different pattern of growth (sometimes referred to as misgrowth) from Western Europe in part because of its dependent industrialization.

Because our focus is on modern Greece as a nation, we will simply glance at the early beginnings of Greek history, ancient Greece, the period of Alexander the Great, the Roman Empire and

* Betty A. Dobratz is the author of this chapter

the Byzantine Empire.[1] Then we will briefly consider selected political and economic aspects of Ottoman rule and early modern Greek history and concentrate upon more recent times up to the 1967 military dictatorship, with the objective of providing a general survey of Greek history rather than a detailed account.

EARLY GREEK CIVILIZATION: PRE-OTTOMAN HISTORY

Although it is difficult to be certain, people may have inhabited Greece as early as 70,000 BC. By about 6000 BC there were probably Neolithic or New Stone Age settlements in which people learned to make stone tools by polishing instead of chipping them. This was followed by the Minoan civilization, which began on the island of Crete about 2600 BC with the migration of peoples from Asia Minor and perhaps Libya and ended about 1100 BC. Its most famous palace was that of Minos in Knossos.

The term Mycenean generally refers to the people and civilization emanating from north-eastern Peloponnesos in the late Bronze Age. Ancestors of the Myceneans were in Greece by 2000 BC, and by the sixteenth century BC their flourishing civilization existed not only in the Peloponnesos but in northern and central Greece as well. Deciphering of the syllabic script (Linear B) of the Myceneans has shown that the language used in the palaces was an early form of Greek. Their Mediterranean commercial explorations as well as Mycenean art, literature, and religion may have provided a strong foundation for the later Hellenes who built classical Greece.

Owing to their country's poor resources and its geographical location in the Mediterranean, the early Greeks often turned to maritime trade and colonization. Writings during the Homeric Age depict a seafaring people and a primitive agricultural and pastoral society. The peoples of ancient Greece can be classified on the basis of their West Greek and East Greek dialects associated with geographic locations before the great migrations (Buck, 1968). The East Greek division contains the 'Old Hellenic' dialects used by people depicted in the Homeric poems, including the Attic–Ionic, Aeolic, and Arcado–Cyprian groups, while the West Greek division contains the north-west Greek and Doric proper dialects.

City-states were important in ancient Greece between the ninth and sixth century BC. A particular city with its surrounding geographic area became the focus of political and social organization with its own form of government and division of labour. The two major city-states were Athens (Ionian) and Sparta (Doric). Athenians stressed intellectual and cultural endeavours as well as the ideal of democracy embodied in the concept of the citizen soldier, while Spartans emphasized physical, militaristic, and oligarchic values. There often was fighting among the city-states and various confederacies were formed at different times. Despite this, the Hellenes showed a sense of unity, sharing a common language, religion, and customs, including national festivities like the Olympic Games. Those outside the Hellenic culture were called barbarians (*barbaroi*), a term applied to foreigners regardless of their level of civilization.

The 'classical' period of Greece during the fifth and fourth centuries BC was the great era of the independent city-state. It began when the Greeks halted the expansionist dreams of the Persians, marking the development of a new era based on secularism and humanism. Some of the renowned individual contributors include the statesman Pericles, philosophers Socrates, Plato, and Aristotle, historians Herodotus and Thucydides, playwrights Sophocles, Aeschylus, Euripides, and Aristophanes, the orator Demosthenes, and sculptors Phidias and Praxiteles.

Athens became the epicentre of the classical period; between 461 and 431 BC, a time known as the Golden Age of Athens, the Athenians produced their greatest sculpture, architecture, and drama. They set the norms and provided the inspiration for the Western world in a wide variety of areas including political democracy, mythology, philosophy, ethics, literature, mathematics, and other arts and sciences. The Greeks touched virtually every aspect of human endeavour. The accomplishments of this age were so great that it would be difficult for them ever to be surpassed. Greeks are proud of this heritage, but they may also understandably be frustrated if they are compared with their classical ancestors or expected to be like them.[2] In view of this, some writers on modern Greece have criticized the Greeks for all-too often looking backwards towards this brilliant historical era rather than forward. Modern Greeks themselves are bothered by this inclination and caution each other about the dangerous effects of uncritical 'ancestoritis' (*progonoplexia*) (Skiotis, 1978: 155–6). Nevertheless, as modern Greeks search for their own identity, some are partially haunted by the legacy of their past.

By 450 BC a series of wars between the Greek city-states had started. In 404 BC the Athenians were defeated by the more militaristic Spartans in the Peloponnesian War, giving Sparta political supremacy although Athens maintained its cultural leadership. Later, Thebes defeated the Spartans and became the dominating force in the region. Athenians at different times aligned themselves with both Thebes and Sparta. After the Theban leader Epaminondas was killed in the battle of Mantinea (Arcadia), Thebes withdrew from its expansionist policy and Athens again became a significant force in the area, though the partially Hellenic outlying Kingdom of Macedonia (north of Greece at that time) hindered Athens from gaining complete dominance.

Eventually the Macedonians became powerful and began a policy of expansionism under Philip II, who conquered much of Greece by 338 BC. In 336 BC Alexander the Great, then only twenty years old, succeeded his father Philip II who had been assassinated. He immediately solidified his control of Greece and then moved on to defeat the Persians. Tutored by Aristotle and influenced by the Greek classical era, Alexander helped spread the culture as far as western India, establishing numerous cities that became centres of Hellenic influence. Alexander advocated the divine right of kings and introduced to the Western world the idea of a widespread empire with a common civilization instead of distinct city-states, each with its own culture. To him, the distinction between Greek and barbarian was no longer significant; the European invaders should not dominate the Asiatics, but both should be perceived as equals and ruled by a monarch (Bury and Meiggs, 1975: 472).

After Alexander's death in 323 BC, the empire was divided into kingdoms and the rising power of Rome came to be felt in the Hellenistic world. By 146 BC the Romans had brought Greece and Macedonia within their empire. Appreciative of Greek culture, they drew upon many Greek ideas during their rule, and applied them in a practical way. The Roman Empire is well known for its statesmanship, administrative abilities, military might, and engineering skill.

When the Roman Empire declined early in the fourteenth century AD owing in part to problems with imperial succession and internal weaknesses in its institutions, Constantine the Great assumed power over the Greeks. Three of his most remarkable accomplishments include: (1) recognition and tolerance of the Christian religion; (2) initiation of a fusion of three cultures—Hellenism, Roman, and the Orthodox Christian—to create the Byzantine Empire; and (3) founding the capital of the Roman Empire at Byzantium (Constantinople). The decision to change the capital to Constantinople marked the beginning of a separation of the empire into the richer, more advanced East and the less secure West, which was more susceptible to Germanic invasions.

In certain ways the Byzantine Empire can be viewed as a continuation of the older Roman Empire in its Greek form. While both the early Roman and Byzantine Empires were basically multi-ethnic and poly-sectarian, the Latin–pagan appearance of the Roman Empire gradually changed to a Greek–Christian form in the Byzantine Empire. Two different cultures developed—one based in Rome, descendant of the Latins and the other based in Constantinople, heir to the Greeks. The multi-sectarian nature of the Byzantine Empire resulted in religious toleration so that much of the Graeco–Roman paganism and Hellenistic mysticism blended with Christianity to create a Byzantine Christian religiosity. The Byzantine Church viewed this Christian synthesis as an enrichment (Constantelos, 1978: 146–7).

The Byzantine or Eastern Roman Empire was in ascendency roughly between 641 and 1071 followed by its decline from 1071 to 1453. Byzantine culture and society were midway between those of the Latin West and Islamic East. Because of the Byzantine historical experience of the Orthodox peoples in the Balkans, they were later more able to adjust psychologically to Westernization than were the Muslims in the East (Vryonis, 1967: 195–6). Unlike the city-state era, the Byzantine period fostered the 'imperial idea' where centralization and Roman imperial bureaucracy were dominant elements in Byzantine political life, and all authority emanated from the emperor. In contrast, the medieval political institutions of the West eventually laid the basis for the nation-state system.

This difference between the East and the West had particular implications for the church. In the West, the papacy gained considerable freedom and political power since there was no powerful centralized state; the Greek patriarchate in the East had less political influence owing to the strong secular power based in Constantinople. Thus the friction between Western and Eastern churches that probably started in the fourth century intensified over time.

During the eleventh century (1054) a great religious schism occurred between the Eastern (Orthodox) and Western (Catholic) branches of Christianity; this placed the Greeks, Serbians, Bulgarians, and Romanians under the Patriarch of Constantinople. The separation developed as a result of debates about dogma and ritual in the two churches and was a formal indicator of the great division between East and West. So, too, did the Crusades illustrate the depth of the religious and cultural conflict between the two. From the Western viewpoint, ideally the Crusades were undertaken to free the Holy Land from the Muslims, but from the Byzantine perspective they represented Western attempts at expansionism by gaining new lands at their expense as well as the Muslims. During the Crusades, Greeks suffered from the Norman sacks of Corinth, Thebes, and Thessaloniki, and most bitterly from the pillage of Constantinople.

Emergent nations of the Western empire surpassed the Greeks in material power and commercial enterprise around the thirteenth century. The Venetians became an important force in the Adriatic, so much so that by 1204 they and the Crusaders sacked Constantinople. For three days in the Byzantine Empire's capital there were murders, rapes, lootings, and destruction of unbelievable proportions. The most dramatic illustration of the hatred of the Crusaders for the Greeks was their desecration of the renowned church of Hagia Sophia, which included not only the destruction of icons and holy books, but the seating on the patriarchal throne of a whore who engaged in vulgar discourse as the Crusaders drank the church's wine from the holy vessels (Vryonis, 1967: 152).

An enduring legacy of bitterness between East and West can be traced particularly to this Fourth Crusade. The potential subjugation of Orthodoxy to the Pope in Rome was viewed at least by some with as much hostility as was the fear of a take-over by the Turkish Muslims. In Constantinople the Grand Duke Loukas Notaras is reported to have stated, 'It would be better to see the turban of the Turks reigning in the centre of the City than the Latin mitre' when faced with the possibilities of subjection either to the Pope or to the Sultan (Doukas, 1975: 210 (annotated translation by Magoulias)). The conquerors appointed a fellow Venetian as patriarch, and a new empire was established in Thrace, Macedonia and Greece.

While the Byzantines eventually regained a certain amount of autonomy, including control over Constantinople, much of Greece remained under Venetian rule. The struggle to regain the empire placed a heavy burden on Byzantine resources. Ironically, though the purpose of the Crusades was supposedly to bring about Islamic defeat, in reality the Crusades so weakened the Byzantine Empire that ultimately the Muslims would be victorious. Yet despite the many negative outcomes of this historical period, it did help to solidify Greek cultural self-perceptions. One of the major developments during the final centuries of Byzantium may have been the emergence of a Greek sense of ethnic identity rather than merely an Orthodox religious identity. At least some inhabitants of Greece came to think of themselves as descendants of the ancient Hellenes (Clogg, 1979: 11).

From the time of classical Greece through the Byzantine Empire, elements of Greek culture had always been part of the ruling-class culture (Vryonis, 1976: 45–6). Clearly when the Greeks ruled themselves during the classical age, their culture predominated. Even under Alexander the Great of Macedonia and his successors this did not change significantly, and Greek culture was spread especially to the East. When Greece was placed under Roman rule, important aspects of Greek culture were integrated into the culture of the Roman ruling classes. So, too, the dominant class in Byzantium gradually incorporated the culture of the Greeks along with major contributions from Roman and Christian civilizations. The period of Ottoman domination would mark the end to this pattern, for the formal culture of these ruling conquerors would be quite different from that of the Greeks (Vryonis, 1976: 46).

OTTOMAN RULE

Constantinople fell to the Ottoman Turks in 1453. In a pattern similar to that of the Crusaders, the Turks indiscriminately murdered people and pillaged churches, palaces, and other buildings. The altar of the church of Hagia Sophia was destroyed personally by the Sultan. Athens was taken by the Ottomans in 1456, and most of the Peloponnesos fell in 1460. These events marked the beginning of the Turkish dominance over Greece that would last for nearly 400 years. The Ottomans had come from central Asia and conquered territories extending to the Persian Gulf, across Northern Africa almost to the Atlantic, and deep into Central Europe. It is estimated that 50 m. people of various nationalities, languages, and religions lived under Ottoman authority. Muslim rather than Christian, the Ottomans were ancestors of the modern Turks.

The Ottomans found it difficult to administer such a large empire. Although the Balkan area included many nationalities, its people shared a common religion, Eastern Orthodoxy. Islam was generally tolerant of Christians and in order to reduce the problems of the Empire a *millet* system was developed by which subject peoples were organized on the basis of religious faith (e.g. Orthodox, Jewish,) rather than ethnic origin. The patriarch of the Orthodox *millet* had control over the administration of civil justice and the education system as well as ecclesiastical affairs. The Orthodox Christian *millet* included Serbs, Romanians, Bulgarians, Vlachs, Orthodox Albanians, and Orthodox Arabs, as well as the Greeks. Greeks, however, were essentially able to control the ecumenical patriarchate and the higher levels of the Orthodox ecclesiastical hierarchy.

Despite the relative religious tolerance of their Islamic conquerors, Christians were subject to various taxes and to military service. Perhaps the most resented policy was the janissary levy placed on the Christians of the Balkans. Christian families were expected to provide a certain proportion of their brightest and best-looking children for imperial service either in a civilian or military capacity. These children were raised as Muslims and indoctrinated with loyalty to the Ottoman Empire.

Ottoman policies such as the regulations and laws that separated non-Muslims from the Muslims and stressed subordinate–superordinate statuses encouraged non-Muslims, such as the Greeks, to maintain their own identity. In addition, the emphasis on the corporate character of each *millet* with its utilization of ecclesiastical organization of civil life and the relatively great degree of communal autonomy given to many villages encouraged the subject group to maintain ethnic boundaries (Bialor, 1971: 49–50; Clogg, 1973).

There were several significant changes that influenced the life of the now subordinate Greeks (Vryonis, 1976). They were politically and legally disenfranchised. Although courts existed for cases involving only Christians, the Christians could not testify in

Muslim courts. Thus, Greeks, like other non-Muslims, were handicapped by the official legal code of the state. Members of previous ruling classes disappeared as political sovereignty went to the Ottomans. Generally, class structure was simplified as most of the ruling dynasty and upper echelons of the military and bureaucracy were killed, fled the region, or converted to Islam. A large mass of Greeks (although certainly not all) suffered economic impoverishment because lands and taxes went to the Muslims. The formal culture of the ruling Byzantine group had ended, so Greek culture became a deformalized popular culture of the people in which Greeks experienced partial cultural isolation from both the Muslim formal culture and Western society. Except for Greeks of the diaspora and those still under Venetian rule, Greece was not exposed to the ideas of the Renaissance or Reformation. Finally, two additional changes, related to each other, occurred—ethnic dilution (proportional decline in the number of Greeks) and religious conversions to Islam from Orthodox Christianity. Both changes were much more likely to occur in Asia Minor than in the Balkans.

Woodhouse (1984) has called this period of Ottoman rule the dark age of Greece. The Ottoman patrimonial system of power centred on the Sultan and a strong state, organized to prevent the creation of a powerful landed aristocracy that could challenge the absolute authority of the Sultan. The weakening of sultanic authority (after the middle of the sixteenth century) did not, however, result in greater aristocratic power within the state. Instead, the local pashas exercised a large measure of autonomy. As Mouzelis (1978: 5) points out, this led to a lack of articulation between the state and the economically dominant classes, which weakened the rule by law. In contrast, among the Western monarchical states there was a greater balance of power between the monarchy and the aristocracy.

During the long Turkish rule client–patron relationships developed in response to Greeks' feelings of insecurity and the need to have mediators to approach the Sultan (and later, local potentates) for favours. Clientelism, a reciprocal personalized political relationship that involves economic or political favours from a notable or politician in return for a person's loyalty and support, led to the emergence of the *cotsambases* or Greek notables who occupied an intermediary role between Turkish rulers and

Greek peasants. Similarly, the Greek Orthodox church was the intermediary between Orthodox subjects throughout the Ottoman empire and the Sultan. Patronage and bribery became the means of controlling one's destiny and limiting the uncertainties of dealing with Turkish bureaucracy. Thus the years under Turkish control created a sense of reliance on the system of clientelism that to some extent persists even in modern Greek society.

As the Ottoman Empire declined in the sixteenth century, the central government's power obviously weakened and imperial expansion could not continue. The local authorities introduced the *chiflik*, or private estate system, which gave them great ownership of land and power over the peasants who now were reduced to serfs rather than tenants. The oppressiveness of the *chiflik* system, combined with disorder and the development of brigands or Robin Hood-type social bandits called *klephts*, resulted in widespread depopulation of the rural area. (The word *klephts* has double meaning—a common bandit, and a resistance fighter against alien rule.)

There was rapid development in commerce, the merchant marine, and industry that stimulated the development of handicraft products. Greek merchants became involved in trading around the Black Sea and Adriatic as well as in internal commerce. Many Greek merchants disregarded the regulations of the weak Ottoman state and specialized in the illegal export of cereals, gaining large fortunes in the process (Stoianovich, 1960). The Greeks, however, lacked the autonomy of Western merchants and played a secondary role to theirs. During the eighteenth century the position of Greek merchants greatly improved for several reasons. First, they were allowed to fly the Russian flag to avoid the very arbitrary and extortionate taxation policies of the Porte (the chief office of the Ottoman Empire). Second, the Phanariot Greeks (an increasingly powerful group of Greeks living in Constantinople) gained key positions in the Ottoman bureaucracy and in finance and banking. And finally, the Greek Orthodox church helped advance Greek economic interests owing in part to the influence of the Greek bourgeoisie on the church (Mouzelis, 1978: 8–9).

During the eighteenth and early nineteenth centuries, a neo-Hellenic Enlightenment spawned a growing secularization of Greek culture as the ideas and books from the Western Enlightenment became known to an intellectual élite. In the process Greek intelligentsia rediscovered their glorious classical heritage (Clogg, 1979: 37). The new emphasis on the idea that modern Greeks descended from classical Greeks meant that many would try to mould their culture and language to the classical model. This resulted, of course, in debate about the fundamental components of Greek identity, a controversy which has never been thoroughly resolved (Kitromilides, 1985).

The neo-Hellenic revival and attachment to classical Greece were limited to a small segment of society and generally were opposed by the Orthodox Church. This nascent national consciousness included a sense of identity with ancient Greece, a desire for freedom from Ottoman dominance, and the belief that the cultural heritage of multi-ethnic Byzantium was a special attribute of Greek-speaking people (although others could share in it) (Petropulos, 1976: 23–4).

Several notable figures contributed to the revival of neo-Hellenism, among them Adamantios Korais, who was born in Smyrna and lived in Paris during and after the French Revolution. Korais supported the Hellenic culture by translating ancient classics into modern Greek, reforming the Greek language, and praising freedom, nationalism, and constitutionalism. Greek schoolchildren even received Korais's nationalistic book, which was donated by two wealthy brothers free of charge. Another important figure was Rigas Feraios who founded a secret revolutionary group in Vienna, stressed the importance of the Greek language and identity, and published revolutionary material including a prospective constitution for Greece. He supported unification of all the Balkan peoples against the Turks. He was arrested and later strangled to death by Ottoman commanders in 1798. His martyrdom helped encourage Greeks to resist.

By the early 1800s there appeared to be seven major groups influencing Greek society: (1) the Phanariots, (2) the church hierarchy, (3) the growing merchant and urban middle class in Greece, (4) the Greeks of the diaspora who were living abroad and adopting liberal and secular ideas including strong nationalist sentiments favouring Greek liberation (through Western support), (5) the peasants who were increasingly being exploited by the *chiflik* system, (6) the local notables whose main function was to levy and collect taxes, and (7) the *klephts* and related naval forces who would form a major fighting force in the struggle for liberation.

The first two groups were divided on the issue of revolution, although the clergy in the village generally supported the fight for liberation. The church had helped maintain Greek identity during the long Ottoman rule. The emerging middle class in commerce and industry was dissatisfied with the imperial government whose officials were constantly exploiting them and forcing them to function in an insecure world. Moreover, the middle-class merchants were impressed by the size and wealth of other European cities, their progress in science and learning, and especially by the rule of law and the safeguarding of individual rights (Stavrianos, 1958: 277), although the richer merchants were often hesitant about vigorously waging revolution. The Greek peasants, however, uniformly had little to lose, having seen their condition deteriorate owing to the *chiflik* system, the embezzlement and corruption of the landowners, and military defeats.

On the eve of the Greek Revolution (1821), then, there were polarized factions within Greek society. On one hand there were the Constantinople Patriarchate and the Phanariots, who had entered the Ottoman service and had gained great power and wealth as administrators, tax collectors, merchants, and contractors. They and the rich families in Greece proper had much at stake if a revolution were to be waged and lost. On the other hand, members of the new middle class provided some of the leadership for the nationalist movements, while leaders emerging from the peasants, especially the *klephts*, provided the needed muscle.

The Greeks were torn by these deep cleavages, the product of revolutionary ideology born abroad and of economic and social differences at home (Stavrianos, 1958: 281). Divisions emerged owing to sectional differences (Peloponnesians vs. mainlanders vs. islanders), varying ideological positions (cosmopolitan Phanariots vs. guerrilla chieftains and high prelates vs. village priests) and conflicting class interests (wealthy shipowners vs. unemployed sailors and powerful primates vs. landless peasants). It was difficult to develop new feelings of loyalty to the country as a whole in place of one's more particular interests in a geographical region or local group. The sea and mountains, after all, had served as forces promoting localism and sectionalism for thousands of years. Thus, rather than a fully fledged modern nationalism, there may well have been a traditional incipient nationalism that involved multiple and perhaps divergent sets of loyalties to various groups in the political sphere (Diamandouros, 1976: 194). Their version of national consciousness focused on the Greek people and could not be equated with the broader bond of religious Orthodoxy that existed throughout the Balkans (Bialor, 1971: 66; Petropulos, 1976; Xydis, 1969).

GREEK REVOLUTION (1821–1828) AND POST-INDEPENDENCE (1829–1875)

The revolution began in 1821 in the Peloponnesos. During the war many regional, kinship, and class conflicts continued. For example, intersectional strife was so great that in 1824 mainlanders (continentals) and islanders joined together to put down the Peloponnesians in a major civil war. The 'traditionalists' with Eastern religious values wanted to overthrow the Turks and simply replace them without changing the structure of political control. The 'Westernizers', on the other hand, were very nationalistic and wanted a strong central state that would reduce regional fragmentation and the autonomy of the local bureaucratic notables (Diamandouros, 1972; Petropulos, 1968). Differences in cultural patterns were great, with the Westernizers dressing in European style (black redingote), sleeping in beds, and living with and sharing meals with their wives. Traditionalists wore white kilts or baggy trousers, slept outside or on mats, and were socially separate from their wives.

Despite these internal conflicts, liberation was ultimately achieved, with many heroes contributing to the victory (e.g. Kolokotronis, Mavrokordatos, Ypsilantis, Botsaris, Androutsos, and Bouboulina). Solomos wrote the 'Hymn to Liberty' in 1824, part of which is used in the Greek national anthem. Philhellenes, including many prominent Americans and British such as Samuel Howe, Daniel Webster, and the lyric poet Lord Byron (who died at Mesolonghi), also contributed to the Greek cause. Before arriving in Greece, many of the philhellenes believed the Greeks of the 1800s would be similar to those of Classical Greece and the Golden Age of Athens. Although they were taken aback by the appearance and culture of the Greek freedom fighters, most remained to help. Both the philhellenes and the Greeks themselves managed to generate support from abroad by portraying Greece as the birthplace of democarcy struggling to overthrow the barbarian Ottoman yoke. During the latter years of fighting, the governments of England, Russia, and France aided the Greek cause. Divisions among the Greeks over which country they supported appeared early with Mavrokordatos favouring the British, Kolokotronis the Russians, and Kolettis the French.

In somewhat simplistic terms there were three possible scenarios that could have been achieved once Greece was liberated from Turkish rule (Petropulos, 1976: 25–6). The first was a multi-ethnic state in which Hellenic ties and sentiment would be the basic criteria and Greeks themselves would be the minority. The Hellenistic Empire of Alexander the Great, the Byzantine Empire during its ascendance, and the Ottoman Empire all provided precedents for this alternative. The second was a nation-state, geographically limited to the area where Greeks would be a large majority of the population. The historical precedent for this would be the contracted Byzantine Empire before its demise. Its inspiration came from the romantic idea of classical antiquity. The final possibility was the creation of several distinct Greek states and reflected what had been happening in the Ottoman Empire during the last century as several provinces on the periphery broke away. The Greeks themselves did not have the strength nor the support of other nations to allow them to achieve the first alternative. Consequently they settled for the second, but not without major implications for the future.

The second alternative meant that liberated Greece proper had only 800,000 people while there were three times that many Greeks in Turkish provinces and the British Ionian Islands. The Great Idea (*Megale Idea*) therefore evolved as the ideal of uniting all Greeks of the Ottoman Empire into one Greek nation with its capital in Constantinople. The Great Idea was the major factor in shaping Greek nationalism and political development during the 1800s. From 1821 to 1923 Greece struggled to unite Greeks inside with those outside the national borders despite foreign forces that wanted to maintain the status quo. The passionate desire to free Greek compatriots from the Turks was especially embodied in the so-called French Party of Kolettis, which was extremely popular with the average Greek. In general, preoccupation with the security and extension of Greek borders has been a significant concern of Greeks throughout their history.

Greece was declared an independent and monarchical state under the guarantee of the three Allied Powers (England, Russia, and France) in the New London Protocol (1828). The foreign powers would consistently involve themselves in Greek politics for years to come. It was quite unlike the example of the American Revolution in which the founding fathers received support especially from the French but framed American politics with little European interference.

The Westernizers were generally victorious in obtaining a centralized government for the new nation. Capodistrias, who was in certain ways eager to modernize Greece, was elected governor. Some of his major contributions included suppressing piracy, organizing the state apparatus, creating a regular Greek army, making provisions for public education, advocating the distribution of state lands among war veterans, and restricting primates and local notables who were trying to become independent potentates in the provinces. Yet his authoritarian style and anti-democratic tendency in carrying out his policies alienated intellectuals, military chieftains, and local notables who were unable to appropriate large amounts of national lands and become major landowners. In 1831 Capodistrias was assassinated and a period of civil strife followed.

Some have contended that Capodistrias's desire to introduce Western political institutions and rationalism was inappropriate for a society just emerging from prolonged Ottoman rule. Tsoucalas (1978: 11) maintains that in Greece there was an 'especially premature institutionalization of bourgeois state structures which were based on the models derived from the French Revolution'. Such 'imported' state structures are not able to function as they do in their countries of origin because they encounter very different social and economic circumstances. Forcing the adaptation of modern institutions to traditional values brought an uncertainty about the nature of the Greek state and strong doubts over the political identity and orientation of modern Greece (Diamandouros, 1983). It was difficult for Greeks to develop a sense of loyalty to the state in the face of competing regional and individual interests.

When the three allied protecting powers agreed that Bavarian Prince Otho should take the throne in 1833, the Greek monarchy was born. Where previously there had been conflicts between Westernizers and adherents of Eastern Byzantine traditions, the monarch now became a third major force in politics. The military would also play an important role in politics as the state engaged in institution-building.

In 1843 the army staged a bloodless coup and forced Otho to grant the people a constitution. This was the first time in Greece's history as an independent nation that the military overtly intervened in politics. As we will see, it would certainly not be the last time. In 1862 a revolution deposed Otho, who had generally ignored the new constitution, and by 1863 the Greeks had a new monarch—Prince William George of Denmark. As a sign of support for the new King, Britain ceded the Ionian Islands, with a population of about 250,000, to Greece. William George largely supported the new liberal constitution of 1864 which essentially granted universal (male) suffrage, the 'most important permanent mechanism of participation in political life and the most fundamental element of the legitimation of government' (Tsoucalas, 1978: 11). During the first eleven years of George I's rule, there were twenty-three administrations. This instability gave the King great power, especially in foreign affairs. Politics remained personalistic rather than issue-oriented.

Economic Conditions

After the ravages of war, Greece was in a poor economic condition, but during the 1830s and 1840s legislation was passed to provide for a relatively equitable distribution of the land previously held by the Turks. By 1870 the average peasant owned a plot of thirteen to twenty-five acres, though the holdings were much smaller in the islands and over-populated mountainous areas (Stavrianos, 1958: 297). The Greek government refused to sell the national lands by auction and thus strongly hindered the emergence of a big landed property class.

From the time of liberation, the Greek ruling class was dissociated from agricultural activities. The large landowners were not able to create a rural wage-earning proletariat. Small land-holding and even some share-cropping predominated. The large landowners thus redirected their attention to more profitable enterprises such as export trade, commerical navigation, purchase of real estate in the cities, and usury. The landowners' gradual loss of interest in agriculture had important consequences for the possible development of class conflict in Greece. The notables no longer engaged in *direct* class conflicts with small landowners. Instead, the families of notables used the system of clientelism to help them maintain their political influence in the rural areas and do so even to the present (Tsoucalas, 1978: 15).

Mouzelis (1978: 15) refers to the period of 1830 to 1880 as one of 'underdevelopment in a pre-capitalist context'. Greece was mainly an agrarian society with very low social overhead capital and virtually non-existent industry (except for handicrafts). According to Sakellariou (1966), in 1840 the middle class was in its very early stages, and there was no proletariat. Of 850,000 people there were only 18,296 merchants, 15,343 artisans, 13,679 seafarers, and 276 bankers and money-changers. Industry did not really start until George I became monarch in the early 1860s. Between the 1850s and 1870s the Greek working class remained small compared to the rising middle class of teachers, lawyers, doctors, and other professionals.

The big capital that existed (foreign, indigenous, and in the hands of the Greek diaspora) was concentrated in finance and distribution/trading rather than industry. While there was some integration of the Greek economy into the world capitalist system during the first fifty years of independence, non-capitalist modes of production prevailed in both agricultural and industrial sectors. The economically dominant merchant and finance capital avoided the production sphere and instead extracted surplus labour through a set of market mechanisms and state policies developed to maintain and promote its own interests (Mouzelis, 1978: 16).

Since the upper class had not been able to maintain dominance as large landowners and had not been able to stop the creation of a centralized state, they decided to try to control the state from within (Mouzelis, 1978; Tsoucalas, 1978). The state's taxation system was the major means of collecting and distributing economic surplus. The control of the state machinery and the imported parliamentary institutions by the ruling class provided the foundation for their economic power. The oligarchic families (*tzakia*) used the representative system of government to protect their privileges by relying on the traditional forms of patronage and clientelism to control the voting process and safeguard their representation in parliament (Mouzelis, 1978: 143).

PRE-WORLD WAR I GREECE (1875–1910)

From 1875 to 1893 Trikoupis was in power ten and a half years. He favoured economic expansion and Westernization and wanted to break up the clienteles and establish a two-party system. Much of his constituency came from the growing professional and commercial classes in part because he tried to restrict brigandage and supported the security forces. Many of his reforms were unpopular because they involved high taxation. On the other hand, his rival Deligiannis (in power 1885–7, 1890–2, 1895–7) appealed more to the rural people of 'Old Greece' and strongly favoured extending Greek borders. There were recurrent crises and fighting in Crete, Thessaly, and Macedonia. In 1881, a settlement was reached that gave Greece Thessaly but only the area around Arta in Epirus. In 1897 Turkey defeated the Greeks, forcing them to pay a war indemnity of 4 m. Turkish pounds and to concede a number of minor frontier forts. An International Financial Control Commission, composed of representatives from various foreign countries, was established to supervise Greece's payment of the interest on its debts. Such a commission was typically regarded as additional foreign intervention in Greece's affairs.

Between the mid-1870s and 1914 Greece experienced a general period of economic growth in part because of the development of a land transport system under Trikoupis. Greece was in transition, moving away from agrarian stagnation and creating necessary preconditions for the development of capitalism (Mouzelis, 1978). Trikoupis especially encouraged private enterprise and Western investment in Greece, yet the typical Greek capitalist invested money in a business that was safe, required little capital, and could be managed personally. This was usually in consumer goods rather than heavy industry which required great capital investment and technical managerial skills. Foreign capital often was invested in mining or railway construction or in loans to the Greek government.

Couloumbis (1983a: 116) describes the 1800s as a period of continuous conflict among foreign powers for influence in Greece. Indicative of this, Greek political parties were even labelled French, English, and Russian. Issues confronting the early Greek government that remained unsolved by the end of the nineteenth century included: (1) foreign influence and domination vs. nationalism and irredentism; (2) the appointed King vs. the elected officials;

(3) military vs. civilian supremacy; and (4) church vs. state authority.

In 1909 the Military League staged a revolt that challenged the parliamentary system, the old political forces, and the dynasty itself. The military tried to introduce new reforms but were frustrated by the political oligarchy. The Military League therefore asked Eleftherios Venizelos, a very popular Cretan politician and nationalist, to assume the premiership. Venizelos and his Liberal Party worked for major changes in Greece's economic, social, political, and military institutions, including the involvement of the state in the management and control of the economy.

WARS AND THEIR CONSEQUENCES: 1910–1923

Under Venizelos, the Greeks formed the Balkan League with Serbia, Bulgaria, and Montenegro to fight against the Turks. Largely owing to the Balkan Wars of 1912 and 1913, Greek sovereignty over Crete was recognized. When Greece acquired southern Epirus and Macedonia, its territory increased by about 70 per cent and its population grew from 2.8 m. to 4.8 m. (Clogg, 1979: 103). Greece thus expanded its borders to the present frontiers. These victories revived national pride and intensified irredentism. Many Greeks from the diaspora (including those in the US) returned to Greece first to join in the fight and later to enjoy the fruits of success.

Economically, Greece began to meet the basic preconditions for the development of capitalism during this time, experiencing territorial and population growth, the influx of foreign capital, the development of an extensive transport system, the creation of a unified internal market, and the establishment of an institutional framework facilitating state intervention in the economy (Mouzelis, 1978: 21). The capitalism that emerged was peripheral and underdeveloped, since much of the original impetus for its growth was from outside interests (foreign and Greek diaspora capital).

World War I brought about a national schism of major dimensions in Greek politics because the leaders could not decide whether to fight in the war or remain neutral. Venizelos and his Liberal Party favoured participation on the side of the Entente (France, Great Britain, Russia, US). Upon King George's assassination in 1913 Prince Constantine, who was sympathetic to the

Central Powers (he was married to Kaiser William II's sister) and advocated neutrality, succeeded to the throne.

Although Venizelos initially persuaded King Constantine to agree to send troops to the Dardanelles Straits to support the Allies, the King changed his decision when his Chief of General Staff John Metaxas refused to move the troops. Venizelos resigned in March 1915, but in the June 1915 elections, he retained his control of Parliament and eventually the King recalled him to office. Matters between the two only worsened, and Venizelos resigned again on 5 October 1915.

A pro-Venizelos coup was staged in Salonica in August 1916 with Venizelos creating a provisional government there in October 1916. Only after the royalist Greek government protested a French and English landing at Athens did Britain and France recognize Venizelos's government. The King resigned in June, and Venizelos returned to Athens on 27 June 1917. He declared war on the Central Powers on 2 July 1917, but it took some time to mobilize Greek forces. In September 1918 the Greeks, along with troops from France, Britain, and Italy, drove the enemy out of Macedonia and moved into Serbia and Bulgaria. The general armistice to end the fighting was signed on 11 November 1918.

Venizelos is well known for his statesmanship and intellectual ability at the peace conference in Versailles where he promoted Greek territorial claims in spite of their conflict with those of other allies. The Sèvres Treaty fulfilled much of Greece's nationalistic ambition. Greece was to receive most of Thrace and numerous islands in the Aegean along with the right to occupy Smyrna for five years, after which there was a possibility of unification with Greece. Unfortunately for Greece, the treaty was never ratified. Turkish nationalists led by Mustafa Kemal (Ataturk) were not willing to give up Turkish rights to various lands.

At about the same time there was internal dissension in Greece leading to Venizelos's electoral defeat and the return of King Constantine. Among the probable factors contributing to Venizelos's defeat were the amount of support for the King and monarchy in general, the hostility engendered by various activities of strong Venizelos supporters who tried to suppress the royalists, and resentment over the allies' involvement in Greek domestic affairs. Moreover the Greeks, mobilized for war for at least eight years, may have become war weary as the Greek army continued to advance to the interior. Many royalists, who had received support from those opposed to the war, changed their minds and decided to pursue the irredentist dream of making Constantinople Greek. The Allies failed to support this royalist initiative which ultimately resulted in the humiliating Greek defeat in 1922 by the Turks, known as the Great Débâcle.

In the wake of the Asia Minor defeat, a group of officers under Colonel Plastiras formed a Revolutionary Committee and King Constantine again abdicated. The committee asked Venizelos to return to head the government. He declined but did consent to use his diplomatic skills to represent Greece at the treaty negotiations. Venizelos and Ismet, the Turkish representative, agreed to a very complex compulsory exchange of populations in most major areas except Constantinople (Istanbul), Imvros and Tenedos, Western Thrace, and Cyprus (then under British sovereignty) in order to reduce tensions and make each nation more homogeneous. In order to resolve the complex question of national identity, it was decided that the basic criterion to determine who was Greek or Turkish would be based on religion rather than language. This meant that many Turkish-speaking Orthodox of Asia Minor, especially women who knew no Greek, were forced to move to Greece. Altogether, about 1,300,000 Orthodox Greeks and 380,000 Islamic Turks were exchanged.

In July 1923 the Treaty of Lausanne resulted in Turkey receiving Eastern Thrace, Imvros, Tenedos and Smyrna, but Greece kept Western Thrace and had its sovereignty recognized in Mytilini, Chios, and Samos. The treaty also revoked the special guarantee that Britain, France, and Russia were to protect Greece, preventing those three powers from using the guarantee as a pretext for interference. The Anatolian disaster signified the end to much of the Great Idea or Greek irredentism (except that regarding Cyprus). The dream of recreating a Byzantine Empire, that first possible alternative for Greeks after official liberation from the Ottomans, was lost forever. The second option, the creation of a homogeneous Greek state, was finally achieved after 100 years of struggle, albeit with the forced uprooting of Greeks from territories outside the formal boundaries of Greece. Greece now turned its attention to internal developments, particularly to the problems associated with the influx of Greeks from Turkey.

INTER-WAR YEARS: POST-*MEGALE IDEA* (1923–1939)

During this period the struggle between monarchy supporters and advocates of a republic continued, and the military increasingly showed its willingness to enter the political arena. Venizelos returned to power briefly in 1924, from 1928 to 1932, and again in 1933. He brought some needed stability, but both he and the middle class that had supported him were no longer very reform-oriented. By the 1930s the middle class wanted to preserve and protect their position rather than encourage change. They viewed the Depression and the accompanying agitation for reforms among the poor with alarm (Stavrianos, 1958: 667). While on the domestic front things were not very encouraging, Venizelos did manage to improve relations with Italy, Yugoslavia, Albania, Bulgaria, and especially Turkey.

The Communist Party in Greece had officially been organized in 1918, but it was of minor consequence until the Depression when it began to attract students, professionals, and refugees as well as workers. Still, the small landowning peasants did not support communism, and even the limited urban working class that had emerged often remained very attached to its village origins. One of the major drawbacks of the Communist Party was that the Comintern (Communist Information Bureau), the international organization of Communist parties, favoured the idea of an independent (rather than Greek) Macedonia, a position that most Greeks found extremely difficult to support.

The period from 1933 to 1935 marked the end of the Greek republic, climaxed by an abortive *coup d'état* that attempted to return Venizelos to power. A November 1935 plebiscite, which may have been influenced by the military's support for the King, overwhelmingly favoured reinstatement of the monarchy. In the 1936 election various royalist and republican parties won 143 and 142 seats respectively so that the Communist Party with fifteen seats held the balance of power. The major parties tried to make deals with the Communist Party, much to the distress of the King and the military. Owing to political problems the Parliament planned to disband for five months. Metaxas, appointed premier by King George II, had numerous people who disagreed with his policies arrested. The Communists especially retaliated by calling strikes so that the King eventually signed a decree suspending various provisions of the Constitution, thus making Metaxas a virtual dictator. All political parties were dissolved, and the police were given extraordinary power.

Metaxas envisaged changing Greek society and reformulating Greek character based on the German corporate spirit and Hitler's Third Reich. He considered himself the creator of a Third Hellenic Civilization that would combine the strong points of the first two Hellenic civilizations: pagan classical ancient Greece and Christian Byzantium. Though the Greek people reacted to Metaxas with a resigned acquiescence rather than either enthusiasm or hostility (Clogg, 1979: 133–4), he remained in power until his death shortly after the beginning of World War II when the Italians attacked Greece.

Economic Conditions

The national economy deteriorated due to the high birth-rate, low agricultural productivity, the inability of industry to absorb the population surplus (1.3 m. refugees came to a country of only 5.5 m.), and the lack of a domestic market adequate to support industrial expansion (Stavrianos, 1958). The world-wide Depression hurt Greece's export of luxury agricultural items (tobacco, currants, wine, olives), so much so that the gross trade decline of 22 per cent in quantity and 70 per cent in value between 1924 and 1934 resulted in a large deficit (Stavrianos, 1958: 666). To meet the trade deficit of about $60 m. annually, Greece relied on its 'invisible exports', which included profits from the growing merchant marine, the tourist industry, and, most importantly, the remittances of Greek emigrants that averaged $30 m. annually in the inter-war period (Couloumbis *et al.*, 1976: 96).

The land reform and distribution in northern Greece, for which Venizelos had laid the groundwork, was extremely important in shaping the structure of the Greek economy. The recently acquired territory in northern Greece constituted 38 per cent of the total cultivatible area of Greece (Stavrianos, 1958: 678–9). By 1936, 425,000 acres had been redistributed to 305,000 families (Mouzelis, 1978: 22), ensuring that small landowning would continue to be the dominant form of cultivation in Greece.

From 1923 to 1930 a great inflow of foreign capital (1162.8 m. gold francs) increased the influence of foreign interests on the

Greek economy (Mouzelis, 1978: 23). The capital itself, a devaluation of the drachma, and the availability of refugee labour and entrepreneurial skills contributed to the development of the Greek economy. Although 92 per cent of the pre-war industries were small workshops employing one to five people using little or no power (Stavrianos, 1958: 679), the small, inefficient, and labour-intensive enterprises did provide a partial solution to the employment problem, and between 1921 and 1929 the value of industrial production multiplied seven times. In 1940 industry accounted for 18 per cent of the national income and employed 15 per cent of the work force (Campbell and Sherrard, 1968: 141). Greece was not, however, able to raise its standard of living from 1830 to 1940 owing to a lack of systematic and consistent economic policy and the administrative inability to implement the few measures passed by progressive politicians (Stavrianos, 1958).

WORLD WAR II AND GREEK CIVIL WAR (1940–1949)

Predictably Greece's strategic location brought quick involvement in World War II. The Italian invasion of Greece was met by strong resistance and humiliating defeats for Mussolini. '*OHI* Day', 28 October 1940, is still celebrated as the day Premier Metaxas said 'No', ('*Ohi*') refusing to surrender to the Italian ultimatum that challenged Greek sovereignty. During the winter of 1940 to 1941 Greece was Britain's only active ally. Metaxas died in January 1941 and King George's appointed Prime Minister, Koryzis, committed suicide shortly thereafter. The Greeks were not able to cope with German forces in 1941, resulting in the occupation of Greece for almost four years during which the King and government fled first to Crete, then Egypt, London, and eventually Cairo.

There was much internal dissension over the pattern that Greek resistance should follow, with those who were vulnerable to economic reprisals tending to be more passive. Another factor resistance fighters had to consider was the Germans' especially harsh dealings with acts of resistance; they often slaughtered many villagers in retaliation, as was the case in the shocking murder of nearly 700 people in the Kalavryta region in December 1943.

The Communists were by far the most experienced and organized group during the war. Most of the active resistance movement centred around the National Liberation Movement (EAM) and the

National Popular Liberation Army (ELAS). Many Greeks who joined the resistance were not actually Communists themselves but strongly supported liberation. The extent of the movement's support and effectiveness is difficult to evaluate because the political persuasions of many authors influence their description of this time period, but estimates of the EAM/ELAS membership range from 500,000 to 2,000,000 people. It does seem safe to conclude (as did Stavrianos, 1958: 788) that this movement was a major force in Greek society. Despite some shortcomings, EAM probably represented Greece as well as any organization could during a period of foreign occupation. In 1944 EAM created the Political Committee of National Liberation (PEEA). There were also other less important organizations of resistance, such as the National Republican Greek Organization (EDES), and the National and Social Liberation (EKKA). In general those who were staging the resistance in Greece did not favour the return of the King and the old political forces.

In 1944 at a conference held in Lebanon, attempts were made to form a national unity government with George Papandreou as premier. G. Papandreou was a well-known Venizelist who had just recently emerged from occupied Greece and replaced Sophocles Venizelos, son of famous Eleftherios Venizelos. EAM leaders at the meeting wanted control of more powerful ministries than they were given, but the Soviet mission encouraged them to be moderate. They accepted a subordinate position in the Greek cabinet and agreed to the landing of British troops. In reality the left wing's representation at the conference was small and did not correspond with the actual power the group had in Greece.

When Churchill and Stalin met on 9 October 1944, they determined that Greece fell in the British and US spheres of influence while Romania and Bulgaria belonged to the USSR sphere. Stalin kept his agreement with the British and offered the Greek Communist Party little support. Hence, with British support, the government of national unity headed by G. Papandreou landed in Greece.

The Greek Civil War, which began with the Battle for Athens in December, 1944, resulted from conflict over which military forces—communist, royalist, or republican—were to disarm. When the Communists staged a mass demonstration in Athens there was shooting, and subsequent fighting lasted for over one month.

British reinforcements from Italy proved to be too much for the Communists, and ELAS eventually accepted a cease fire on 11 January in part because Churchill, who actually came to Athens on Christmas Eve 1944, had agreed to a plebiscite to decide on the return of the King. In addition, G. Papandreou was replaced by General Plastiras on 3 January 1945. The Varkiza Peace Agreement, signed in February, provided that the Communists surrender their arms, but a number of reforms were to be introduced and amnesty was to be granted for political crimes.

After the Varkiza Agreement Greece faced various crises including the first Communist rebellion, economic problems (particularly inflation), and an inability to form and maintain governments. Although Italy ceded the Dodecanese Islands after World War II, Greece's failure to acquire Cyprus produced frustration. The British pushed for early elections which the royalists won in 1946 with the Communists refusing to participate. These elections marked the first official US involvement in Greece as part of the Allied Mission observing the election in which a plebiscite brought back King George II.

By early 1947 the Greek Civil War had accelerated greatly. The non-communist political leaders encountered difficulties in making the government functional, and the economy was near paralysis. It seems that Greece was in such poor condition that even the request for US aid was drafted in America by US officials (Couloumbis *et al.*, 1976: 11). On 12 March 1947 the Truman Doctrine was announced, its main objective being to prevent Greece and Turkey from becoming Communist. The Greek government appears to have realized that US support would mean interference in internal affairs but believed it was necessary (Xydis, 1963: 479–80).

Substantial military hardware (74,000 tons) including artillery, dive-bombers, and stocks of napalm were sent to Greece in the last five months of 1947 (Barnet, 1972: 150). American involvement in Greece from 1947 to 1949 included supplying weaponry, equipment, and military advisers. It was at least as great as, and possibly greater than, British involvement from 1944 to 1947 (Clogg, 1979: 162). The Greek Communists received some assistance from Tito and Yugoslavia, Bulgaria, and Albania. By late 1948 martial law had to be proclaimed in Greece owing to the Communist success. Greece had again become a major battlefield for the big powers, this time in the Cold War. When the Tito–Stalin rift resulted in Tito's expulsion from the Cominform in 1948, Tito closed the Yugoslav–Greek border (officially in July 1949 but in reality earlier), cutting off aid to Greece and eliminating an escape route for Greek guerrillas. The Stalinist faction in Greece led by Zakhariadis purged many of the Titoists headed by Markos in early 1949.

The tide of the war changed early in 1949, but the war continued until the Communists were defeated at their stronghold in the mountains of Grammos and Vitsi. The Communist Party call for a temporary cessation of fighting in October 1949 turned out to be permanent. The heavy costs of Civil War included 80,000 casualties, 700,000 refugees (10 per cent of the population), and shocking atrocities committed by both sides against their fellow Greeks. Macrides (1968) suggests that the pro-Western forces in Greece won the Civil War because of American aid to Greece, the refusal of many Greeks to aid the Communist guerrillas, the closing of the Yugoslav–Greek border, and the use of US prestige and propaganda to convince people that political, economic, administrative, and military reforms would occur. From that time on, the US would play a major role in the political developments of Greece. Seventeen different governments ruled Greece from the Battle of Athens until the formation of the Diomedes cabinet in June 1949. The parties ruling Greece were generally right of centre, and the right firmly maintained control of the state machinery. In addition, the Greek army, which the US had trained and supported, was given a free hand to police, intimidate, and control the citizens and government. Until 1962 the army and police issued the 'certificates of civic loyalty' needed to gain employment, move, or register to vote. The Greek military served as a major power-bloc quite independent of the traditional political structure (Legg, 1969: 190–1).

Obviously economic disaster resulted from the war and the internal fighting. During three-and-a-half years of war 30 per cent of the nation's wealth was destroyed and 7 per cent of the population (500,000 of 7,000,000) died from fighting or starvation (Stavrianos, 1958: 787). Stavrianos suggests that the utter destitution of the Greek people drove them into the national resistance as a means of self-preservation. After the war, the thirty-three-day Battle of Athens alone resulted in $250 m. in property destroyed and 11,000 people killed (Stavrianos, 1958: 828).

In summary, the Truman Doctrine and the aid associated with it eventually resulted in the Greek Communist defeat, a conservative government for Greece, and American involvement in Greek affairs. Couloumbis *et al.* (1976: 119) estimate the massive US military and economic aid at over $2 b. while Stavrianos (1952: 192) points out that American appropriations between 1947 and 1949 for military purposes totalled close to $400 m. with another $300 m. for economic aid. Much of the economic aid went toward reconstruction, advanced farming technology, and an anti-malaria programme. Inflation ran rampant so that by the spring of 1948 no less than one-third of the population was destitute and on relief. By 1949 Greece reached only 70 per cent of its pre-war output in agriculture and 86 per cent in industry (Stavrianos, 1952).

POST-WAR GREECE (1950–1963)

In general, the political labels of left, centre, and right that had existed before World War II were still appropriate after the war. The defeat of the Communist forces in the Civil War resulted in the weakening of all leftist forces and the outlawing of the Communist Party until 1974. The military continued to play an important role in maintaining order in Greece. In the 1950 election the Populists lost most of their strength, winning only 62 of 250 seats. The centre was divided into three groups: the Liberal Party led by Sophocles Venizelos won 56 seats, the National Progressive Union of the Centre won 45 seats, and George Papandreou's centrist party won 35 seats. Since the Communist Party had been outlawed, the left was represented by the Democratic Front, which won 18 seats and had 10 per cent of the vote. In 18 months 5 weak, unstable coalition governments were formed.

In 1951 new elections were held. Papagos, a former Army general, formed the National Rally Party, a right-leaning party, and secured 114 seats out of 258. The divided centre received 131 seats, and Plastiras formed a coalition government that lasted only until 1952. The United Democratic Left (EDA) became the legitimate party of the left. Then in elections called in 1952, Papagos and the Rally Party won 247 of 300 seats. A new constitution took effect in 1952, and Greece joined NATO. The US government supported Papagos because it wanted stable governments that were clearly opposed to Communism. During the time Papagos was in power

(1952–5), many measures such as a devaluation of the drachma, state loans, and special laws for attracting foreign capital were passed.

Constantine Karamanlis succeeded Papagos and renamed the party the National Radical Union Party (ERE). Between 1952 and 1963 the right maintained a decisive parliamentary majority and a popular vote ranging between 44 per cent and 50 per cent. After the first six years of conservative government, clients of the right were in control of the public services and the armed forces. Many Greeks came to believe Karamanlis could not lose (Campbell and Sherrard, 1968: 260). In general, law and order were maintained because the right was willing to use repressive measures when necessary.

Near the end of Karamanlis's rule, leftist deputy Gregorios Lambrakis, a physician and former Olympic athlete, was murdered, a historical event depicted in the famous film *Z*. His assassination by right-wing thugs, as he went to speak at a peace rally, generated a great deal of controversy and a movement for peace. Although Karamanlis was not involved, officials high in the Greek government were implicated.

The 1950s can be characterized as a time of heavy American influence that promoted a pro-Western stability. Unlike the Civil War years, this period brought some negative Greek reaction to American interference, especially concerning Cyprus. There was a steady decline in US economic aid, but military aid increased (Couloumbis *et al.*, 1976: 126). In the early 1960s the Kennedy administration indicated its willingness to support a centre government if it were united enough to maintain stability (Campbell and Sherrard, 1968: 264). In 1961 George Papandreou succeeded in bringing together various factions of the centre into the Centre Union Party, and although it did not win the election of that year, the party did win 100 seats in Parliament. The assassination of Lambrakis, a mounting balance of payments problem, and the disputes between the royal family and Karamanlis led Karamanlis to resign in 1963 and call for new elections. Karamanlis had objected to King Paul and Queen Frederica accepting an invitation to visit London because demonstrations had occurred against the Queen on her private visit there a few weeks before.

Despite the fragmentation of the Greek political system, one can identify some pattern of durability in the major political formations over time. The left, centre, and right have taken somewhat different stands on such issues as the monarchy, foreign policy, and the nature and extent of internal socio-economic change. In addition, the political groupings do have certain differences in their social bases of support although this is not as clear cut as in most Western European countries. For example, during the 1960s, ERE was generally the party of those who owned businesses or stores and of farmers, particularly those in Old Greece mainly Peloponnesos. Salaried employees, civil servants, and people living in rural areas that traditionally had favoured Venizelos tended to support the Centre Union. The left has drawn its support from discontented intellectuals, industrial workers, and lower-paid service employees, especially among families of Asia Minor refugees.

Economically Greece grew quite rapidly owing in part to American aid. By the early 1950s the Greek economy was back to its pre-war level of production. In 1959 the volume of industrial production doubled that of 1938 and tripled it by 1964. Production of agricultural products increased also, but the most important growth was in tourism (increasing five times from 1938 to 1961) and in shipping (the merchant marine). In spite of this growth, there were many signs of underdevelopment, including a growing, highly parasitic tertiary (service) sector, a small stable manufacturing sector, a low labour absorption capacity, and a large but inefficient agricultural sector (Mouzelis, 1978). In 1960 more than half of the labour force was still engaged in agriculture, while only 19 per cent were craftsmen, production-process workers, and labourers, 3 per cent technical, professional, and related workers, and 1 per cent administrative (National Statistical Service of Greece, 1971).

The labour ministers under Papagos and Karamanlis tried to break the power of the trade unions by using governmental interference in the policies of the unions. Some suggest that Karamanlis attempted economic development without adequately considering social development. For example, the government spent a great deal of money to promote tourism and introduced a liberal credit policy that encouraged private enterprise and industrial development, yet it did little to improve social welfare or provide wage and salary increases. According to Jecchinis (1967: 159), the middle and upper-middle classes were gaining the benefits of economic progress, but the existing inequality in income distribution actually widened. In the cities there was considerable urban unemployment and underemployment owing to an influx of workers from rural areas. At the same time, the difference between average incomes in the cities and those in the depopulated countryside widened.

Through the late 1950s manufacturing was very underdeveloped since the bulk of the Greek capitalists invested in non-manufacturing sectors. The tertiary economy expanded rapidly while manufacturing stagnated (Mouzelis, 1978: 120–1). Greece, which had been far ahead of its Balkan neighbours Yugoslavia, Bulgaria, and Romania according to the index of manufacturing production in 1938, had fallen behind by 1959. The Karamanlis government's attempt to attract foreign investment by granting large economic advantages during the latter part of its administration succeeded in increasing the amount of foreign capital from $11,683,700 in 1960 to $50,026,290 by 1963 (Mouzelis, 1978: 28). Gradually the emphasis changed from production of consumer goods to capital goods. During this time Greece officially began the process of becoming a full member of the European Economic Community (EEC).

TRIUMPH OF CENTRE UNION AND FALL TO MILITARY DICTATORSHIP (1963–1967)

George Papandreou generally continued to maintain unity within the Centre Union Party. The November 1963 election resulted in a rather indecisive victory for him over Karamanlis with the Centre Union winning 138 seats as compared to 132 for ERE. EDA captured 28 seats and the Progressive Party of Markezinis had only two seats. In 1964 G. Papandreou called for new elections, which his party won easily with 173 seats to 98 for ERE, 22 for EDA, and 7 for the Progressives. Greece seemed to be moving toward political liberalization and economic progress.

The G. Papandreou government introduced many changes that would benefit the lower income groups, including improved social services, free education at all levels, and wider distribution of income. The average increase of wages in manufacturing in 1964 was 11 per cent compared to 6 per cent in 1963 and 4 per cent in 1962 (Jecchinis, 1967: 169; Campbell and Sherrard, 1968: 308). G. Papandreou's son Andreas, an economist who had taught at Berkeley, and other government officials tried to increase industrial development while improving social conditions at the same time—a difficult combination to achieve. In 1964 and 1965 there were important increases in the GNP (9 per cent in 1964 and 7 per cent in 1965), and for the first time the value of industrial production exceeded that of agriculture. At the same time though, the growth of imports greatly exceeded that of exports. The adverse balance of trade grew from $57 m. in 1963 to $172 m. in 1964 (Campbell and Sherrard, 1968: 307–8).

Between 1946 and 1963 the US gave Greece $3,285.5 m. of which 45 per cent was military and 55 per cent economic aid. In addition, companies such as Esso, Reynolds Metal, Dow Chemical, and Chrysler invested private US capital in Greece during the Karamanlis and G. Papandreou governments, but the flow of foreign capital was not great in absolute terms. Between 1954 and 1963 $398.5 m. was authorized, but only $110.1 m. entered the country. Still, such investments are important given the narrow base of Greek industry and the fact that total investment in 1963 was estimated to be only $628 m. Between 1963 and 1966 another $160 m. was invested (Campbell and Sherrard, 1968: 315).

Both King Paul and Sophocles Venizelos died in 1964, and Karamanlis departed to France leaving G. Papandreou in the political spotlight. Yet by mid-1965 the Centre Union forces were badly divided, and G. Papandreou resigned, ostensibly owing to the conflict with King Constantine concerning who had the right to replace the Minister of Defence. A clandestine organization of leftist officers known as ASPIDA, in which A. Papandreou was alleged to have been involved though it was never officially proven, had been exposed by the Minister of Defence. When G. Papandreou resigned, he called for elections that were postponed numerous times, but in the meantime Greece was run by caretaker governments.

G. Papandreou was unpopular with the right because he considered reducing expenditures for the military and had released over 400 political prisoners. Yet he accepted Greece's role in NATO and refused to recognize the Communist Party. Control of the rural police over the countryside was reduced, and the power of security forces that had maintained files on many Greeks was diminished. In addition, the government renegotiated some of the contracts with large foreign monopolies and obtained terms that were more favourable to Greece. Pilisuk (1972: 179–80) maintains that G. Papandreou's downfall was due to his failure to weaken the organization of the right wing military establishment, the appointment of his son Andreas as Minister of Co-ordination, and his pro-

Greek position in the Greek–Turkish dispute over Cyprus, an island republic with a population that is more than three-quarters Greek Cypriot. Regarding the latter he upset the US because he supported Makarios who accepted aid from the Communists and sent Greek military troops to Cyprus. Couloumbis *et al.* (1976: 130) believe that internal problems of the mid 1960s were the result of the unwillingness of ERE and the Centre Union politicians to respect each other as 'legitimate members of the same political establishment'.

Regarding external factors, G. Papandreou broke with ERE's NATO-oriented policy in trying to solve the problems over Cyprus. He tried to realize a more politically advantageous settlement through the UN rather than through the US and NATO. The US pushed for partitioning Cyprus, but Papandreou tried to explain to the US President that the Greek Parliament and people would never accept such a policy and Greece would have to reassess its position in NATO. President Johnson is reported to have replied first to Papandreou: 'Maybe Greece should rethink the advisability of a parliament that could not make the right decision' and later to the Greek ambassador: 'America is an elephant. Cyprus is a flea. Greece is a flea. If those two fleas continue itching the elephant, they may just get whacked by the elephant's trunk, whacked good . . . We pay a lot of good American dollars to the Greeks, Mr. Ambassador. If your Prime Minister gives me talk about Democracy, Parliament and Constitutions, he, his Parliament and his Constitution may not last long' (quoted from Iatrides, 1983: 165). During 1965 and 1967, the US tilted in favour of King Constantine rather than G. Papandreou (Couloumbis *et al.*, 1976: 134).

Legg (1973) has suggested that the two Papandreous tried to accomplish societal modernization by reforming the Centre Union Party through weakening political clientelism. They were unsuccessful, but the threat of a modernized Centre Union Party helped provoke a military coup. During the interim after G. Papandreou's resignation the Papandreous became more and more critical of the King, the economic oligarchy, the American CIA, and the military. While the top military leaders in Greece were seriously considering a coup, younger military officers led by Colonel Papadopoulos somewhat unexpectedly pulled off a successful military coup on 21 April 1967. For the next seven years Greece would remain under authoritarian military rule, first under

Papadopoulos and later Ioannides. Both internal weaknesses in the Greek social structure and American interference and interests have been cited as causes of the Greek dictatorship.

Couloumbis *et al.* (1976: 135) maintain that at a minimum American diplomatic and intelligence services expected extra-constitutional military intervention in Greek politics during 1967, and Washington chose not to oppose it actively. The US was among the first to recognize the military government. Indeed the Greek coup-makers used the NATO contingency plan in the take-over. Anastaplo (1968) contended that the US allowed itself to be identified in Greece as a force against a fairer distribution of the growing wealth in the country and encouraged the continuing perception among Greeks, especially within the military, that Greece was threatened by Communism. According to Craig (1976) during the military regime there was a period of political stability and a continuing alignment of Greece with the US. In both cases when conservative parties were in power and when the military ruled, the US successfully maintained American and NATO bases in Greece with a minimum of restrictions along with a secure south-eastern flank for NATO.

The Greek military ruled from 1967 to 1974 and were followed by a return to democracy led by Constantine Karamanlis and his New Democracy Party. Then in 1981 Greeks elected the first socialist government headed by Andreas Papandreou. The following chapters provide additional information on the events from 1967 to the present.

Notes

1. For a thorough consideration of the historical beginning of Greece through the time of Alexander the Great, see Bury and Meiggs, 1975. For a detailed history of Greece from the conquest by the Romans to 1864 (in 7 volumes) see Finlay, (1970). Vryonis (1967, 1978, 1981) provides valuable information on the Byzantine Empire. Zakythinos (1976) examines the factors related to the formation of modern Greece from Byzantium to official independence.

2. There is a great deal of controversy about whether modern Greeks are actually descendants of the ancient Greeks. Some continuity in culture and in physical type does exist as well as a belief among Greeks in a shared historical experience (Vryonis, 1967: 80–2; Woodhouse, 1984: 11–13). The controversy itself is beyond the scope of this book, but see Vryonis (1978) for an excellent review of it.

3

GOVERNMENT AND POLITICS*

ONE of the main features of Greek society is the changing and unpredictable nature of its politics, including frequent military involvement, political crises, and conflicts between and within the parties. Since 1900 Greece has experienced five international wars, two civil wars (1917–18 and 1946–9), three periods of military/authoritarian rule, ten major military revolts, and periods of foreign occupation during World Wars I and II (Couloumbis, 1980: 24). Although there has been political instability and turmoil in modern Greece, a partial pattern of continuity persisted through the early to mid-1960s among the major political formations in Greece (right, centre, and left) in spite of frequent changes of party labels. Since the 1960s, major changes have occurred in the political parties of Greece. In the previous chapter we examined the political and economic aspects of modern Greek history until the late 1960s. In this chapter we will explore the political developments since the military coup of 1967 by specifically focusing on civil–military relations, the formal and informal political structure (particularly the 1975 Constitution and the patron–client system), and party politics.

CIVIL–MILITARY RELATIONS

In some societies the military élites respect the 'civilian political authority' while in others the military élites assume both political and military roles and become actively involved in national politics. Praetorianism or military political activism is by no means a novel phenomenon. Frequent military involvement in politics characterizes many nations outside the core of developed ones. Indeed the literature on military praetorianism and civil–military relations is extensive.

Historically and in more recent times, the Greek officer corps has

* Betty A. Dobratz is the author of this chapter except for the section on civil–military relations written by Yorgos A. Kourvetaris.

been directly and indirectly involved in national politics. Actual military coups and counter-coups occurred in 1908, 1922, 1926, 1933, 1935, and more recently in 1967. Our purpose here is not to discuss the historical role of the military in politics but rather to look briefly into the most recent praetorian regime in Greece which began 21 April 1967 and lasted until 1974.[1]

Under the leadership of veteran liberal politician George Papandreou, the Centre Union party rose to power in the 1963 national elections. The military thought he was too unreliable and lenient toward the left despite the fact that he was pro-western and anti-communist. In 1964 Andreas Papandreou, the son of George Papandreou, was elected to Parliament. His open criticism of the crown, NATO, and the United States' foreign policy toward Greece alarmed the military. The young Papandreou was seen by the officers as pro-communist.

Uneasiness within the army came to a climax when Prime Minister George Papandreou attempted to remove the Minister of Defence, Petros Garoufalias, a man loyal to the army and the King, but not necessarily to the elected government. An alleged conspiracy within the army known as ASPIDA, which implicated the younger Papandreou, was another reason for the military to distrust the Papandreou government. The ASPIDA conspiracy was thought to be a left-wing movement within the military, but Papandreou's involvement has never been proved.

A contributing factor to military intervention was the Cyprus situation, which reached such dangerous proportions that it almost brought Greece to war with Turkey in 1964. Cyprus became the sore point in Greek–Turkish and Greek–American relations. Especially among the left political forces in Greece, it evolved into an anti-NATO and anti-American issue, which continues to this day. Many officers perceived the anti-NATO and anti-American stand of Andreas Papandreou as a threat to the corporate interests and the *raison d'être* of the military itself. A proposed reduction of the military budget by the Papandreou government also alarmed the military. In retrospect, then, the popularity of the elder Papandreou and the fear of his victory in the scheduled 1967 national elections were important reasons for the coup.

National elections scheduled for May, 1967 never took place owing to the military coup staged one month earlier by a triumvirate of middle-ranking army officers. The staging of the coup was rationalized as a response to perceived communist threats, political corruption, and the decadence of society. The coup-makers adopted the rising phoenix as their symbol, suspended the Constitution, banned the political parties, and ruled by decree. They made an effort to legitimize their rule by naming the new regime the National Revolutionary Government. Although only a small conspiratorial group of officers were actively involved in the actual coup, many more were sympathetic to the goals of the coup. The coup-makers and those who supported them saw themselves as the saviours of Greece and the military as the repository of Greek ideals and Greek Orthodox Christian values.

The seven-year military dictatorship hurt Greece both at home and abroad. Internationally, Greece became isolated in the world community because of its military dictatorship. Its European participation was minimal; it was forced to withdraw from the Council of Europe, and its entrance into the EEC was slowed. The United States, however, was among the first countries to recognize the military junta. Vice-President Agnew visited Greece and praised the National Revolutionary Government; the United States government continued to support the praetorian regime despite Greek and American pressures not to do so. At home, the regime was repressive and torture of dissidents was widespread. Communists, liberal politicians, and critics of the military junta were arrested and imprisoned or exiled in remote Greek islands and villages. In addition, military morale was undermined in the early stages of the junta when widespread purges of some of the brightest officers weakened the cohesion and effectiveness of the armed forces. Efforts to topple the military regime in December 1967 by royalist officers and the King were unsuccessful. King Constantine failed to rally any support among the Greeks, fled to Italy, and later settled in England with his family.

Many officers felt the military dictatorship of 1967 and its attempted coup against Cypriot President Makarios undermined the armed forces' image at home. The military junta in Athens saw Makarios as an obstacle to the union of Cyprus with Greece. On 15 July 1974 the Cypriot National Guard assisted by Greek officers staged a coup against Makarios which encouraged the double invasion of Cyprus by Turkey. Even many Greeks perceived their military leaders as responsible for provoking the Turkish invasion of Cyprus. The Turks claimed they intervened to protect the

Turkish–Cypriot minority. After the 1974 coup they invoked the Treaty of Guarantee of 1959 (part of the Zurich and London Accords) that had designated Turkey, Greece, and Great Britain as protecting powers of Cyprus.

The demise of the Greek military junta was a culmination of various factors. Some of the major ones were foreign criticism, domestic unrest especially as exemplified in the student uprising at the National Polytechnic School, the internal dissension within the military, the abortive coup against President Makarios, and the subsequent Turkish invasion of Cyprus. Since 1974 organizational changes in the armed forces have improved discipline and professional integrity and have restored civil authority over the military. A partial list of those changes includes the imprisonment of the 1967 coup-makers, the forced retirement or dismissal of several officers actively involved in the coup of 1967 and who participated in the military government, and the reinstatement of some officers dismissed during the dictatorship.

Danopoulos (1985a) argues that praetorianism in Greece has not followed the common pattern in which one military intervention succeeds another. Since 1974 both the political and military leaders have played a significant role in keeping the military out of politics. One reason for this is that continuing disputes and tensions between Turkey and Greece over Cyprus and the Aegean have made the military more prudent and have united both political and military leadership. In addition there is the fear of reprisals against coup-makers. Greece is one of the few countries that has tried and punished those officers responsible for the seven-year military dictatorship. Despite the extreme right's effort to release the major coup-makers, the protagonists of the 1967 coup are still in jail. Finally, the post-1974 restoration of parliamentary democracy and the adoption of a new constitution re-established the supremacy of civilian authority over the military.

Since the restoration of democracy in Greece, all civilian governments have supported the corporate interests of the military. In fact, the socialists have turned out to be as supportive of the military's role in defence as were the conservatives. Prime Minister Papandreou, who at one time was also the Minister of National Defence, has made it clear that the military's place is in the barracks. Its role is to defend the nation from external attack, and not to become involved in domestic politics.

Although the military's image has been tarnished, its institutional legitimacy has not been challenged. Civil–military and public opinion about the armed forces is positive. The universal conscription of males, the voluntary enlistment of women into the military, the lack of aristocratic tradition, and the broad social base of the officer corps of the Greek armed forces make civil–military relations relatively harmonious. Greek nationalism and the Turkish threat have contributed to wide support for the Greek armed forces as long as they stay out of politics.

FORMAL POLITICAL STRUCTURE

The military rule of Greece from 1967 to 1974 collapsed when the Greek junta encouraged the Greek–Cypriot military coup against Archbishop Makarios and Turkey invaded Cyprus. In July 1974 the discredited Greek military invited former premier Constantine Karamanlis to return from voluntary exile in France and form a transitional government until elections were held. One of the main concerns was to begin to formulate a new Greek Constitution, which was the caretaker government's first official act. After considerable debate in the newly elected Greek Parliament, the Constitution was approved on 9 June 1975. It follows certain provisions of the 1952 Greek Constitution but incorporates ideas from many liberal constitutions. As a result of a referendum on the return of the monarchy held in December 1974 in which 69 per cent of the Greek people favoured a crownless democracy, the form of government specified in the Constitution is a parliamentary republic. Because of previous restrictions on human rights, the constitution attempted to expand individual freedoms and strengthen social justice. Greek men and women were to have equal rights and equal obligations. The Constitution also tried to make the complicated state bureaucracy more efficient.

In Greece voting is compulsory, universal, and by secret ballot, with all parliamentary elections held simultaneously. Members of Parliament are elected for four years although parliamentary elections may be called more frequently. The size of the Parliament can vary from 200 to 300 members and is currently 300. Members are elected by constituencies based on the population according to the most recent census. Parliament is essentially responsible for the legislative functions. As in the British system, the executive branch or cabinet must maintain the confidence of the Parliament. All laws must be passed by Parliament, including the state budget and the Five-Year Development Plans.

The Prime Minister and the appointed cabinet form the executive branch, referred to as the Government in the Greek Constitution. Generally the leader of the party with the absolute majority of seats in Parliament is appointed Prime Minister. If no absolute majority exists, the leader of a party with the relative majority tries to form a government that will gain the confidence of Parliament. Constitutionally, there are a total of twenty-one ministries that form the cabinet, including national defence, interior, co-ordination, justice, foreign affairs, commerce, finance, agriculture, labour, industry, and energy. (Recent modifications in the number of ministries will be discussed later.) Local Authority Agencies (OTAs) govern municipalities and communities. Administratively the OTA is independent, but the central administration still influences its finances.

There is also provision in the Constitution for a President of the Republic who is elected by Parliament for a five-year term and may be re-elected only once. The President needs a two-thirds majority of the members of Parliament on the first or second ballot; if a third ballot is necessary a three-fifths majority is sufficient. If the candidate does not receive this, Parliament dissolves and new elections are called. The President, a national figure who is to be 'above politics', is involved in many ceremonial functions and charged with regulating the function of the institutions of the republic (Article 30).

The Constitution actually gave considerable powers to the President. In 1985 the socialist party PASOK called for constitutional changes that would transfer power from the President to the Parliament or Prime Minister. All constitutional amendments must be passed by two successive Parliaments before they are official. These changes were endorsed by the Parliament before the June 1985 elections and again by the new Parliament in March 1986. The President no longer has the authority to dismiss the Prime Minister, to dissolve Parliament, to declare a state of emergency, to call for a national referendum, or to grant amnesty for political crimes.

The Supreme Court, composed of eleven judges, is the highest court of appeal. The courts are separated into administrative, civil, and criminal. Civil courts have jurisdiction on all private disputes.

A Council of State makes decisions on administrative disputes, can reverse final rulings of administrative courts, and decides on revisions of disciplinary matters concerning civil servants. A Special Supreme Tribunal serves as final arbiter of conflicts about parliamentary elections and referendums, disputes between courts and administrative authorities, and constitutionality of the laws. The judicial system also includes justices of the peace, magistrates' courts, fifty-nine Courts of First Instance, and two courts of appeal. The Ministry of Justice appoints judges to the Supreme Court, courts of appeal, and the Courts of First Instance. Retirement is compulsory for judges at sixty-five or sixty-seven depending on their positions.

FORMAL STATE BUREAUCRACY VERSUS INFORMAL CLIENTELISM

Two major factors have strongly influenced the development of Greek politics since independence: Greek politics function under the shadow of foreign interference/dependence and the state has emerged as a powerful force used by the parties in power to consolidate their position and expand clientelistic ties (Lyrintzis, 1984). While the two are related, the former will be discussed more thoroughly in the next chapter while the latter will be considered here.

With some outside pressure in the 1800s, Greeks adopted European (Western) formal and rational bureaucratic structure but with less success than many other Western European nations. From the time of the Ottoman Empire, Greeks often relied upon informal, personal means known as client–patron relations rather than on a formal bureaucratic structure to achieve what they wanted. Western Europeans, on the other hand, have tended to accept as legitimate the generalized rules and procedures of bureaucracy.

Ideally 'civil servants shall be the executors of the will of the State and shall serve the people' (House of Parliament, Article 103, Constitution of Greece, 1979: 72–3). In reality state bureaucrats act like mini-czars, manipulating the state for private benefit (Gianaris, 1984: 66). Our interviews with Athenians (Kourvetaris and Dobratz, 1984) showed that many of them feel that public servants are not responsive to citizens' demands: 'The state favors a few of its citizens and does not care about the average Greek citizen'; 'The Greek citizen does not always find his rights fulfilled'; and 'The state authorities do not listen to or grant the rightful demands of the Greek citizen.'

The Greek state bureaucracy has been criticized for being extremely large, centralized, and burdened by enormous amounts of procedural red tape. The great centralization of government authority has led to inefficiency and the waste of valuable resources. Bureaucracy in Athens moves very slowly and is often unable to implement local projects with any degree of efficiency. The framers of the 1975 Constitution recognized this problem and called for decentralization (House of Parliament, Article 101, Constitution of Greece, 1979). Now the state is to supervise local government agencies without infringing their initiative and freedom of action.

The public sector in Greece has had increasing demands placed upon it by members of Greek society to provide jobs and perform a wide range of economic and social services. Some of these pressures are due to the system of clientelism in which the patron or politician is expected to provide a job or a short cut through bureaucratic red tape in exchange for the client's support. To accommodate their loyal supporters, bureaucrats and politicians have filled the public service sector with unneeded personnel. Out of twenty large public and semi-public enterprises, twelve to fourteen had large deficits in recent years primarily through high labour costs, low productivity, and bureaucratic inertia (Gianaris, 1984: 52–3). They are the price of nepotism, favours, difficulty in dismissing civil servants without serious cause, and managerial inefficiency.

When a political party is in power, it may find clientelism an effective means to help maintain and perhaps increase its support. The political party thus in a sense becomes a collective patron (Lyrintzis, 1984). The right was consistently in power from the post-World War II period to the early 1960s and found clientelism to be particularly useful. In the mid-1960s George Papandreou tried to modernize the Centre Union party and weaken political clientelism by creating a modern political organization. In order to accomplish this, debates about policy alternatives rather than on political personalities should take precedence. Loyalty to the party ideology rather than to a person was needed. Trying to transform the Centre Union resulted in both the military and the monarchy feeling threatened. This then helped contribute to the 1967 military coup (Legg, 1973).

Lyrintzis (1984) maintains that the conservative New Democracy Party, in power from 1974 to 1981 and headed mainly by Karamanlis, also wanted to modernize itself but was not able to create a well-structured mass organization. Therefore it remained mainly a party of notables communicating with the people through its clientelistic network. PASOK, the socialist party now in power, may have a better chance of reducing and restricting clientelistic politics. Featherstone (1983) maintains that PASOK has consciously attempted to break away from the traditional party practice of organizing client networks based on an internal hierarchy of dependence. It has tried to establish control over the civil service by terminating about 300 director-generals because they were said to be right-wing appointments. At the same time Papandreou has appointed a similar number of new political advisers who are expected to resign when the government changes. The 'preference cross' which allowed voters to choose between candidates from the same party has recently been abolished. This change increases the power of the party leader, minimizes the voters' choice of candidates from a particular party, reduces the personal power of Members of Parliament, and lessens the extent to which candidates can establish clientelist networks.

PASOK has introduced various packages of legislation to reform the civil service. These measures call for a unified structure of administrative authority to replace the multi-headed one, a reduction of the number of grades in the hierarchy from six to three, the establishment of a unified structure of grades and salaries, and the elimination of multiple employment in the public sector. In spite of this, Lyrintzis (1984: 114) contends that PASOK has failed to institutionalize itself completely and may possibly adopt clientelistic politics as it tries to purge the state machinery of the right-wing elements.

Various reasons have been cited for the development of clientelism in Greek society including the nature of the Greek culture, the perceived atmosphere of scarcity and insecurity, and structural and economic constraints. In addition it has been suggested (Kaufman, 1974; Berman, 1974) that the patron–client model is an extension of world systemic dependence relations. If one looks at Greece within the international world system framework, a pattern of Greek dependency upon protecting powers is apparent, somewhat similar to that of the Greek client depending on the patron.

To a great extent, this foreign dependency has been imposed upon Greece. According to Petras (1977), Greece's position as a client-state within the world capitalist system and the ruling class's dependence upon the West may well limit politicians' ability to develop reformist politics. As Greece moves towards more independence, urbanization, and what may be labelled 'modernization', clientelism appears to be weakening. Yet while clientelism is more fragile than it used to be, it remains a force that influences the political and bureaucratic structures of Greek society.

PARTY POLITICS AFTER 1974[2]

Since the fall of the junta and the return to democracy in Greece, electoral politics have been relatively stable in spite of various problems that have occurred and the changeover to Greece's first elected socialist regime in 1981. Karamanlis laid the groundwork for the elections so fast that the leftists criticized him because they had little time to organize, a necessity because Greek politics is a multi-party affair with great emphasis on dramatic speech-making, sloganeering, and colourful party banners.

The political spectrum can be divided into left, centre, and right with some combinations. Karamanlis, heralded as a saviour of Greek democracy, called his party New Democracy (ND). It is mainly a descendant of ERE, Karamanlis's old party. Karamanlis campaigned on a platform that favoured national unity, strong armed forces, Balkan co-operation, increased trade with Arab countries, independence and territorial integrity for Cyprus, and eventual membership in the European Economic Community (EEC). The EEC application process had been halted during the military junta. One of the slogans that was used during the campaign was 'Karamanlis or the tanks', drawing on the notion that Karamanlis was the only leader strong enough to insure that Greece would remain a democracy and not fall victim to another military junta. The party platform emphasized ND's commitment to achieving a balance between freedom and order and re-establishing parliamentary procedures. ND is conservative and pro-Western, and believes in a unified Europe.

George Papandreou's old liberal Centre Union party of the 1960s was split. Drawing on some of the party's previous support, George Mavros formed the Centre Union–New Forces, a moderate but generally pro-Western party. This party stressed its liberal heritage and continuity by emphasizing its historical ties with Eleftherios Venizelos, the founder and leader of the Liberal Party (1910–36). On many domestic issues it did not differ much from ND although it did use terms like 'participatory democracy', 'Greek social democracy', and 'checks imposed on capital' (Veremis, 1981: 91). It generally agreed with ND on NATO and the EEC, but it emphasized the need for Greece to act more independently, yielding less to foreign pressures. While Karamanlis was neutral on the question of the monarchy, Mavros and the Centre Union–New Forces alliance were against its return.

Andreas Papandreou, imprisoned during the junta and then released due to international outcry, chose to form a new party, the Panhellenic Socialist Movement (PASOK) rather than stay within the old Centre Union fold. While exiled, he had formed the international Panhellenic Liberation Movement (PAK) against the military regime. His party was presented as a new socialist one advocating radical change in Greek society. PASOK tried to integrate three forces in Greek society: (1) the war-time resistance EAM movement, (2) the centre–left faction of the Centre Union, and (3) the forces that developed to fight the junta. The strongest element was probably the PAK group followed by the centre–left of the Centre Union, with EAM membership being the weakest. PASOK may best be described as 'a new force in Greek politics which both achieved an extensive renewal of political personnel and brought new ideas and practices to the Greek party system' (Lyrintzis, 1984: 110). It advocated a Greek road to socialism different from that of the mainstream Western European socialist parties and the communists. In his 3 September 1974 'Declaration of Aims and Principles', Andreas Papandreou proclaimed PASOK to be a movement of the working and underprivileged people of Greece that wanted 'national independence, the sovereignty of the people, social liberation, and democratic processes' (quoted in Featherstone, 1983: 238). He also blamed the US and other foreign countries for Greece's low level of development: 'The root of our holocaust lies in the dependence of our country . . . The economy has been infiltrated and eroded by US and Western multinational companies in cooperation with domestic comprador capital' (quoted in Axt, 1984: 193).

Initially PASOK also rejected membership in the EEC and considered collective self-reliance through the establishment of a common Mediterranean Market, but later it dropped this idea. The party was emphasized as a movement with a populist and third world orientation. The type of socialization PASOK favoured did not necessarily mean nationalization or state ownership, but more often the development of co-operatives, worker self-management, decentralization, and government management of certain enterprises on behalf of the interests of the Greek people.

On the political spectrum PASOK is a new phenomenon representing a centre–left position that is non-Communist in orientation. Also at the left were several segments espousing some elements of Communism. While the Communist movement had certainly been strong as a resistance effort during World War II, the loss of the civil war created grave ideological and organizational problems. The Communist Party (KKE) was outlawed in Greek politics, resulting in the creation of the United Democratic Left (EDA) which still retained links to the Communists who remained in the country and to those who were abroad in Eastern Europe. Conflict within the party often flared between those who remained inside Greece and those outside. During the junta all parties were abolished, and most of the Communists who were able to leave or escape ended up abroad. The ideological differences then became very obvious, resulting in a break in 1968. The KKE leadership retained its pure hard line of pro-Soviet Communism and dependence on Moscow while the dissident group labelled itself the KKE-Interior Party and was more open to Eurocommunism and the unique characteristics of the Greek situation. In spite of these differences, the KKE, KKE-Interior, and EDA did form a coalition for the 1974 election. They advocated an anti-imperialist foreign policy (eliminating NATO and US bases, internationalizing the Cyprus problem, and strengthening Greece's relations with the East) and swifter democratization and dejuntification.

The 1974 election was the first in ten years for the Greek people. Table 3.1 presents the results of the Greek national and European Parliament elections for 1974–84. Karamanlis and New Democracy accomplished a major victory, winning 54 per cent of the vote and 220 seats of the 300-seat Parliament. Karamanlis represented the

TABLE 3.1. *Results of Greek National and European Parliament Elections, 1974–1984*[a]

Political Parties	National Elections 1974 %	Seats	1977 %	Seats	1981 %	Seats	European Parliament 1981 %	Seats	1984 %	Seats
New Democracy (ND)	54.37	220	41.68	172	35.87	115	31.34	8	38.11	9
Panhellenic Socialist Movement (PASOK)	13.58	12	25.31	93	48.07	172	40.12	10	41.58	10
Centre Union/Union of Democratic Centre (EDEK)	20.42	60	12.00	15	0.40	0	1.12	0	0.28	0
Communist Party of Greece (KKE)	9.47[c]	8	9.29	11	10.93	13	12.84	3	11.62	3
Communist Party of Greece Interior (KKE-Es)			2.70[d]	2	1.34	0	5.29	1	3.42	1
Party of Dem. Socialism KAE – Agricultural Party (KODISO)[b]					0.70	0	4.25	1	0.80	0
Nat'l Dem. Union[e] (EDE)	1.08	0								
Nat'l Alignment[e] (EP)			6.84	5						
Neoliberals[b] (KNF)			1.09	2						
Progressives[e] (KP)					1.68	0	1.95	1	0.17	0
Party of Liberals[b]					0.36	0	1.04	0	0.35	0
Christian Democracy[b]					0.15	0	1.14	0		
Nat'l Political Union[e] EPEN									2.29	1

[a] Only parties receiving at least one per cent of the vote in one of the elections are listed.
[b] Indicates a moderate party.
[c] In 1974 these two Communist parties and the EDA combined together.
[d] In 1977 the Communist Party of Greece Interior was allied with four small centre-left groups.
[e] Indicates a party of the extreme right.
Sources: Dimitras, 1983, 1984a; Clogg, 1982; *Yearbook* 1982; Dobratz, 1985.

idea of stability that most Greeks seem to have wanted after the uncertainties of the 1965–7 period and the seven-year military regime. Second in terms of support was the Centre Union–New Forces, with 20 per cent of the vote and sixty seats in Parliament. PASOK could probably be considered a disappointing third with about 13.5 per cent of the vote and twelve seats. The United Left, combining the Communist elements, received about 9.5 per cent of the vote and the remaining eight seats in Parliament.

Karamanlis and ND thus formed the first elected government after the fall of the junta. Parliament ratified the Constitution of 11 June 1975, and then elected Constantine Tsatsos, a distinguished philosopher, academic, and ND politician, Greece's first President of the republic after the passage of the Constitution. Michalis Stasinopoulos had been President before the adoption of the Constitution. The ND government basically concentrated its efforts on four areas: (1) solidifying and strengthening democracy, (2) bringing about economic development, (3) reforming the educational system, and (4) dealing with foreign policy issues particularly over Cyprus, Greek–Turkish relations, and entry into the EEC (Loulis, 1981).

Karamanlis was quite successful in re-establishing democracy in Greece. Instead of adopting a simplistic anti-Communist repressive approach that ERE, his previous party, had taken, Karamanlis legalized the Communist Party, making it a legitimate force in Greek society. Holding a referendum in which the issue of the reinstatement of the monarchy was voted down seems to have signalled the end to this divisive feature of Greek politics. The military was disengaged from politics and generally the major torturers and the leaders of the coup, the military regime, and the violence at the National Polytechnic School, were arrested and tried. After the election of Karamanlis there were some junta attempts to seize power, principally the 'conspiracy of the thirty-nine' in 1975 February, but all these failed.

Greece faced socio-economic problems that were severe, deep-rooted, and difficult to solve: inflation, overdevelopment of the construction sector and underdevelopment of manufacturing, over-expansion of the public sector, low productivity, and widening balance of payments deficit (Loulis, 1981: 67). Reforms in taxation policies and income distribution were introduced. Inflation was temporarily reduced to 13.3 per cent during 1975–6, and industrial production increased by 4.4 per cent in 1975 and 10.6 per cent in 1976. Because of the perceived need for a strong military, Greece was spending about 6.5 per cent of the national income on defence (Loulis, 1981: 65). Some progress was made in education although problems remain (see ch. 6 for more detail). No real advances were made on the Cyprus issue, but Karamanlis was able successfully to lay the groundwork for full accession to the EEC.

In spite of its accomplishments, ND encountered various problems. Organizationally Karamanlis had wanted ND to transform itself into a modern mass party similar to those of other Western European nations. Instead ND continued to rely on clientelistic ties to the people and failed to develop a grass roots organizational structure. Power remained in the hands of the party leadership (Loulis, 1981; Lyrintzis, 1984). Karamanlis requested that elections be held early (in three years rather than four) because Greece faced major national problems especially over Greek–Turkish relations and EEC membership, and the government thus needed a new mandate from the people. Most likely, Karamanlis realized his support was declining and wished to stage elections while his party and personal appeal were still relatively strong. Critical forces from both the extreme right and the left were mounting.

The left wing of the political spectrum was faced with decisions about whether to unite in opposition to ND or to be independent elements. While originally there were attempts to unify around PASOK, Andreas Papandreou broke them off, claiming that the other parties tried to minimize the class and political contradictions in Greek society. KKE then rejected other overtures from various parties of the left and decided to run independently. The other significant remaining force was KKE-Interior, which did align with four smaller parties—EDA, Socialist Initiative (former members of the Centre-Union–New Forces), Socialist March (former members of PASOK), and Christian Democracy (Christian intellectuals with left leanings).

As the campaign for the votes of the Greek people intensified, everywhere one could see PASOK's green and white posters, banners, and stickers, and ND's blue ones followed by the red campaign material of the Communists and finally the Union of Democratic Centre's orange and blue. The Centre Union–New Forces had changed its name to the Union of the Democratic Centre (EDIK). Each party presented slogans and held rallies to capture the attention of the people. ND had the image of Karamanlis, its relatively moderate ideology, and its record to support it. ND's lack of grass-roots organization and its static image were perhaps its major handicaps. Two of ND's slogans illustrating its static tendency were 'ND: The Great Guarantee' which stressed security and 'ND Found Chaos. It Created a State', which emphasized the past (Loulis, 1981: 75). One of Karamanlis's favourite statements —'Greece Belongs to the West'—also did not sit particularly well with many nationalistic Greeks who were very concerned about the failure to make any progress in Cyprus.

EDIK suffered also from disorganization, compounded by internal disputes and the lack of a charismatic leader. Mavros, a respectable gentleman and a highly-regarded politician especially in the area of foreign affairs, could not finally compete with the wise Greek father or saviour image of Karamanlis or the challenging son–redeemer image of Andreas Papandreou who was taking his case to the people (Veremis, 1981; Elephantis, 1981). EDIK's clearest difference with PASOK was over EEC membership with EDIK strongly favouring it and PASOK still questioning it. Mavros's major attack on the government was over Cyprus which he saw as an international problem that should be referred to the UN rather than handled as a Greek–Turkish matter. EDIK's slogan 'For change with certainty/security' seemed contradictory and did not capture people's imagination (Veremis, 1981).

PASOK appeared to be the one force that offered something new. Petras (1977: 23) viewed it as the 'newest and most dynamic of the leftist forces'. It stressed nationalism and was critical of US domination through NATO, American military bases in Greece, and European domination through EEC. 'Greece Belongs to the Greeks' was one of its slogans. Unlike ND and EDIK, between 1974 and 1977 PASOK had developed strong grass roots support at the central, regional, local, and cell levels. In spite of this, many (Elephantis, 1981; Featherstone, 1983; Lyrintzis, 1984) suggest that the policy and decision-making process rested in the hands of one individual, Andreas Papandreou.

In the mid-1970s the party platform of the Panhellenic Socialist Movement (1976) proposed restructuring Greek politics and society. It advocated: (1) the application of the UN charter on human rights to the citizen's basic rights; (2) equality of both sexes in social and economic sectors; (3) participation of all citizens in the country's political life; (4) the right of work for all citizens; (5) greater autonomy of trade unions; (6) the separation of church from state with monastic fortunes being socialized; (7) the socialization of the financing system, banks, and the major import and export trade organizations; (8) the decentralization of the country into regions; (9) the right to reject participation in economic, political, and military coalitions which undermine Greece's national independence and the Greek people's sovereign rights; (10) cancellation of previous international agreements and contracts disadvantageous to Greece; (11) free and compulsory education; and (12) socialization of health care with all Greeks enjoying free medical, pharmaceutical, and hospital treatment, as well as pensions.

Although PASOK continued its strong nationalistic appeal and remained critical of the US and NATO, it generally moderated its position before the 1977 elections. While PASOK had originally called itself a socialist movement that used Marxist theory and method while rejecting Leninist principles, references to Marxism declined as the election approached. Although Andreas Papandreou referred to 'socialization of monopolies', the word socialism was used less and less.

KKE directed much of its campaign toward its communist or formerly communist membership. It displayed red flags with the hammer and sickle, sang revolutionary and resistance songs, and made constant reference to the heroes of the resistance and civil war. It strongly opposed NATO and EEC membership and favoured the claims of the workers. The bulk of its vote came from the working class, especially trade union members and students. The alliance centring around KKE-Interior stressed unity rather than polarization of the left and the right. KKE-Interior was critical of the 'isolationism' of KKE and of PASOK's 'anti-unity' strategy. At times it seemed to support ND. Thus it in turn was criticized as the 'Karamanlist left' with a policy based on 'unity without principles' (Papayannakis, 1981: 154).

Table 3.1 shows the election results for 1977. ND remained the party in power with 42 per cent of the vote and 172 parliamentary seats. However, it lost about 13 per cent of its vote, most likely to both PASOK (on the left) and the newly-formed right-wing Nationalist Front (EP). The latter won about 7 per cent of the vote and five seats. PASOK almost doubled its vote and increased its seats dramatically from twelve to ninety-three. EDIK declined, especially in terms of its parliamentary seats. It was the KKE that showed its dominance over the other left-wing forces receiving more parliamentary seats and almost the same percentage of votes as the United Left coalition in 1974.

Karamanlis and ND would therefore remain in power while Papandreou and PASOK became the primary opposition. ND continued to rely on bureaucratic clientelism, plagued by internal divisions and failure to generate a workable and dynamic new programme (Loulis, 1981; Lyrintzis, 1984). Greece could do little to bring about change in the Cyprus tragedy, and resentment toward the US continued particularly in relation to the presence of American bases and NATO. The socialist party under Andreas Papandreou was clearly gaining ground, and it was extremely unlikely that Greece would rejoin the military side of NATO if Papandreou were in power. Achieving the reintegration of Greece into NATO was not easy, however. Turkey as well as the other member nations had to consent. Only after a successful military coup did Turkey accept the controversial 'Rogers Plan', which allowed the reintegration of Greece into NATO but did not settle the question of NATO command and control of the Aegean. Greece wanted the operational command established as it was before 1974, but Turkey refused, having challenged Greek rights to certain islands and the continental shelf. PASOK and Andreas Papandreou criticized the agreement as one that hurt Greek sovereignty. By the time Greece was reintegrated into NATO, Karamanlis had resigned his position as Premier and had become President of the Republic (May, 1980). Rallis was elected head of the ND and became Premier. ND negotiated Greece's full membership in EEC effective 1 January 1981. The leftist parties remained critical of the pro-Western stance of ND.

In line with the Constitution, elections were called for October 1981, almost four years after the previous elections. ND had lost its charismatic leader Karamanlis, who as President of the republic chose to remain above politics. ND under Rallis failed to offer the people anything new. Papandreou and PASOK capitalized on ND's stagnant image by using the slogan 'Change' (*Allaghi*). At the same time PASOK continued to moderate its position on numerous issues. Andreas Papandreou portrayed himself as champion of the non-privileged against the privileged, and offered assurances to

Greeks with a house, car, and perhaps a small business that they would not lose anything if a PASOK government were elected. In general, PASOK can be characterized as follows: (1) its leader/founder has great charisma and continues to dominate the party; (2) it has an extensive grass roots organization; (3) it has cross-class nationwide appeal resulting in heterogeneous support; and (4) the party ideology can be labelled flexible, eclectic, and sometimes inconsistent owing in part to its attempt to appeal to a broad spectrum of people (Featherstone, 1983).

Given its previous success KKE remained an independent political force on the left. After 1977 EDIK continued in disarray. George Mavros (who eventually joined PASOK) was replaced by John Zigdis, a deputy from the island of Rhodes. He, however, came into conflict with some of the other politicians in EDIK. Some joined ND and others formed the Party for Democratic Socialism (KODISO). Results of the October 1981 elections show that the Greeks, probably owing in large part to the continuing unsettled problems over Cyprus and the Aegean and the worsening economic situation, moved toward the left and elected their first socialist government. As again shown in Table 3.1, Papandreou-led PASOK received 48 per cent of the vote and 172 of the 300 seats in Parliament, followed by ND with 36 per cent of the vote and 115 seats and the Communist Party with 11 per cent of the vote and thirteen seats. No other party received any seats in the Parliament.

EDIK did not even receive 1 per cent of the vote. For several reasons, the bottom fell out of the centre. It suffered for its inability to distinguish itself adequately from both ND to the right and PASOK to the left, the internal divisions between the old Centre Union notables and the newer elements entering the party, the lack of charismatic leadership, and the absence of an effective organization and political machine to make contact with the people and bring about reform (Veremis, 1981).

During the national elections Greece, as a full member of EEC, participated for the first time in the European Parliament voting. These results show somewhat different voting patterns, most likely because of the different electoral voting systems used (Table 3.1). The Greek national election uses the reinforced proportional system which heavily favours the larger parties. For example, in the 1977 election ND got 42 per cent of the vote but 57 per cent of the seats while in 1981 PASOK got 48 per cent of the vote and 57 per cent of the seats. The system is rather complicated with three distributions of the seats[3] and another twelve seats being reserved for state deputies. In the 1981 elections only parties that received at least 17 per cent of the vote were eligible for the second and third rounds of distribution and for the state deputies. Candidates for state deputies do not belong to a particular geographical district nor do they compete *per se* in the elections. They are elected in proportion to the nationwide success of the party that nominated them. Table 3.2 shows the results of the 1981 election according to the three allocations and for the state deputies. Only PASOK and ND participated in the second and third distribution of seats. While certain electoral reforms were passed for the 1985 election, one of the messages implicit in a reinforced proportional system is that voting for small parties in the national elections may not have much impact on the final results.

TABLE 3.2. *Distribution of Seats in the Parliamentary Elections of 1981*

Political Parties	First Distribution	Second Distribution	Third Distribution	State Deputies	Total
PASOK	140	19	6	7	172
New Democracy	95	12	3	5	115
Communist Party of Greece	13	—	—	—	13

Source: Clogg, 1982: 97.

This, however, is not the case for the European Parliament elections which use a simple proportional representation system. Thus, again looking back at Table 3.1 and comparing the results of the two 1981 elections, one can see that ND and especially PASOK received a lower percentage of votes in the European Parliament elections. PASOK's vote declined by about 8 per cent and ND's by about 4.5 per cent. KKE increased its support about 2 per cent while two other small parties gained significantly. KKE-Interior increased its strength fourfold and KODISO-KAE, a coalition of the Party of Democratic Socialism and the Party of Peasants and Workers, increased sixfold. While PASOK had ten seats, ND had eight, KKE three, and KKE-Interior, KODISO-KAE, and the extreme right KP one each.

THE PASOK PROGRAMME

The transition of power to PASOK and Andreas Papandreou went quite smoothly. Papandreou (1981: 1) announced his programme to Parliament on 22 November 1981: 'National independence, territorial integrity, popular sovereignty and democracy, self-supporting economic and social development, a cultural revival, the revivification of the countryside, the radical improvement of the quality of life in the towns and in the villages, social justice and, finally, social liberation are the targets of our government and set the course we are to follow. The course of change will be a long one.' Andreas Papandreou and PASOK have had to confront the problem of 'realizing far-reaching goals and a radical change without social, economic, and political disruptions' (Axt, 1984: 196). One of the more novel and interesting features of PASOK's programme was the idea to 'socialize' entire segments of the economy, although quite a large proportion of them were already under direct or indirect state control. The purpose of socializing these enterprises was to make them more responsive to both consumers and employees. Reforms were initiated in education, social welfare, labour unions, wages and salaries, and the state machinery (Papandreou, 1981; Clogg, 1982).

Some problematic industries near bankruptcy, and the pharmaceutical and arms industries, have been socialized. In 1982 legislation was passed enlarging the rights of workers and trade unions and forbidding lockouts, although in 1983 another law made it particularly difficult for trade unions to strike. Wages were increased but later, a wage freeze was introduced, and then a wage and salary indexation policy was implemented. In 1985 the economic austerity measures limited the use of the indexation. Supervisory councils, referred to as consultative councils, have been established to give workers some participation although the system is different from the self-management found in Yugoslavia (Axt, 1984: 199).

In foreign affairs Andreas Papandreou (1981: 19) called for 'an independent and truly multidimensional Greek foreign policy'. The idea is that Greek strategic, economic, and political concerns rather than loyalty to one nation or alliance should influence Greek foreign policy. Since the return to civilian government in 1974 Greece has probably reduced its dependency on America and improved its relations with many nations, including Yugoslavia and other Balkan states and the Soviet Union.

Greece's relations within NATO under the Andreas Papandreou administration have been tense. In 1981 the Prime Minister described the relations in these words: 'For Greece, NATO has an altogether different meaning than for the other European countries. For us NATO is associated with the bitter experiences of US intervention in Greek affairs, the apostasy of 1965, the 1967 military coup, the Turkish invasion of Cyprus in 1974 and steady support to Turkish aggressiveness for all these years' (Panhellenic Socialist Movement, nd: 36 [from *To Vima, 23* April 1981]). Andreas Papandreou went on to note that NATO assumes that the threat to various countries comes from the Warsaw Pact to the north of Greece. However, for Greece the perceived threat is clearly from the east, that is from Turkey, another NATO country.

Another major Greek–American controversy has centred upon the American bases in Greece. Negotiations on the bases were completed in July 1983. Andreas Papandreou (Committee on Foreign Affairs, US House Hearing 1983: 41) noted that the agreement was 'literally unique', proved Greece's national independence, and fulfilled the fundamental goals of PASOK. The agreement extended the lease of the American bases but made the lease terminable after five years by either party upon written notice to the other. Should it be terminated, the US would then have seventeen months to withdraw. The Greek leader thus maintained that the agreement had an expiration date and a time schedule for removal of the bases. He told the Greek people (Committee on Foreign Affairs, US House Hearing, 1983: 43): 'The signing of this agreement constitutes a historic step in safeguarding our country's national independence, in establishing the principle that—irrespective of the size or power of countries—Greece is an equal member of the international community.'

Although Andreas Papandreou initially favoured a Mediterranean economic community and later maintained that EEC membership should be put to the Greek people in a referendum, he seems now to have accepted Greek membership and is pushing for Greece to have a special relationship within the EEC. Indeed, he recently stated that from an economic point of view, withdrawal of Greece from the EEC would be a disaster. In 1982 the Greek government sent a memorandum to the EEC asking for greater financial assistance and for modification of Greece's status, including exemptions from Community regulations that would restrict its development. In a partial response in February 1983 the EEC Commission permitted Greece to block imports of eight categories of products from its members. In March 1983 the Commission responded quite favourably to the memorandum although some differences remained. The Commission accepted PASOK's five-year economic plan, which included certain protections to small Greek businesses which were contradictory to the EEC rules about competition. The Greek government then announced it would remain in the EEC. Some problems still need to be settled within the context of EEC policy on Mediterranean countries, particularly with the admission of Spain and Portugal.

While PASOK initially developed a platform that stressed national independence and identified the enemy as foreign (especially American) multinational capital and imperialism, the volatile issues of withdrawal from NATO and the EEC and the removal of US military bases from Greece have toned down. The government recognizes that transitional periods are necessary before the bases can be dismantled or Greece can leave NATO. Greece will remain in NATO as long as it benefits Greek interests; ideally both NATO and the Soviet military bloc will be abolished in the future.

THE 1984–1986 POLITICAL SCENE

After Rallis's defeat in the 1981 election, ND had a new election for its party leader resulting in the victory of Evangelos Averoff on 9 December 1981. Like Rallis, the former Minister of Defence Averoff was not a particularly charismatic leader. ND and Averoff were tested politically in the June 1984 European Parliament election that was the forerunner of the 1985 national elections. Averoff campaigned that there was to be a choice between 'the forces of progress, welfare, democracy and freedom' and those 'of darkness and totalitarianism' (Dimitras, 1984a). ND used the slogan disengagement (*apallaghi*), meaning an end to the changes of PASOK. PASOK, on the other hand, continued to capitalize on the charismatic appeal of Andreas Papandreou and reminded the people of the negative aspects of the previous conservative governments. Slogans such as 'Greece comes first' and 'Greece for the Greeks' appealed to Greek nationalism. While the previous elections had involved vigorous campaigning, these included some elements of physical and verbal violence reminiscent of the pre-junta period.

In the June 1984 European Parliament election neither of the two major parties did as well as they had probably hoped (Table 3.1). PASOK retained ten seats, ND gained one to achieve a total of nine, and KKE kept its three seats. The main three parties continued to show their dominance of the political scene, gaining more than 91 per cent of the vote. KKE-Interior and the National Political Union (EPEN) each won a seat. EPEN is an extreme right party headed by George Papadopoulos, who is the former military junta leader still in prison. PASOK again received the highest percentage of the vote—41.6 per cent, almost 1.5 per cent higher than the previous European Parliament election but less than its 1981 national election total. ND gained almost 7 per cent more of the votes than it did in the 1981 European Parliament election and 2 per cent more than in the 1981 national elections. It still, however, remained second.

Owing in part to ND's dissatisfaction with the European Parliament election results, the party held another election for president in September 1984. This resulted in a victory for Constantine Mitsotakis, who was first elected to Parliament in 1946. Athenian public opinion polls (Dimitras, 1984b) show him to be more popular than his predecessors Rallis and Averoff although not as popular as Andreas Papandreou and Karamanlis. One questionable part of Mitsotakis's past is his role in the events of 1965 when George Papandreou resigned as prime minister. Forty deputies, including Mitsotakis, who had been Minister of Finance in 1963–4, left the Centre Union party and supported the new government appointed by the King. Those loyal to George Papandreou and the Centre Union labelled them 'apostates'. In 1965 Mitsotakis became Minister of Co-ordination under Stefanopoulos's caretaker government. In an October 1984 survey, 63 per cent of the Athenians interviewed felt Mitsotakis's role in the events of 1965 was a disadvantage while only 8 per cent believed it an advantage, 27 per cent neither, and 2 per cent didn't know (Dimitras, 1984b). Andreas Papandreou was upset with Mitsotakis's election victory and labelled him a 'traitor'.

The ND platform has remained similar to the one Karamanlis

expounded although it also reflects Mitsotakis's political orientation. It includes the idea that 'the place of Greece is in the Western world, with which it has long had political, economic and defence ties' (Nea Domokratia, 1984: 2) and also advances the 'principles of the pluralistic parliamentary democracy as developed and applied in the West' (Nea Demokratia, 1984: 1). Regarding economic policy ND recognizes the importance of private initiative and the need to encourage it to meet the public interests. Some state intervention in the economy is necessary in areas where private initiative is lacking and where it is essential to develop the national economy.

The possible re-election of Karamanlis as President of the Republic became a controversial issue within PASOK because according to one opinion poll less than half its supporters wanted to see Karamanlis re-elected. Those who favoured ND almost unanimously supported his re-election, but the Communists unanimously criticized it (Dimitras, 1985b: 13). In early March 1985 President Karamanlis resigned when PASOK decided to nominate Supreme Court Judge Christos Sartzetakis for President of the Republic. According to the Constitution a two-thirds vote of parliament for President is needed in the first two ballots for President while on the third ballot 60 per cent is needed. On 29 March in the controversial third balloting Sartzetakis received exactly 60 per cent or 180 votes of 300. New Democracy protested the vote of Acting President of the Republic Yannis Alevras. ND claimed this Member of Parliament could no longer vote because he had become acting president. Initially Mitsotakis refused to recognize the election of Sartzetakis. In spite of this, Sartzetakis became the fourth President of the Republic since the restoration of democracy in 1974 and the third since the 1975 Constitution was passed. Sartzetakis, the investigator in the Lambrakis murder on which the film *Z* is based, is well known for his honesty.

As previously noted, PASOK and Papandreou proposed amendments to the Constitution to limit the President's discretionary powers. Constitutional changes require two separate votes in one Parliament followed by a vote in the next (new) Parliament before they are officially ratified. Votes in April and May 1985 supported the amendments. After that, Prime Minister Papandreou requested that Parliament dissolve and that new elections be called in June owing to the Cyprus crisis and the need for these constitutional amendments.

For approximately one month the Greek election campaign was in full swing with electioneering and colourful rallies throughout Greece. Typical for the Greek press, the campaign reporting was extremely partisan. Various Greek newspapers can be categorized according to their political preference (e.g. pro-government, opposition, conservative, communist). The Greek television and radio system (ERT) is state-controlled. Each party was allotted a certain amount of TV time depending upon the party's strength. Political advertising is not allowed on television. In this election the parties also agreed to limit posters and banners, the honking of horns, and use of loudspeakers.

The new 1985 PASOK platform stressed that during the first four-year term great leaps and innumerable small steps had been made and a new four-year term of change was needed to bring about a greater sense of national independence, a consolidated democracy and stronger popular sovereignty, and a welfare state that provides care for the individual and improves the standard of living (Panhellenic Socialist Movement, 1985: 1). The socialist search for Greek identity could best be expressed as follows: 'We are struggling for a Greece in which the decisions will be taken by the people themselves, without foreign dependencies, influences or interventions, for a just society, where the exploitation of man by man and his estrangement from the product of his toil will cease. A society which will allow individuals to reach self-realization intellectually and culturally, and to creatively develop their initiatives'. (Panhellenic Socialist Movement, 1985: 2.)

Mitsotakis tried in his campaign to portray ND as a liberal party and thus to attract voters from the centre. PASOK, however, countered with the slogan 'The people know what the right wing means'. The New Democracy (1985) platform called for a free economy, freedom of choice in the market, and the abolition of both state and private monopolies. It recommended competition between the state and the private sector over provision of social services and public utilities. The party favoured membership in NATO, but advocated that Lemnos must be part of NATO military manœuvres in order for Greece to participate. EEC membership was viewed as a political as well as an economic alliance. Probably in an attempt to gain votes, ND proposed substantial tax reductions in all income categories and raising the tax-free income limits.

Florakis (1985), the leader of KKE, criticized PASOK for abandoning its 1981 platform that called for removing nuclear weapons, nationalizing basic sectors, and having a referendum on membership in the EEC. He argued that Greeks should not support one of the two main parties, but rather should vote for KKE which is the only party of true change. KKE continues to favour withdrawing from NATO and the EEC and removing nuclear weapons from Greece. It wants to annul the 1983 bases agreement between the US and Greece. The public sector is to be the key element developing an economy that should be anti-monopolistic and anti-imperialist (Communist Party of Greece (KKE), 1985).

For this election, the smaller parties tended to ally themselves with the two major parties. EDIK and its leader Zigdis as well as former leader Mavros supported PASOK. So did EDA led by M. Glezos and the Christian Democractic Party headed by N. Psaroudakis. The KODISO party of Democratic Socialism and its founder I. Pezmazoglou co-operated with ND although its youth group did not.

TABLE 3.3. *Results of the 1985 Greek National Elections*

Parties	Results		
	Total Votes	%	Seats in Parliament
Panhellenic Socialist Movement (PASOK)	2,916,450	45.82	161
New Democracy (ND)	2,599,949	40.85	126
Communist Party of Greece (KKE)	629,518	9.89	12
Communist Party of Greece Interior (KKE-Es)	117,050	1.84	1
Other parties	102,073	1.60	0

Source: Embassy of Greece, Press Office, Washington, DC, 10 June 1985: *Greece The Week in Review*, 1.

Election results of 2 June 1985, generally were favourable to Papandreou and PASOK (Table 3.3). PASOK received nearly 46 per cent of the vote and 161 seats of the 300-member Parliament. This did, however, represent a decline of about 2 per cent of the vote from that of the 1981 national elections. New Democracy gained several seats and about 5 per cent of the vote making its total 41 per cent and 126 seats. The Communist Party lost one seat and about 1 per cent of the vote. The Communist Party of the

Interior was the only other party to win a seat. The juntist EPEN was able to gain only .6 per cent of the vote.

PASOK continued to appeal to a wide variety of people. It received about 45 per cent of the vote in urban and semi-urban regions and 47 per cent in the rural areas. The residents of the islands of Greece were particularly likely to support PASOK, while the socialist losses (from 1981 to 1985) were most likely in or near Athens and in Salonica. ND, on the other hand, gained increasing support from urban areas and was especially strong in southern and eastern Peloponnese, central Greece, southern Epirus, and northern Greece (Macedonia and Thrace). Although voters for KKE are most likely to be from the islands, Greater Athens, Greater Salonica, and Thessaly, the overall Communist support in these areas declined from 1981 to 1985. KKE did manage to increase its strength in certain areas where it had previously been quite weak. As before, KKE-Interior's strength was in urban areas (Dimitras, 1985c).

This national election marked two firsts: eighteen-year-olds participated, and people voted for party lists rather than individual candidates. PASOK's margin of victory was sufficient for it to capture a majority of seats in the Parliament and thus not need to form a coalition with another party. PASOK's areas of strength appear to be in health and welfare, foreign policy, increases in salaries and pensions, improvement of information on radio and television, and education. While most Greeks did not believe that PASOK was very efficient in fighting unemployment or inflation, they felt ND would be even worse (Dimitras, 1985b).

On 5 June 1985 the Papandreou-led government was sworn in by President Sartzetakis. The new cabinet consisted of nineteen ministers and under-secretaries serving only on a provisional basis until Parliament passed legislation to limit substantially or merge the fifty-two ministerial posts. On 17 June the new 300-member Parliament was sworn in, and then on 22 June Prime Minister Papandreou presented his government policy to Parliament. After debate about the policy statement, the government was given a vote of confidence of 161 votes to 138.

In July Parliament passed legislation for a smaller and more efficient governmental structure that included the Prime Minister, Vice-Premier, Minister to the Prime Minister and eighteen other ministry positions as well as several alternates and under-secretaries. The ministry for the Aegean was a newly created position to highlight the importance of that region. Papandreou remained head of Defence. The restructured government had ten fewer people than the previous one, with eleven persons holding government offices for the first time. Some major changes included former Foreign Minister Yannis Haralambopoulos becoming Vice Premier while K. Papoulias became Foreign Minister. G. Arsenis was replaced as head of the Ministry of National Economy by former Agriculture Minister Kostas Simitis. The government was sworn in on 26 July 1985. In April 1986 Papandreou again reshuffled the cabinet and relinquished the portfolio of defence. Haralambopoulos was named Defence Minister and the public order position which had been joined with the Interior Ministry in 1985 was again separated, probably reflecting the government's concern with incidents of violence. No changes were made in foreign or economic posts.

In August 1985 the ND party encountered internal dissension, particularly over the scheduling of the national party congress. Mitsotakis resigned from the party leadership but was re-elected, receiving eighty-two votes with thirty-seven abstentions. Kostas Stephanopoulos, generally regarded as a conservative, and several others resigned from the party and formed the Democratic Renewal Party. Stephanopoulos called for improving relations with the west and preserving Greek cultural traditions and the Greek Orthodox faith. The split of the Democratic Renewal Party from New Democracy indicates one source of dissension and fragmentation within Greek politics.

In October 1985 Papandreou announced a series of stabilization measures for the economy to deal with Greek economic problems. His economic programme met with opposition from both right and left parties. There were mass protests against the measures, but PASOK generally has remained committed to fighting inflation and reducing the balance of payments problem. Results of a November 1985 opinion poll in Athens show a decline in support for the government probably in large part due to its austerity measures (Dimitras, 1985e). A slight majority (52 per cent) of the Athenians surveyed believed that the measures were unjustifiable while 46 per cent believed they were unavoidable because of the economic problems (2 per cent didn't know).

In February 1986 ND held its second Congress in Thessaloniki and supported Mitsotakis's position. Mitsotakis expressed his doubts about the government's economic policy and claimed there would be no recovery in spite of the favourable international economic situation (reduction of oil price and decline of the dollar). He predicted that an economic crisis would be inevitable in the next year or so because PASOK is destroying confidence and possibilities for investments (Athens News Agency, 1986a: 1–2).

In order to draw on the possible discontent of the Greek voters due particularly to the economic austerity measures, New Democracy put forth very strong politicians in the October 1986 municipal elections where candidates needed to achieve a majority of the votes to be declared the winner. Since Greece has a multi-party political system, it is often difficult for a candidate to gain 50 per cent of the vote on the first round so run-offs between the top two candidates occur a week after the initial electoral contest. In 1986 215 of 303 municipalities had run-off elections.

New Democracy was able to win in Athens, Thessaloniki, and Piraeus—the three largest Greek cities. In Athens Miltiades Evert gained nearly 55 per cent of the vote in the run-off against Dimitris Beis, the socialist mayor of Athens since 1978. Evert had been a Member of the Greek Parliament since 1974 and served as Minister of Manufacturing from 1977 to 1980 and of Finance from 1980 to 1981 when New Democracy was in power. In the prefecture capitals, PASOK won 31 (61 per cent), ND 13 (25 per cent), KKE 5 (10 per cent), and others 2 (4 per cent). Nationwide, citizens in other municipalities elected 146 mayors from PASOK (48.2 per cent), 78 candidates from New Democracy (25.7 per cent), 53 from the Communist Party (17.5 per cent), and 26 who were independents or supported by the Communist Party Interior (8.6 per cent) (Greek Press and Information Office, London, 1986: 1). The ND party charged the government distorted the election results claiming that it had supported 93 mayors who were victorious (Athens News Agency, 1986b). In the run-offs the Communists, particularly in Athens, did not support the socialist candidates in part owing to PASOK's unwillingness to amend the national electoral laws that still favour the two largest parties. Many blank ballots were cast especially in the larger cities. Shortly after the municipal elections, Florakis, the leader of the Communist Party, met Prime Minister Papandreou to stress concern about the standard of living of the low income earners, problems in the trade union movement, and the need to establish a simple proportional representation.

While municipal elections are not typically very accurate

indicators of national parliamentary election results, still it is apparent that many voters, particularly in urban areas, were not satisfied with PASOK's policies. Mitsotakis, the leader of New Democracy, claimed that the municipal election results were not simply a vote of protest but also one of condemnation of the present government policy. On the other hand, Prime Minister Papandreou noted that the municipal results signalled 'significant messages from the people to the government, but not solely to the government'. In spite of the difficult economic conditions, he assured each citizen that 'we will respond to his desires, and expectations, and we will proceed decisively to the completion of the course towards the great change with new, fast and decisive paces' (Athens News Agency, 1986c: 2). The cabinet was restructured with changes in the Ministries of Industry, Energy and Technology, of Labour, of Transport and Communications, and of Commerce. Numerous under-secretary posts were eliminated reducing the total membership of the cabinet from 49 to 36. The changes were hoped to lead to greater administrative efficiency and greater contact with the public. However, Papandreou indicated there would be no major changes in the government's foreign or domestic policies including the economic stabilization measures.

Accomplishments and Criticisms of PASOK

In general PASOK has made several significant changes in politics and society which, although not necessarily radical transformations, have had liberalizing effects:

The development of relatively good relations with the military through assurance that they had nothing to fear from the socialist government and emphasis on their importance *vis-à-vis* the threat from Turkey. Military expenditures are a major part of the national budget.

The recognition of the National Resistance Movement during World War II and the contributions of the Communists and others including extending them pension rights.

Promotion of decentralization and popular participation through provisions for local self-government and the establishment of prefectural councils and popular conventions.

Although not always consistent, measures to work toward freer and more independent trade unions.

The greater participation of youth in social, educational, and political processes, including recognition of students' rights to participate in educational decision-making and the legalization of the right to vote for eighteen year olds.

Laws providing for equality of the sexes and the modernization of the Family Code. Civil marriages and divorces are now possible; adultery is no longer a criminal offense.

The establishment of a national health system and control of the production and distribution of medicine. By October, 1985, there were seventy-two health centres in operation with another eighty-two near completion.

The raising of pensions and improvement of the social welfare system.

Provisions for the development and organization of the farmers' cooperative movement.

The abolition of the 'preference cross' in voting that should reduce clientelistic ties and enhance the party's power.

The formulation of a new electoral law and representation system for the 1985 elections which allows all parties to participate in the first two distributions of seats.

Gaining some recognition of Greece's special economic position and problems from the EEC.

Negotiating the five year agreement with the US concerning American bases in Greece.[4]

In spite of these achievements, various criticisms have also been levelled against Andreas Papandreou and PASOK. PASOK has not put forward a clearcut, consistent, and coherent policy, and it has centred around the charisma of its leader in spite of its grass-roots organization. Andreas Papandreou has expelled dissidents from his party and has been accused of being an authoritarian leader (Featherstone, 1983). Since the introduction of the austerity measures, Papandreou has expelled numerous prominent union leaders and his former finance minister G. Arsenis.

Lyrintzis (1984: 116) considers PASOK to be a 'party still in search of its political identity' having failed to fully institutionalize itself. While the rhetoric has been radical and patriotic, often creating high expectations, in reality the policy has at times been confusing and subject to change (Featherstone, 1983). The opposition has criticized PASOK's inconsistency for frightening away investors in the economy. That inconsistency may in part be due to PASOK's diverse base of support and its catch-all strategy. Its support is drawn from both the centre and the left, and is well balanced between males and females. It also draws widely from various social classes, except the very élite. The only well-marked difference seems to be in terms of age, with younger people more likely than older to support PASOK. This mixed coalition, however, may make it difficult to please all the varied elements.

These criticisms have to be placed within the framework of Greece's political history including its clientelistic elements and its past dependence on the west. Various factors that could be cited for the discrepancy between PASOK's ideal 'radical' goals and its real accomplishments include Greece's underdevelopment, structural economic problems, deficits in balance of payment, large public debts, fear of military intervention, lack of strong independent movements among the peasants, small working class, long-time history of conservative regimes, and its system of ideological formalism (Axt, 1984). The latter refers to the fact that while a great deal of radical debate and criticism of the system may occur, it is of little consequence because changes are not implemented (Mouzelis, 1978).

CONCLUSION

A poll of Athenians in January 1985 provides some idea of how Greeks view their political leaders from 1922 through 1985. A total of fifteen prime ministers that governed Greece for at least eighteen months were evaluated. Respondents were asked if each leader contributed a great deal, enough, a little, or nothing to Greece. Four leaders emerged as well-regarded (contributed a great deal or enough) by the Athenians: Eleftherios Venizelos (65 per cent), George Papandreou (54 per cent), Constantine Karamanlis (52 per cent), and Andreas Papandreou (46 per cent). As illustrative perhaps of a sign of the times, three of the four belong or belonged to centre or left of centre parties with only Karamanlis from the right. Venizelos had the most broad and diverse support based on age and party preference. He received positive evaluations by 61 per cent to 73 per cent of Athenians in all age groups and party affiliations except KKE where he achieved only 43 per cent (Dimitras, 1985d: 2–3).

It seems important to consider whether the political formations in Greece have changed since the time of the 1960s. One thing is clear: the traditional centre has collapsed. But one may ask does PASOK represent a new kind of centre. Featherstone and Katsoudas (1985) found that PASOK has gained support in certain new regions where the old Centre Union did not fare well, but it has also done well in many, although not all, of the areas where the Centre Union was successful. PASOK has experienced a quicker and more balanced rate of growth in attracting supporters than did the Centre Union. Also according to a 1981 pre-election poll, PASOK has broad support across classes, but is more popular among the young, males, and those with a secondary education. In some aspects the Greek party system has returned to the 1963 mould with a centre–right party (New Democracy), a populist centre–left party (PASOK), and a left party (KKE). It may be different than the 1960s, however, because PASOK's ideology is not that similar to the former Centre Union. One segment of PASOK supporters considers itself Marxist–Socialist (Featherstone and Katsoudas, 1985: 30, 39).

PASOK supporters tend to be internally divided among themselves on both foreign policy and domestic issues. Using discriminant analysis Tsokou, Shelley, and Dobratz (1986) find it is much easier to classify supporters of left and right parties correctly by knowing their foreign and domestic issue orientations than it is to classify PASOK supporters. Attitudinal factors are generally more important than demographic traits in influencing partisan preferences.

PASOK has emerged as a new party in the centre–left of the spectrum that has a very wide base of support. Its continuing strength depends upon its ability to keep those diverse elements of its coalition together. If PASOK were to lose ground, it would seem that New Democracy would need to become more attractive to those who occupy the centre of the political spectrum or that the KKE or KKE-Interior would have to appeal to the more leftist members of PASOK. Another possibility, which does not appear very likely for the time being, would be the creation of a new centre party; instead, what recently occurred was the creation of a new right party. PASOK, unlike New Democracy, is attractive to the young, who grew up during the 1950s and 1960s when the right engaged in repressive policies, G. Papandreou encountered pressures in maintaining his government, and the military came to rule. In many people's minds the US was associated with the problems over Cyprus and the military junta. Even as these young people mature, it may be difficult for them to find New Democracy attractive unless the party changes substantially.

Couloumbis (1983a: 95) has suggested that Greece, like many other nations, has been experiencing a protracted 'identity crisis'. Is it or should it be a part of the west, the Mediterranean, NATO, EEC, a developing semi-peripheral nation, capitalist, socialist or what? The 1985 nationwide parliamentary elections provide some indication of the direction Greece is taking in its search for identity. According to the Panhellenic Socialist Movement (1985: 6) programme: 'We have permanently reoriented the country from the policy of WE BELONG TO THE WEST to WE BELONG TO GREECE, a policy that determines, promotes and safeguards national needs and priorities, our national interests.'

While it is too early to determine how 'permanent' the reorientation is, the road to change appears to be a Greek one with socialist elements.

Notes

1. The military dictatorship in Greece became an international issue. For additional background information, there are numerous publications including studies by Stockton, 1971; Holden, 1972; Katris, 1971; Kourvetaris, 1971a and b; 1977b; Papandreou, 1970; and Danopoulos, 1985a and b.
2. This description and analysis of electoral politics in Greece relies extensively on Axt, 1984; Clogg, 1982; Dimitras, 1983, 1984a; Dobratz and Kourvetaris, 1981; Featherstone, 1982 and 1983; Kohler, 1982; Lyrintzis, 1982 and 1984; and Penniman (editor), 1981.
3. For the 1981 election there were fifty-six constituencies with the number of deputies each constituency elects based on population. In each constituency the quotient of the number of votes cast to the number of seats plus one gives the number of votes needed to elect a deputy. In the first round typically many of the seats are not filled. In the second and third rounds only parties with 17 per cent of the vote at the national level could compete. This politically favours large parties making it easier for one party in a multiparty system to gain majority

control of Parliament. For more detail see Lyrintzis, 1982 and Vegleris, 1981. For the 1985 elections the new electoral law provided another version of reinforced proportional representation allowing all parties to participate in the second distribution of seats where few seats are likely to be distributed. In the third distribution, the party with the most votes is strongly favoured (Dimitras, 1985a).

4. For more detail see Papandreou, 1984, and General Secretariat of Press and Information, 1983.

4

INTERNATIONAL RELATIONS*

GREECE, at the crossroads of three continents and cultures, has long been searching for its national identity and independence in the face of foreign intervention in its political affairs. While ch. 3 dealt primarily with domestic political processes, in this chapter we will examine the position of Greece in international politics. Greece's geo-strategic location in the eastern Mediterranean defines to a large extent its importance in international affairs. It has been the 'apple of discord' in the international arena throughout its history. It has been invaded, occupied, and dominated by foreign powers twenty times since 1825 (Psomas, 1974).

When international relations are viewed from a world system perspective that defines the present capitalist system as one in which peripheral and semi-peripheral countries are dependent on and dominated by core countries,[1] Greece typically is classified as being in the semi-periphery. Since Greece is not economically autarkic, an independent posture in international politics is difficult. Given its semi-peripheral position, Greece's identity is problematic—it identifies fully with neither the Western capitalist democracies nor the countries of the Third World; rather it has characteristics of both. Greece, however, in its political and economic structures is closer to Western democracies than to Eastern European socialist nations or Third World countries.

From the 1950s to the early 1970s, Greece's foreign policy largely followed an anti-communist ideology with a strong pro-Western and pro-American orientation. The Truman Doctrine (1974), which was designed to provide foreign aid to Greece and Turkey to prevent communist take-overs, marked the beginning of US penetration into Greek politics. Greece shortly thereafter joined the North Atlantic Treaty Organization (NATO) in 1952 and with Turkey formed NATO's southern flank. Greece became an associate member of the European Economic community (EEC) in the early 1960s, and a full member in January 1981.

* Yorgos A. Kourvetaris is the author of this chapter.

For the last 40 years, US and NATO strategies basically have not changed; they seek to prevent communist domination in the Middle East and eastern Mediterranean. While Greeks perceived this communist threat during and after the Civil War (1944–9), the perception of that threat was considerably weakened by the mid-1970s. At present Greece believes the immediate and long-range threat to its national security comes not so much from communist subversion or from its northern neighbours, but from Turkey, a fellow NATO member.

The Panhellenic Socialist Movement's (PASOK's) assumption of power in 1981 put in motion a new approach to foreign affairs in Greece. The socialist government has been trying to adopt a less pro-Western and more independent posture in international relations. At present it professes to follow a multidimensional foreign policy that includes EEC membership, Balkan co-operation, *détente* with the USSR, and friendly economic and political relations with the countries in the Middle East and the rest of the world. Greece is linked with many countries by bilateral and multilateral agreements concerning economic, cultural, trade, and transport arrangements and has diplomatic relations with 150 countries, 60 of which have embassies in Greece.

Before its 1981 victory, PASOK pledged to take Greece out of NATO, terminate American bases, and hold a referendum on whether or not Greece should join the EEC, but during the 1985 campaign, PASOK slowed down its anti-Western rhetoric. Greece continues to be in NATO, remains the tenth member of EEC, and US bases have not been removed although their status, established by the US and Greece in 1953, has been renegotiated recently. The 1983 agreement provides a five-year extension for the American bases after which Papandreou has said he is not in favour of a renewal.

In discussing the nature of foreign relations in Greek politics, one has to consider not only Greece's relationship with its traditional Western allies but its commitments resulting from current political realities and the socialist government of Greece. Analysis of modern Greece's foreign policy for the mid-1980s and beyond must then include an assessment of the major issues preoccupying Greece in the area of international relations as well as the relationship between domestic and foreign affairs. In doing so we look at the principal nations and issues involved, mainly from the Greek point of view.

The United States, Turkey, NATO, the EEC, and Cyprus are primary actors in Greece's foreign policy arena. The major powers' influence in the eastern Mediterranean and the Middle East have made Greece and Turkey junior partners in the asymmetrical equation of international geopolitics and regional big power politics (Couloumbis, 1983b). In addition, a score of secondary issues also preoccupy Greece, among them its regional relationship with its Balkan neighbours and the Middle East especially in terms of trade and commerce, tourism, transport, and a nuclear-free zone. Finally, Greece is concerned with its international image in general, especially over terrorist activities. Recently Greece has been used as a springboard for international terrorism as exemplified by the two skyjacking incidents involving planes leaving the Athens airport and a terrorist attack that took place on an airline en-route to Athens. These incidents have had negative economic and political consequences for Greece, especially for tourism. Greece along with other countries in the Mediterranean region is vulnerable to international terrorism.

GREEK-AMERICAN AND NATO RELATIONS

The US decision to support Greece and Turkey both militarily and economically against communist insurgence following World War II marked the beginning of American active political penetration in the region. This policy decision known as the 'Truman Doctrine' originally served the strategic interests of both the US and Greece. At present, though, the Greeks are sceptical of that doctrine. An illustration of this is the decision by the Socialist mayor Beis and City Council of Athens not to re-build the Truman statue destroyed by anarchists in Athens in early 1986.[2] In the words of Iatrides (1983), US-Greek relations are strained. He outlines six stages leading to the current state of affairs: abandonment of US non-involvement (1945–6); active US intervention (1947–51); close US–Greek partnership despite Cyprus (1952–63); partnership in decline (1962–7); an embarrassing partnership during the military dictatorship (1967–74); and since 1974, a new possible relationship. The breakdown of democracy in Greece in 1967, the seven-year military dictatorship, the Turkish invasion of Cyprus, the collapse of the military junta, and the restoration of democracy in Greece in 1974 and related political events are many of the reasons for the troubled relationship between Greece and the US. Since 1974 this relationship has been aggravated further by the unresolved Cyprus issue and the Turkish threat in the Aegean where Greece senses a US tilt toward Turkey.

The US had formulated its foreign policy toward Greece during the cold war period following World War II based on the notion of anti-communism, and Greece was considered decidedly vulnerable to communist threat from both its northern neighbours and from within. While the US continues to hold this position, the consensus of all major political parties in Greece is that the most immediate threat comes not from Greece's northern neighbours but from its NATO ally to the East.

In order to understand the deterioration of US–Greek relations, we have to look at the real and perceived factors that have aggravated them. Reviewing US policies toward Greece and Turkey in the post-Truman Doctrine period, Couloumbis (1983b) has characterized the three countries' relationship as a 'troubled triangle'. Despite original US intentions to establish friendly rapport with both Greece and Turkey, it has managed to alienate Greece and, to some extent, Turkey too. US and NATO diplomats, prompted by strategic considerations and particularly US–Soviet competition in the oil-rich Middle East and Eastern Mediterranean, have failed to understand the seriousness of Greek–Turkish disputes over Cyprus and the Aegean. As Couloumbis (1983b: 202) put it: 'Missing has been an understanding that the Greek–Turkish disputes for the two countries . . . are matters of the most vital importance involving considerations of security and territorial integrity.'

In assessing the US role in the Cyprus affair, Dr Sakellarides, a former US State Department official, best summarizes the overall theme of what Greeks perceive to be a tragedy: 'American or world public opinion cannot be deceived by the United States' specious arguments that the Turkish aggression was made to protect the rights of the small Turkish minority on Cyprus, or to prevent its annexation by Greece.' He continues, 'What the world saw was an act of brutal aggression aiming at the destruction of the overwhelming Greek majority of Cyprus. Nor can the people of the U.S. justify such colossal injustices and crimes committed by Turkey on the basis of what Dr. Kissinger perceives to be the U.S. national interest in our foreign policy' (quoted in Kourvetaris, 1976b). US

Senator Kennedy concurred: 'The Turkish invasion turned the island of Cyprus into shambles. In political terms, it violated the integrity of an independent state; in economic terms, it shattered the island's flourishing economy; and in human terms, it brought personal tragedy to thousands of families and turned half of the population into refugees, detainees, or beleaguered people caught behind the ceasefire lines' (quoted in Kourvetaris, 1977a).

On 28 August 1974 Constantine Karamanlis, Prime Minister of Greece following the restoration of democracy, decided to withdraw Greece from NATO as a protest against what Greeks saw as the US government's indifference to, and indeed tacit support of, the Turkish invasion of Cyprus. His decision was also based on the fact that Turkey, a NATO member, disregarded international agreements and remained a threat to Greek national sovereignty.

Under Prime Minister George Rallis, Greece later asked for its readmission into the military structure of NATO. The conservative government hoped that by re-establishing this relationship with NATO and thus the West, a just solution to the Cyprus issue could be reached. It is interesting to note that the only country that objected to Greece's re-entry was Turkey, which demanded instead an expansion of its own airspace responsibilities in the Aegean. Such an expansion would mean that Greece's national sovereignty over the airspace of the Greek islands in the eastern Aegean would be violated. Greece's re-entry was the result of the so-called 'Rogers Plan', an interim arrangement which left the question of NATO command and control of the Aegean to be worked out between NATO military authorities. The basic issue of contention between Greece and Turkey which has prevented resolution of command and control of the Aegean is Greece's insistence on the re-establishment of its pre-1974 NATO area of operational command and control of the Aegean.

The problems in Cyprus and the Aegean are still unresolved, thus rendering the southern flank of NATO ineffective. Most US policy-makers and strategists seem to view Turkey, along with Israel, as the bulwark against Soviet penetration in the Middle East. Greeks feel that the Pentagon and makers of long-range US foreign policy have supported Turkish claims because of its strategic importance and have overlooked Greece's concerns about its sovereignty in the Aegean. Yet the notion that Turkey is indispensible to NATO and the Western alliance in general is not shared by all US policy-makers. Retired US Admiral Jene R. LaRocque, for example, strongly challenges the assumption that Turkey is essential to NATO. He totally disagrees with the Pentagon's assessments and questions the idea that Turkey is important in the defence of the West (Vlavianos, 1984). He believes that Turkey does not have the military capacity and the resources to defend NATO and US interests. The Greek alternate minister of defence argues that Greece is the link between Turkey and Europe. If Greece was lost to the West, Turkey would be isolated. Also it is Greece that provides the main avenue for support for Yugoslavia and the logical base for NATO operations in Eastern Europe (Kourvetaris, 1987).

The US and NATO need Greece for major military installations and bases in the eastern Mediterranean and south-eastern Europe. In Greece, the US uses the Hellenikon Air Base in Athens, the Nea Makri Communications Station near Marathon, and the Iraklion Air Station and the Souda Bay Complex in Crete. By far the most important facility is the Souda Bay Complex, which can accommodate the entire sixth fleet. Both the US and NATO forces use it.

The average Greek was as aware of the strained Greek–American relations in the early 1980s as was his/her government. As mentioned before, many Greeks believe that the US, particularly through the CIA and NATO, had something to do with the 1967 military coup and the 1974 Turkish invasion of Cyprus, since they believe nothing would happen in the Greek and Turkish militaries unless the US and NATO had prior knowledge. A Eurodim poll taken in April 1984 shows that out of six countries, Turkey and the US[3] are very likely to be perceived as threats to Greece (91 per cent and 55 per cent respectively). The other four countries—the Soviet Union, Albania, Bulgaria, and Yugoslavia—that were the *raison d'être* of NATO's inclusion of Turkey and Greece were much less frequently viewed as threats to Greece. Twenty-two per cent saw the Soviet Union as a threat and 19 per cent saw Albania in this light. Fewer than 10 per cent of the respondents believed Bulgaria or Yugoslavia were as dangerous. Somewhat similar mistrust is expressed against NATO. Eurodim polls show that the majority of Greeks are not willing to entrust the national security of Greece to NATO or any other supranational organization (Dimitras, 1984c). Criticism of the NATO alliance has been widespread among all segments of the Greek population (Carmocolias, 1981; Kourvetaris and Dobratz, 1981). More recent Eurodim polls in 1985 do show some change in the Greek attitudes toward the US with a larger number of Greeks favouring the improvement of Greek–American relations and the keeping of American bases.

As leader of the socialist government, Papandreou has been outspoken and critical of the West and especially the US for its pro-Turkish position which, Greeks feel, has been particularly evident since the collapse of the Shah of Iran. Greeks wonder how the US and the West can support Turkey, a country that has one of the worst records on human and minority rights, including the genocide of Armenians, Kurds, Syrians, and Greeks. In addition Greece has been a proven ally of the US and the West in general in both World Wars and the Korean War while Turkey was against the West during World War I and neutral during World War II.

While the United Nations all but universally condemned the double Turkish invasion of Cyprus in 1974, the US has either abstained or voted against the UN resolutions. In addition, the US has not exercised its influence against what many Greeks perceive to be the intransigent and expansionist Turkish policies in Cyprus and the Aegean. On the contrary, the US increased military aid to Turkey and supported its claims to the Aegean airspace and continental shelf which are contrary to the international law of the sea.

In 1976, while campaigning for the US presidency, Jimmy Carter stated: 'We would be negligent of the moral issues and courting longer-range disaster if we fail to couple the improvement in relations with Turkey with increased fair progress on the Cyprus issue.' And in a news release later in the autumn of 1976 he declared: 'The impasse on Cyprus must be broken. The United States must be prepared to work with others, including the United Nations, to insure the independence, territorial integrity, and sovereignty of Cyprus . . .' (Makrias, 1980: 2). While the majority of Greeks in the US took Carter's pronouncements at face value and supported his candidacy, they soon became disillusioned and frustrated for rather than carrying out his promise, he actively pressed Congress to increase military aid to Turkey in spite of the US law prohibiting military aid for aggressive purposes.

President Reagan has made similar pronouncements about Cyprus. In one of the periodic reports on the Cyprus issue required by US law, he stated: 'The tragic situation in Cyprus must not continue. The foreign military forces [meaning Turkish forces] on the island should be substantially reduced, and Cypriot refugees, be they Greek or Turkish, should be permitted to return to their homes and land' (Makrias, 1980: 3). Like Carter, President Reagan has disappointed Greeks at home and abroad by not helping to obtain a just solution for the Cyprus issue. Promising one thing but failing to carry it out, according to many Greeks, reflects American foreign policy-makers' *realpolitik*.

On 15 November 1983 the Turkish-Cypriots declared an independent pseudo-state in the conquered northern part of Cyprus. Although ostensibly the US condemned this illegal act, the next day Reagan's administration persuaded Congress to increase military and economic aid to Turkey. Many Greeks feel that as long as the US and NATO do not press Turkey to withdraw its forces from Cyprus, Turkey has no incentive to settle the Cyprus issue. Meanwhile, a large portion of military aid given to Turkey is going toward maintaining armed forces in the northern part of Cyprus which support the pseudo-state of the Turkish minority on the island.

In addition to feeling that the US favours Turkey in Cyprus, most Greeks and the government of Greece believe that the US and NATO tend to support Turkish expansionist claims over the Aegean. For example, the US plan drafted first by General Haig and later by General Rogers, both US commanders of NATO in Europe, has been construed as recognizing Turkish claims over the operational control of the Aegean and the Greek islands, which impinge on the national sovereignty and territorial integrity of Greece. According to Prime Minister Andreas Papandreou, it has become more and more apparent that NATO, Turkey, and the US interpret General Rogers's agreement in such a way that vindicates all Turkish claims (Blueline Greek and Mediterranean Intelligence, 1984).

At a NATO meeting Prime Minister Papandreou suggested that NATO and the US should guarantee each member protection from attack from any direction, even from another NATO country. However neither NATO nor the US will guarantee Greece's eastern frontier because they believe it would be an affront to Turkey to do so. Greeks clearly feel threatened by Turkey, and many of them think that if Turkey attacks, Greece will have to fight all alone. It is rather paradoxical that NATO, a collective military organization formed to defend any member state against communist external aggression, will not state that it is willing to protect its members' national security and territorial integrity from a fellow member. In a meeting of NATO defence ministers, Papandreou made it clear that Greece intends to shift its troops from its northern frontier, where they are at present stationed as NATO strategy requires, and place them along the eastern Aegean to face the 4th Turkish Aegean army which is deployed along the coast of Asia Minor opposite the Greek islands in the Aegean.

NATO's inability[4] to resolve the Greek–Turkish conflict has escalated an arms race between the two countries. In the wake of the 1974 crisis, Greece and Turkey have registered the highest increases in military expenditures among the countries in NATO. In 1976, for example, the defence budget of Greece amounted to 26 per cent of its total or $1,249,000,000; Turkey spent 29 per cent of its budget or $2,800,000,000 on defence (Clogg, 1983). This tremendous military build-up has a negative impact on the economies of both countries. In 1982, except for the US, Greece and Turkey had the highest defence expenditure as percentage of gross national product among the sixteen members of NATO, 6.7 per cent and 5.2 per cent respectively. Meanwhile, the US Congress has maintained the ratio of military aid to Greece and Turkey at 7: 10. In other words, if Greece receives $7 m. in military aid then Turkey will receive $10 m. Neither the US Pentagon nor the Reagan administration supports the 7: 10 ratio. Greece contends that only a military balance between Turkey and Greece and equal aid packages from the US will assure peace in the region.

The socialist government of Papandreou is more critical of US policies toward Greece than previous conservative governments were. Yet Papandreou maintains that he is neither anti-American nor pro-American; rather, he is pro-Greek. In an interview on CBS's '60 Minutes' programme on 6 January 1985, Prime Minister Papandreou explained his position: 'I am in disagreement with the foreign policy of the Reagan Administration, that is clear', he said, 'This I am prepared to accept. But that I am anti-American, no.' And Papandreou further reiterated: 'A democracy such as the United States which has fought in two World Wars and played the decisive role in winning them for the forces of freedom cannot and should not be identified with supporting or creating regimes that are oppressive.'

Despite the tensions in US–Greek relations, there are signs that they are improving, particularly since the 1985 Greek national elections. For example, a number of high level American officials have visited Greece recently including Secretary of State Schultz in March 1986. Two additional indicators of improvement are the decline in anti-US rhetoric and the approval of the sale of forty F-16 fighter planes to Greece. Even Papandreou speaks of calmer waters and is refraining from confrontation with Western allies. Nevertheless, Greece, like several other European allies, did not support the US economic sanctions or military reprisals against Libya, although it went along with other EEC members to limit the size of the Libyan diplomatic corps. Moreover, the issue of renewing the agreement allowing the US to maintain bases in Greece is provoking considerable debate between the two allies since in 1988 the agreement could be terminated.

GREEK-TURKISH RELATIONS

The Cyprus Conflict[5]

For 3,000 years Cyprus has been a major arena of contention among the great powers primarily because of its strategic location in the eastern Mediterranean. But despite successive conquests and occupations by a number of foreign invaders—Persians, Arabs, Franks, Byzantines, Turks, British—Cyprus has retained its essential Hellenic character since antiquity. Cyprus is the third largest Mediterranean island, with an area of 3,584 square miles and a population of about 660,000 inhabitants. Before the invasion the majority or 80 per cent of the population were Greek Cypriots, 18 per cent Turkish Cypriots, and 2 per cent other minorities. Likewise 86.5 per cent of the land (by value) was owned by Greek Cypriots, 13.1 per cent by Turkish Cypriots, and 0.4 per cent by others. Because Greeks were the dominant ethnic group on the island, they pursued a policy of union with Greece, which was vehemently objected to by Turkey. In 1960 Cyprus gained its independence from Britain, but England, Greece, and Turkey were designated the three guarantor powers of Cyprus.

A number of writers (Markides, 1977; Kitromilides, 1979) argue that the cause of the Cyprus conflict can be traced back to the irredentist nationalisms of both Greek and Turkish Cypriots and the politics of unreason of the radical right as promulgated by the

EOKA (the National Organization of Cypriot Fighters) movement led by General Grivas. While originally both Archbishop Makarios and Grivas had embraced the notion of unification (*enosis*) with Greece, the 1960 accords of London and Zurich precluded either unification of Cyprus with Greece or partition (*taksim*) of Cyprus between Greece and Turkey. Eventually Makarios and his followers felt that union was unrealistic, but the more extreme right elements led by Grivas and later by others continued to struggle for unification.

In July and August of 1974 Turkey, a NATO country equipped by the US, invaded Cyprus, a small, sovereign, and independent island republic in the eastern Mediterranean and a *bona fide* member of the UN. Turkey's rationale for launching a massive seaborne and air attack against the republic of Cyprus was that it wanted to protect its ethnic minority in Cyprus. The invasion took place following the abortive coup of 15 July 1974, against President Makarios. The Greek military junta engineered the coup which was carried out by members of the Greek Cypriot national guard and Greek officers from the mainland. The coup-makers saw Makarios as an obstacle to the resolution of the Cyprus issue, and similar efforts to assassinate him had been attempted before. Greek officers were part of the contingent stationed in Cyprus in compliance with the 1960 accords of London and Zurich which gave Cyprus its independence. This time Makarios fled unhurt and the coup failed ultimately, leading to Makarios's return.

Turkey saw the coup as an attempt by the military government in Greece to declare the union of Cyprus with Greece and used the Treaty of Guarantee as a pretext to invade the island. However, the second military invasion of Cyprus in August of 1974 occurred after the constitutionality of the Cyprus government had been re-established. In retrospect, some Greek scholars believe Turkey's real reason for invading Cyprus was not a genuine interest in peace, justice, and the welfare of the people of Cyprus, but rather that Turkey invaded the island to gain, as a *fait accompli*, by the force of arms, what it had failed to gain at the negotiating table in Geneva. In fact some argue that the invasion of 1974 was the first phase of Turkey's long-range goal to annex Cyprus. Kourvetaris (1986), for instance, believes the first three phases of invasion, partition, and colonization have more or less been accomplished.

The inability of the UN peace-keeping forces on Cyprus to stop the Turkish onslaught and enforce the repeated ceasefires violated by Turkish invading forces has cast doubt upon the effectiveness of the UN itself. Compounding this, Britain's failure as one of the three guarantor powers to protect Cyprus and dissuade Turkey from invading a commonwealth member nation has contributed to the present Cyprus tragedy. Moreover, it seems that NATO's unwillingness to discourage one of its members from invading Cyprus, coupled with US foreign policy, has contributed to the present stalemate. Finally, the Greek military junta is accountable for engineering the coup against President Makarios which Turkey used as a pretext to invade the island in the first place.

The Greeks are greatly concerned about the Turks colonizing the northern part of the island, especially since Turkey has not withdrawn its troops from Cyprus more than a dozen years after the invasion. The continuing colonization is changing the demographic and cultural character of the island by increasing the number of Turkish Cypriots from the mainland Turkey. In addition Greeks feel that Turkey's flagrant violations of human rights in Cyprus hardly reconcile with Turkey's professed interest in peace, justice, and the welfare of all the Cypriot people. Furthermore the 2,000 or more Greek Cypriots who have been missing since the Turkish invasion remain unaccounted for and many Greeks suspect that they may be in Turkish prisons.

Polyviou, a Greek-Cypriot legal scholar, has vividly likened the Cypriot tragedy to a 'catastrophe of Biblical dimensions', while Christophorides, the former Foreign Minister of Cyprus, suggests the 'peace soldiers' of Mr Ecevit, the prime minister of Turkey at the time of the invasion, are reminiscent of the 'macabre glory of the Medieval Attila'. In summing up, Hitchens (1984) argues that the Cyprus issue can only be understood within the context of both inter-communal and inter-ethnic conflicts resulting from international intrigue and manipulation.

The Aegean Dispute

Parallel to the Cyprus issue and an extension of what Greece perceives to be Turkey's expansionist policy is the so-called 'Aegean dispute' that began in late 1973. The historical, ethnic, and cultural identity of the Greek islands as the cradle and repository of Hellenism is well documented by Greek and non-Greek scholars.

Despite numerous invasions, the continuity of Greek ethnic identity in the Aegean has not been seriously questioned. Hellenic roots can be traced back to at least 2000 BC. The Aegean Sea, beyond territorial waters as prescribed by international accords and the law of the sea, is an open sea and navigation is free. There are five basic interrelated issues involved in the so-called Aegean dispute: territorial waters, the continental shelf of the Greek islands, air traffic control over the Aegean, NATO operational control, and fortification of the islands.

Territorial Waters. Territorial waters refers to the waters over which the sovereign nation has complete control except for the right of innocent passage. According to the international law of the sea, the islands and mainland of any country have the right to territorial waters. At present both Greece and Turkey claim six miles of territorial waters in the Aegean based on the idea of equidistance (overlapping distances between two countries divided equally).

Greece would like to extend its territorial waters from six miles to twelve, and the Convention of Montego Bay, held in Jamaica in December 1982, recently reaffirmed Greece's right to do so. Turkey has similar rights and has extended its territorial waters in the Black Sea and along its southern coast. However, Turkey refuses to recognize that Greece, in turn, can do the same in the Aegean. Turkey adamantly opposes Greece's right to extend its territorial waters in the entire Aegean and has threatened war or *casus belli* if Greece exercises its right. Turkey's objection stems from its view that the Aegean is a semi-closed sea and other special circumstances. Even if this is the case, Kozyris (1985) argues that this position is not relevant since it would call for co-operation on the environment and management of living resources, rather than for changing territorial waters. The majority of nations including those in the Mediterranean are already exercising the twelve-mile right of extension of territorial waters. Greece advocates that both countries extend their territorial waters to twelve miles. Such an arrangement would not solve the disagreement over the continental shelf to Greece's satisfaction but will reduce its importance.

The Continental Shelf Issue. A second issue of contention in the Aegean is the so-called continental shelf particularly as it affects the

Greek islands. More specifically, it involves the extent of the continental shelf for Greek islands and whether it is equal to that of the mainland. This issue received great attention when, on 1 November 1973, the Turkish government *Gazette* published a map showing that it had unilaterally demarcated the north-east Aegean continental shelf and issued exploration rights to the Turkish Petroleum Company. Two days before the first invasion of Cyprus, another licence was granted to the Turkish Petroleum Company to explore a section of the south-east Aegean claimed by Greece. Greece denounced Turkey's claims as arbitrary and unlawful and appealed to the International Court of Justice at the Hague both in 1976 and 1978. While Turkey originally agreed to co-operate, it later refused to have the case adjudicated. Turkey insists on direct negotiations with Greece to settle the issue of the extent of the continental shelf. Greece believes that Turkey used the continental shelf issue as a starting-point for an expansionist policy directed at sovereign Greek territory. To reinforce its demands, Turkey proceeded to form the Aegean army including landing craft in April 1975, with headquarters in Izmir (Smyrna) and deployed it all along the coast opposite the Greek islands. Again in March 1987 Turkey and Greece came to the brink of war over Aegean oil exploration rights off the continental shelves of the northern Greek islands.

According to the 1958 Geneva Convention, islands have their own continental shelves. A continental shelf has both a geological and legal definition to it. The legal definition is the seabed and subsoil of sea areas outside the territorial waters to a depth of 200 m. or to the point where it is still possible to exploit the natural resources. Following this definition, the Greeks interpret their continental shelf as an almost unbroken entity because the Aegean Sea is not very deep (50 to 500 m.) and with modern techniques virtually all the area can be exploited for resources.

The geological definition of the continental shelf is the extension of the coast with a slight incline below the surface of the sea. When the incline becomes steeper, it forms the continental slope which goes to the bottom of the sea or the sea-bed (The Journalists Union, 1984). In terms of the geological criteria, the Greeks argue that the Aegean continental shelf is an extension of the Greek mainland and island coasts of Greece while the Turks claim that the continental shelf is an extension of Anatolia. Greeks provide evidence that the islands are extensions of Euboea and the Mount Athos peninsula, and they also say that every island, not just mainland Greece, is entitled to its own continental shelf. The Greek position that the islands have both continental shelf rights and territorial waters is strongly supported by international law of the sea.

The Turkish arguments are based on 'special circumstances' and the 'equitable principle' as defined in the law of the sea. Turkey claims the islands are simply rounded projections on the Turkish continental shelf and thus the continental shelf between the mainlands of Turkey and Greece should be divided on the basis of 'equitable principles' (not equidistance) to arrive at a reasonable solution based on geography, geomorphy, and other characteristics such as population, economic importance, and size of the islands *vis-à-vis* the Turkish mainland. If Turkey's conception was to be followed, it is likely that Turkey would have continental shelf rights relatively near to the Greek islands in much of the eastern half of the Aegean. This interpretation concerning continental shelves is not generally accepted by either Greece or the international community.

Air Traffic Control over the Aegean. On 7 December 1944, in Chicago, thirty-seven countries signed the International Civil Aviation Law, which regulated international air communications and established an International Civil Aviation Organization (ICAO) that would deal with all problems concerning civil aviation on a world scale. Control and responsibility over the Aegean airspace were assigned to the Athens Flight Information Region (FIR) by two international agreements of ICAO, one in Paris in 1952 and another in Geneva in 1958. The Athens FIR corresponds with the eastern borders of Greece, that is the eastern coasts of the Greek islands. A country's FIR is not always similar to its airspace, but the FIR-Athens covers the whole of Greece's airspace plus scattered sections of international airspace.

Without warning and contrary to international conventions, in August of 1974, Turkey issued NOTAM 714 (a warning issued to aviators in a given airspace) claiming that its own FIR authority extended as far as the area of its expansionist designs in the middle of the Aegean, i.e. to the region that includes the Greek islands of Samothrace, Lemnos, Lesbos, Agios Efstratios, Psara, Antipsara, Chios, Icaria, and the entire Dodecanese. All these Greek islands are populated by Greeks, and they are an integral part of Greece's national sovereignty. Turkey demanded that any aircraft flying over the Aegean follow instructions from Turkish ground control regarding traffic movement and not report to FIR Athens. Greece responded with NOTAM 1155 which closed the entire Aegean as a dangerous area. Therefore the world's airlines stopped using the Aegean and diverted aircraft flying to or from Turkey. Many violations of Greek airspace by Turkish military aircraft which were intercepted by Greek fighters increased the tension (The Journalists' Union, 1984). On 22 February 1980 Turkey withdrew NOTAM 714 because it gained nothing from the disruption and hurt its own tourism.

NATO Operational Control. Before the 1974 withdrawal of Greece from NATO in protest of Turkey's invasion of Cyprus, operational responsibilities for Aegean airspace were assigned to the command of the Greek Chief General of Naval Staff. In 1980 Greece re-entered the military wing of NATO and asked to resume the status it occupied in NATO before its withdrawal in 1974. Despite Turkey's objection, Greece joined the military structure of NATO, but it did not resume the original operational responsibilities that it had requested. According to the so-called 'Roger's Plan' under which Greece re-entered NATO, two simultaneous commands were to be created, one in Larissa under Greek command and another in Izmir (Smyrna) under Turkish command. This plan is not yet in operation. Meanwhile, both NATO and Turkey violate Greek airspace during their exercises in the Aegean despite protest from Greece. NATO consistently refuses to include in its manœuvres and exercises the fortified Greek island of Lemnos, because it supports Turkey's view that Lemnos should not be fortified. The island is fifty miles from the straits of Dardanelles controlled by Turkey. Greece has refused to participate in NATO exercises in the Aegean as long as this island is not included.

Fortification of the Islands. Closely related to the debate about NATO Operational Control is the issue of fortification of some of Greece's Aegean islands. Coufoudakis (1983) points out that the fortification of the Greek Aegean islands off the Turkish coast must be seen against the context of the Turkish invasion of 1974 and the Aegean dispute in general. Greece has fortified the islands on the grounds of national defence against a perceived Turkish threat which has been further aggravated by the fact that Turkey in 1975 created the Fourth Aegean Army which is stationed across from the Greek Aegean islands. Turkey also has the second largest fleet of landing craft among NATO countries, most of which are in the naval bases off the Aegean coast of Anatolia. This growing threat and perception of threat in the Aegean has given rise to conflicting legal interpretations of three treaties—the Lausanne Treaty of 1923, the Montreux of 1936, and the Paris Treaty of 1947 with each country trying to advance its own position, maximize its advantages, and sway the allies in its favour.

Both the islands of Lemnos and Samothrace were dealt with in the Treaties of Lausanne in 1923 and of Montreux in 1936. Under the Treaty of Lausanne Samothrace and Lemnos were to be partially demilitarized, and only local defence forces were allowed to be on the islands. Turkey claims this treaty is still in effect for these islands. Greece counters this by arguing that the Treaty of Montreux supersedes that of Lausanne and does not call for the demilitarization of these two islands. Originally even many official Turkish documents and statements accepted this interpretation. For example, on 31 July 1936, during a debate in the Turkish National Assembly on the ratification of the Treaty of Montreux, Rüstü Aras, minister of foreign affairs in the government of Inonu, made the historic statement: 'The provisions concerning the demilitarization of the islands of Lemnos and Samothrace which belong to our friend and neighbour, Greece, and which had been demilitarized by the Treaty of Lausanne in 1923, are abolished by the Treaty of Montreux and we are particularly pleased about this.' It was not until recently that Turkey protested against the presence of military installations. Greece argues that even the United Nations Charter Article 51 recognizes its right to fortify its islands as a defence measure. Under the Montreux Treaty Turkey also has remilitarized the Straits and its islands of Imvros and Tenedos (Kozyris, 1985).

The second group of islands comprises the Dodecanese which is covered under the Treaty of Paris of 1947 to which Turkey is not a party. Under this treaty Italy ceded the Dodecanese to Greece and did not give Turkey any rights to them whatsoever. Again, under international law and the UN Charter (Article 51) Greece has the inherent and inalienable right of fortification of these islands for self-defence which supersedes any conventional demilitarization obligations. In short, Greece believes that it has the right to fortify the Greek islands to defend them from external aggression or threat of aggression (Kozyris, 1985).

Not long ago the Turks conducted an exercise observed by Kenan Evren, the Turkish President, opposite the Greek island of Chios in the eastern Aegean. This exercise was carried out with real fire and use of all the landing vessels of the Turkish Navy that had been concentrated along the coast of Turkey, opposite the Greek islands in the Aegean. Greece interpreted such a manœuvre as a real threat to its own sovereignty. Another crucial issue concerning sovereignty is that the Turks wish to move the line of operational control of the seventh Allied Tactical Air Force westward. This would mean that the protection of many Greek islands would fall into the hands of the Turkish Air Force and more than 500,000 Greek people living in those areas would be put under Turkish control.

Greek–Turkish relations have been further aggravated by continuing violations of the human rights of the Greek minority in Turkey. These include restrictions imposed on the Greek Orthodox Patriarchate, on the Greek populations of Tenedos and Imvros, and on the Greek minority in Constantinople (Istanbul). Turkey has violated articles 14 and 38–44 of the Lausanne Treaty (1922) which protects the human rights of Greek minorities. About twenty years ago, there were 100,000 Greeks living in Turkey; by the 1980s only 5,000 were left. On the other hand, the 150,000 Turkish Muslims living in Greece are still thriving and increasing in numbers.

The crucial question is to what extent are the perceptions of Turkish threat justified? Greece believes that the behaviour of Turkey in both Cyprus and the Aegean constitutes a real threat to its national sovereignty. The evidence, Greece argues, is overwhelming and includes: (a) Turkey's double invasion of Cyprus in 1974; (b) the creation of the fourth Turkish Aegean Army which is outside the NATO command structure; (c) the belligerent statements and pronouncements by Turkish officials; (d) the continuing challenge of Greek rights in the Aegean; (e) the refusal of NATO and the US to guarantee the defence of the Greek islands if attacked by Turkey; and (f) the militarization of the Straits and the islands of Imvros and Tenedos.

The deterioration of Greek–Turkish relations has made the southern flank of NATO ineffective. Because the US and NATO have failed to address themselves to Greece's national security concerns, Greece believes they have capitulated to Turkey's expansionist policies in Cyprus and the Aegean. While Greece desires peace with its neighbour, Turkey, Prime Minister Papandreou has made it clear that: 'The status of the Aegean is not negotiable for any reason whatsoever or under any circumstances.'

EEC AND GREECE

In January 1981 Greece became the tenth member of the European Economic Community (EEC) after being an associate member since the early 1960s. The Treaty of Greece's associate membership in the European Community had been suspended during the seven-year military dictatorship, but following the restoration of democracy in Greece in 1974, the Karamanlis government renewed Greece's interest in joining the EEC as a full member.

The decision to join the EEC was as much political as it was economic. One of the main reasons Greece joined the community was to strengthen its own parliamentary democracy and identify itself with Western institutions. It was thought that full membership would give Greece an international and equal status with the rest of Western Europe. This also can be argued to hold true for Spain and Portugal. All three countries experienced authoritarian regimes and joining the community was perceived to be a guarantee against future dictatorships.

Another more pressing reason why Greece joined the community was the perceived Turkish threat especially following Turkey's invasion of Cyprus in 1974. Since neither NATO nor the US prevented the invasion, Greece had to seek a new framework for protecting itself from Turkey's military aggressiveness. The EEC tried to maintain an even-handed policy towards both Greece and Turkey from the late 1950s on. The original reaction to Greece's application to the EEC was rather negative for the EEC did not want to upset Turkey. Rather it urged Greece to maintain its links with Europe through NATO (Tsakaloyannis, 1980). Greece's eventual accession to the EEC further intensified the Greek–Turkish problem in the view of EEC members who did not want to be involved in the disputes over Cyprus and the Aegean, but Greece saw its membership as a means to restore its shattered security and as a deterrent and a shield against Turkey's further aggression.

Since the socialists' ascent to power, Greece has taken diametrically different positions from other member nations of the EEC in practically every foreign-policy issue. Greece remains a strong advocate of greater equality between the more developed northern European states and the less developed southern European oncs.

While the EEC today is primarily an economic supranational organization of twelve European nations, its long-range goal is the political integration of Europe. Under the Treaty of Rome, Article 238, the community established the European Parliament in which all member states of the EEC are represented in proportion to their population. The power of the European Parliament is growing in international affairs. At present it is mostly a forum for discussing international issues, particularly those affecting the member states of the EEC, but it does not have any binding power on the member states. Many believe that the EEC eventually will become a third independent power between the two superpowers, the US and USSR.

GREECE AND THE BALKANS

Geographically Greece is closer to south-eastern than western Europe since it forms part of the Balkan peninsula along with Yugoslavia, Romania, Albania, Bulgaria, and European Turkey. Since 1974 Greece has developed closer relations with the socialist countries of eastern Europe especially in the areas of commerce, cultural exchange, transport, tourism, and business in general. Greece's entry to the EEC may be helping extend the community's influence in the Balkans due to the fact that Greece maintains good relations with its northern neighbours.

Greece also has promoted the freeze of nuclear weapons to make it, along with the other Balkan countries and the Mediterranean in general, a zone free of nuclear stockpiles. On the issue of nuclear proliferation and deployment in Europe, Greece joined with Argentina, Mexico, Sweden, India, and Tanzania to promote peace and the freeze of nuclear weapons in the world.

Greece has resolved the major issue of Greek political refugees in Eastern Europe by allowing them to repatriate, and many former guerrilla fighters have returned to Greece and have rejoined their families, friends, and relatives. Despite the fact that the Karamanlis government initiated the policy of Balkan co-operation, the socialist government of Andreas Papandreou has generally seen it through. Prime Minister Papandreou visited many Eastern European countries including Poland, the Soviet Union, Bulgaria, Yugoslavia, and East Germany. Greece and Albania have re-established relations in a number of areas such as cultural exchange, commerce, and trade. There are still some areas of concern, however. While Albanians have allowed the teaching of modern Greek, they have not allowed much religious expression or worship among the Greek Orthodox faithful, nor have they encouraged the continuation of Greek ethnic identity in the younger Greek generations. Albania also has established a policy of changing Greek-sounding names to Albanian-sounding ones.

GREECE AND THE MIDDLE EAST

Greece lies in close proximity to the Middle East and the Arab world. Indeed, many students of international politics and development sometimes include Greece in the Middle East. Historically and culturally Greece along with the rest of the Balkan nations, has traditional ties with the Middle East that reflect Byzantine, Greco-Roman, and Ottoman influences in the region.

The Greek presence in Egypt goes back to ancient times. In the early part of the twentieth century, the Greeks of Egypt were prosperous and educated, much like the Greeks of the US. Greek Egyptians have been interested in the politics of Greece, but were not active in the political events and processes taking place in Egypt especially during the 1920s. Then the rise of Nasser in Egypt in 1952 and the growth of Egyptian nationalism changed the standing of the Greeks in Egypt. The nationalization of businesses owned by Greeks and other Europeans resulted in the flight of the majority of Greeks from Egypt. Many of them returned to Greece, others migrated to the US, and the Greek–Egyptian community, like that in Turkey, declined. Only recently have there been some efforts to revive the traditional ties between Greece and Egypt and indeed the rest of the Middle East. For example, former President of the Greek Republic, Karamanlis visited Egypt, as did Prime Minister Papandreou in February, 1986 and Egypt's Prime Minister Mubarak reciprocated. There are now Greeks working in Egypt and Egyptians working in Greece.

Greece has good relations not only with conservative nations in the Middle East but also with the more progressive and radical regimes in the region including Iraq, Syria, and Libya. In 1986 a direct line of communication between Volos and Latakia in Syria was established. Greece, as a member of the EEC, has pledged to work as a 'go-between' to promote resolution of the Middle East conflict. Greece supports the legitimate aspirations of the Palestinian people for self-determination and a homeland while supporting the existence of the Jewish state within secured borders. It also supports the UN resolutions for the return of all Arab territory captured by the Israelis in the 1973 war. Greece played a mediating role between France and Libya over the dispute of Chad in Africa. It provided humanitarian assistance during the evacuation of Palestinians from Lebanon in the summer of 1983, and Greece has repeatedly appealed to Arab state governments to exert influence on their citizens to refrain from using Greece as a location of terrorist activities. The repetition of terrorist activities in Athens has aggravated Greek–Arab relations. Despite the Greek socialist government's support of the Arab/Palestinian cause, the Arabs collectively have not embraced Greece, nor have they made great investments there.

Relations between Greece and Israel are not as warm and friendly as Greece's relations with the Arab states, although recently some improvement has been noted. Greece is the only country in the EEC that has not fully recognized Israel because Greece objects to Israel's expansionist policies and criticizes its refusal to abide by the UN resolutions to withdraw from Arab territory. Many Greeks believe there are some similarities between the Turkish invasion and occupation of Cyprus and the Israeli invasion and occupation of Lebanon and other Arab lands, among them the Golan Heights in Syria and the West Bank in Jordan. Greece argues that unless the Palestinian issue is resolved there will be no real peace in the Middle East.

In conclusion, Greece, having experienced many wars and conflicts in the past, wants to live in peace with its neighbours and all nations. However, at the same time it is not willing to give up its territorial integrity and national sovereignty at sea, on land, or in the air. It is against the bipolar superpower domination of the world. Traditionally it has sided with the West, but this does not mean that Greece should not develop friendly relations with the

East, North, and South. Since 1974 Greek leaders have pursued a multi-faceted foreign policy. Greece wants to be treated with respect, not as a protectorate of any superpower, but as an equal partner, not as a dependent nation, but as an independent and/or interdependent one. In other words, Greece feels it should not be taken for granted by its allies. It is a nation striving to maintain its own national identity and pursue its own national interests.

Notes

1. According to world system theory the capitalist system has a core, a periphery, and semi-periphery. The core countries include Western Europe, Japan, and the United States. The periphery is those countries collectively known as the Third World, such as nations in Asia, Africa, and Latin America. The semi-periphery includes those countries which are in between the two poles of development. The implication here is that the core countries dominate those countries found in the periphery and semi-periphery not only in the economic sphere but in the international arena of politics as well.
2. This decision not to rebuild the statue angered the leadership of the American Hellenic Educational Progressive Association (AHEPA) which had originally given the statue to Greece during the Karamanlis era to show its appreciation for US military aid to Greece during the Civil War. The AHEPA Supreme Lodge has asked the Greek government to return the statue to the US. More recently the Government has said it plans to rebuild the statue. The Athenian Mayor Evert of New Democracy who was elected in October 1986 pledged that the statue of President Truman would be re-erected.
3. A Euro-barometer survey of Greece as well as other EEC countries in April 1982 revealed the following: On the question of trustworthiness, 53.7 per cent of those who answered believed Americans are not at all trustworthy. On 'the over-all opinion of the U.S.' question, 33.5 per cent were very unfavourable, 39.5 per cent somewhat unfavourable, 20.5 per cent somewhat favourable, and 6.4 per cent very favourable. On whether the US was able to deal responsibly with world problems, 48 per cent replied not at all, 39.1 per cent indicated not very well, 9.1 per cent to a fair extent, and only 3.8 per cent to a great extent.
4. In an October 1985 meeting of the Inter-University Seminar on Armed Forces and Society, an American military officer from NATO headquarters (Belgium) argued that the dispute between Greece and Turkey over Cyprus and the Aegean are matters to be solved by the United Nations and not by the US or NATO. However, Turkey refuses to abide

by any UN resolutions. For example the resolutions concerning the Cyprus conflict urging Turkey to withdraw from Cyprus and allow the Cypriots to return to their homes and properties have been consistently ignored.

5. This section on the Cyprus issue draws heavily on the articles by Kourvetaris 1976b and 1977a. The literature on the Cyprus issue is voluminous. See especially writings by Van Coufoudakis (1985), Markides (1977), Hitchens (1984), and a selective bibliography by Kourvetaris, (1976).

5

THE ECONOMY*

THE state of international affairs has strongly influenced the economy as well as the politics and foreign relations of Greece since it is a small nation, not particularly rich in natural resources and not industrially advanced. Our earlier historical chapter noted this lack of industrial base in comparison with many Western European countries. The Greek economy has been labelled as an 'under-development/dependent type of industrial capitalism' in which simple commodity production and small family businesses and crafts exist side by side with the dominant capitalist mode of production (Mouzelis, 1978). Since Greece lacks indigenous sources of growth and relies on investments from foreign sources, including Greeks of the diaspora, its economy has been particularly vulnerable to influence from first Western Europe and then the US. Mouzelis (1978: 153–4) argues that development in Greece should not be an issue of catching up or imitating the West but rather of finding and implementing new developmental strategies.

Greece's accession to the European Economic Community (EEC) has opened its somewhat fragile economy to the competitive policies of the other EEC countries. The generally homogeneous EEC economies are being affected by Greece's admission and by the more recent admission of Spain and Portugal. The number of loans and concessions made in recognition of Greece's own particular economic problems provides some evidence of this, and it is also telling that Greek per capita income in 1984 was equivalent to $3,330 while the EEC average was $7,300 (Economist Intelligence Unit (EIU), 1985a: 9).

The Greek economy is now going through what Prime Minister Papandreou (1984: 7) calls a 'period of transition to socialist restructuring' or a *mixed* economy with some capitalist and some

* Betty A. Dobratz wrote the introductory section and those on the occupational structure; primary, secondary, and tertiary sectors; public and private sectors; and natural resources and sources of energy. Yorgos A. Kourvetaris wrote the sections on Greece and the EEC; taxation; invisibles; and foreign trade and the balance of payments.

socialist elements. Further Papandreou (1984) maintains that the Greek economic programme provides a Third Road to Socialism,[1] which is different from existing forms of socialism and from the model of social democracy, and employs a strategy of transition which rejects various blocs of power, involves a partisan pluralism, and takes into consideration the sovereignty of particular national characteristics. Such a programme is intended to allow Greece to maintain its national identity.

Greece, throughout its history, has had considerable state ownership and involvement in its capitalist economy, but the socialist government has introduced measures that could alter certain aspects of the economy. Its Social and Economic Development Plan is broadly concerned with the quality of life and calls for decentralization of economic activities with emphasis on regional development, worker participation, and stimulation of private investments for increased productivity and employment. The government's programme has tried to promote a better distribution of income, encourage the vertical integration of industrial production, support the exporting sector, and improve services in health and education (Gianaris, 1984: 116–17). However, major economic changes are unlikely to occur quickly in Greece owing to the limited radicalism of the middle classes, a small working class, a weak trade union movement, and the lack of a socialist tradition (Axt, 1984: 196).

In the face of severe economic problems, the socialist government introduced major stabilization measures in October 1985. Papandreou cited the need for a national effort to bring the Greek economy out of its crisis and to lay the groundwork for self-sufficient economic development; he argued that in order to maintain its territorial integrity and independence, Greece must have a strong economy (Blueline: Greek and Mediterranean Report, 1985a: 1). Too much economic dependence on other nations is perceived as a threat to Greek identity.

The major economic problems are a significant balance of payments deficit, very high public sector borrowing, high inflation, low productivity and profitability, and stagnant investment. Among the changes implemented by the stabilization measures were the devaluation of the drachma[2] by 15 per cent, the imposition of a four-month wage freeze on the automatic wage adjustment system, followed by severely limited adjustments during

1986, and restraints on imports. In order to import goods, a mandatory non-interest-earning six-month deposit must be made with the Bank of Greece for a percentage of the value ordered. For luxury items such as automobiles it is 80 per cent (EIU, 1985b: 8). In short, the government policy makes it more difficult to import goods but should make Greek exports cheaper. Critics of the stabilization reforms have referred to them as austerity measures.

Why is the Greek economy encountering such enormous problems? Greece's position within the global economy helps shed light on many of the difficulties. According to world system theory countries can be classified as core, semi-peripheral, and peripheral.[3] Core societies (i.e. US, Japan, most of Western Europe) are economically diversified, rich, strong, and relatively independent of outside controls while peripheral societies are over-specialized, poor, weak, and often manipulated by the core nations. Semi-peripheral societies are economically between the core and periphery and may be trying to industrialize and diversify. This latter term best describes Greece's location in the world system because of its relatively large although declining primary sector (e.g. agriculture), its client–patron relations, limited industrial development, and external dependence on trade in primary commodities. Greece does not have a very developed capital goods industry, part of its limited manufacturing is foreign owned, and many enterprises are small, family-oriented businesses. The economy has been bolstered by receipts from tourism and remittances from emigrants abroad but has been adversely affected by its need to import many of its technological and energy resources. Therefore the nation has often been characterized as politically and economically dependent upon bigger and more industrialized countries, but at the same time Greeks display strong feelings of national identity and independence which are deeply rooted in their culture.

Petras (1983) points out that an analysis that places Greece in the semi-periphery is not adequate, and that one must also consider non-industrial roads to development such as shipping, wholesaling, retailing, banking, and fixed income (e.g. lands, bonds) which are complementary to industrial capitalism. Greek shipping facilitates the flow of goods throughout the world while tourism provides leisure and travel for people. Greek development is thus qualitatively different from that in much of Western Europe and has been adversely affected by the worldwide shipping crisis, the decline in emigrants' remittances, and the decrease in receipts from tourism.

In addition to Greece's being in the semi-periphery of the world system, a second form of core–periphery relations exists *within* Greece based on the differences between its urban (core) and rural (peripheral) areas. The rural areas suffer from declining employment, depopulation (especially of the young), inadequate roads and health services, and poor education facilities. Although the exodus from the countryside has slowed during the last few years and the government has attempted to bring about greater urban–rural balance through decentralization and greater incentives to invest, major problems still remain in the less developed regions.

In the remainder of this chapter we give a brief profile of the Greek economy by focusing on selected economic aspects which are germane to understanding some of the key problems Greece is encountering. Major dimensions of the economy we examine are its occupational structure, work environment (primary, secondary, and tertiary sectors), and public and private sectors. Also we consider natural resources and sources of energy, relations with the EEC, taxation, balance of payments, and foreign trade.

THE OCCUPATIONAL STRUCTURE OF GREECE

The composition of the Greek labour force is given in Table 5.1 which provides the occupations of employed persons in 1961, 1971, 1981, and 1984. The most obvious change shown over time is the decline in agricultural and kindred workers from 54 per cent in 1961 to 30 per cent in 1984, but still nearly one third of the labour force is in agriculture which illustrates the continuing importance of farming and the slow industrial development in the Greek economy. There have been problems of agricultural productivity which can be traced back to the small size of the farms, although the continued development of agricultural co-operatives has been advocated as one means to increase the productivity and efficiency of agriculture.

As a result of increasing urbanization and industrialization, the percentage of production workers, operators, and labourers increased from 22 per cent to 30 per cent between 1961 and 1971, but since then, this percentage has remained about the same. The percentage and number of professional, technical, and kindred workers more than doubled between 1961 and 1984 while the

TABLE 5.1. *Occupations of Employed Persons, 1961, 1971, 1981, and 1984: Thousands of Persons and Per cent of Total Employed*

Occupation	1961		1971		1981		1984[a]	
	'000	%	'000	%	'000	%	'000	%
Professional, Technical and kindred workers	125	3	183	6	332	10	374	10.5
Managerial and administrative workers	27	1	20	1	62	2	51	1.4
Clerical and kindred workers	144	4	244	8	336	10	328	9.2
Sales workers	222	6	233	7	301	9	349	9.8
Service workers	247	7	239	7	278	8	319	9.0
Craftsmen, Production workers, operators and labourers n.e.c.	787	22	966	30	1,119	32	1,045	29.4
Agricultural and kindred workers[b]	1,974	54	1,313	41	973	28	1,065	30.0
Occupation Not Determined	113	3	36	1	53	2	22	0.6
TOTAL[c]	3,639	100	3,234	100	3,454	100	3,553	99.9

[a] The 1984 statistics refer to persons employed who are 14 years old and above while the other data are based on the economically active population of 10 years old and above.
[b] Includes workers in farming, forestry, lumber, fishing, hunting and mining.
[c] Columns may not add to total due to rounding.

Sources: *Statistical Yearbooks of Greece, 1964, 1981, 1984,* National Statistical Service of Greece, 1965, 1982, 1985 and personal communication with Director of the National Statistical Service of Greece (letter of A. Dimitras, 14 January 1987, Ref. No. 2556/IST-2647).

number of managerial and administrative workers more than doubled between 1971 and 1981[4] but still is a small proportion of the labour force. Clerical, sales, and service workers also increased although not as rapidly as professionals and managers. In spite of these increases, Greece lacks personnel trained in the technical skills needed for development. Some believe that Greece has too many professionals i.e. doctors, lawyers, and architects but needs nurses, skilled workers with industrial training, and personnel to implement the socialist programme—e.g. to appraise investors' proposals and to institute self-management (Carson, 1983; Gianaris, 1984).

When one looks at the employment structure broken down in terms of workers, owners, and the self-employed, one can see why Greece has been labelled a country of small shopkeepers and owners. In 1981 self-employed and family workers still made up 46 per cent of the labour force (down from 52.9 per cent in 1971), 3 per cent were employers, and 51 per cent wage and salary-earners (Centre of Planning and Economic Research, 1984: 14). The individual's occupational life-cycle (especially for males) is often characterized by early wage or family employment with gradual changes to farm ownership or self-employment in trade, transport, restaurants, and other services (Petras, 1983). Most Greek enterprises are small firms which depend on paid or unpaid family members who work extremely long hours.[5] Almost 90 per cent of them employ ten or fewer people and tend to be in food, fats, canning, ceramic, cosmetic, and shoe industries. These small owners may be reluctant to lose ownership and control and to participate in larger-scale agro-industrial co-operatives which use more modern technology and mass production methods.

The majority of the labour force is now either salaried or wage-earning with white collar employees as well as blue-collar workers belonging to labour organizations. Historically the state has dominated trade unions so that paternalism has generally characterized the relationship between the state and unions (Jecchinis, 1967; Katsanevas, 1984). Thus, trade unions overall are not an independent entity in Greek society. The potential for growth of unions is limited owing to the large agricultural sector and the limited industrialization, which has resulted in a small pool of workers, small industries and factories, and the general lack of employment opportunities. Instead a parasitic service sector of vendors, peddlers, and others who buy and sell merchandise on the streets has developed. Further, certain Greek cultural values reflect a very individualistic orientation that encourages persons to own their shops and be independent rather than to organize collectively. On the political scene, repression of leftists, dictatorships, and governments using divide-and-conquer strategies have encouraged fragmentation and the dependence of union leaders on the state (Katsanevas, 1984).

The largest trade union is the General Confederation of Greek Labour (GSEE) with forty-five federations, eighty-five local unions, and 800,000 workers. Altogether there are about 3,000 registered trade unions grouped in various federations including the General Confederation of Employees (130,000), the Federation of Bank Employees (40,000), and the Federation of Secondary School Teachers (36,000) (Centre of Planning and Economic Research,

1984: 37). Labour unions in public corporations and enterprises are very well organized and have often obtained concessions that would be impossible to achieve in the private sector. From 1974 to 1981 the unions were dominated by conservative forces associated with New Democracy, the political party in power, but left unionism was represented by various political organizations which aligned with PASOK, KKE, and KKE-Interior.

With its election victory in 1981, PASOK gained ascendance in the overall trade union movement, and its PASKE organization has been especially strong in white collar unions. While PASOK has made efforts to liberalize the trade unions, at times it has also tried to dominate them (Featherstone, 1983). While Law 1264/1982 gave trade unions greater freedom and protection, and forbade employers to hire strike-breakers and engage in lock-outs, Law 1365/1983 made it more difficult for the public sector to strike at all. Although workers benefited from PASOK's earlier income and wages policy, the recent stabilization reforms have led to widespread protest and strikes by wage and salary earners who are now experiencing cuts in real wages because of the government's anti-inflationary policy.

PRIMARY, SECONDARY, AND TERTIARY SECTORS

In addition to examining the labour force, one can look at the work setting which can be divided into sectors: the primary that gathers and extracts natural resources including fishing, mining, farming; the secondary that turns raw materials into manufactured goods, or industry; and the tertiary that provides needed services such as teaching, merchandising, health, banking, and tourism. Some of the traditional literature on economics has suggested that Western nations in the early stages of development have a large primary sector, then industrialize and emphasize the secondary, and finally stress the providing of services. Greece does not fit this pattern very well. Although there was some industrial growth, especially during the 1960s, it has been suggested that Greece skipped over part of the second stage, changing, from a nation whose primary sector was strong to one that emphasized the service sector.

The Greek economy had to recover from severe disruptions engendered by World War II and the Civil War. Pre-war figures show the share of agriculture in total output to be about 60 per cent and that of the secondary sector to be less than 20 per cent (Krimpas, 1982: 223–4). From 1963 to 1973 the contribution of industry to gross domestic product increased from 25 per cent to 35 per cent while agriculture declined from 25 per cent to 16 per cent. Even in 1963 services already were at 50 per cent of the GDP. Since the first oil crisis and the slowing down of the rate of growth, there has been limited change which has favoured the service area. In 1983 the sectors' percentages of gross national product were 17 per cent agriculture, 24 per cent industry, and 59 per cent services (EIU, 1985a: 10).

The primary sector had 969,000 workers or 28.6 per cent of the employed labour force in 1981, secondary sector workers comprised 29.8 per cent and the tertiary sector 41.6 per cent (Centre of Planning and Economic Research, 1984: 13). One of the major problems with the Greek economic structure has been its emphasis on services at the expense of industry. The public sector (public works, utilities, and state sector services) rather than manufacturing has expanded the most.

Production in manufacturing remains slow with a 1.6 per cent decline during the first five months of 1985 in comparison with the first five months of 1984 (EIU, 1985b: 10). To some extent it can be argued that Greece is experiencing a process of deindustrialization. Reasons for the decline in manufacturing include the increasing foreign competition that has followed Greece's entry into the EEC, an unfavourable international environment, poor management, and failure to adjust to changing production and world trade patterns (Organization of Cooperation and Economic Development (OECD), 1986: 37). Unlike other OECD countries, the recovery in Greek manufacturing output has been very modest with its level in 1985 still about 4 per cent below the 1980 peak. In the three years to 1985 employment in manufacturing declined by around 2.5 per cent with a modest increase in 1984 being followed by another fall early in 1985. While manufacturing has remained generally stagnant in the three years to 1985, the *importing* of manufacturing products has increased by roughly one-quarter in the same time period (OECD, 1986: 8). In spite of pressures by various Greek governments and producers to exert Greek identity by buying Greek products, the psychology of the consumers is definitely biased in favour of foreign products which are viewed as more reliable and durable.

There is a great overconcentration of national employment (more than half) and manufacturing (about half) in the Athens area, and only small scale handicrafts tend to be widely dispersed throughout Greece. The countryside needs more small or medium-sized factories to process olives and grapes and produce flour, shoes, pottery, and cloth. Because of the lack of jobs and industries in the Greek periphery, the population in the countryside has declined.

PUBLIC AND PRIVATE SECTORS

In the centralized Greek state a large proportion of the economy is under state control, including banks, public utility companies, transport, communication, energy, and education. The public sector includes public enterprises and social insurance institutions as well as the central, state, and local governments. Greece's very large public sector has been growing at the expense of the private sector. One means of maintaining the work force has been through government-sponsored projects. The public sector (general environment) expenditures increased from 19 per cent of GDP in 1960, to 22 per cent in 1970, and 32 per cent in 1980. The central government expenditures went up from 62 per cent of the total public expenditures in 1960 to 70 per cent in 1980. The deficits of the public sector totalled 210 bn. drachmas in 1980, 304 bn. in 1981, and 337 bn. in 1982 which was 70 per cent of the total tax revenue. They are much higher in Greece (13 per cent of GDP) than in France and West Germany (both 2.5 per cent) (Gianaris, 1984: 71). One of the most expansionary demand components of the domestic economy during 1984 and 1985 has been public sector investment. This steep upward trend of public investment in recent years illustrates the need to deal with major deficiencies in the economic structure, for it is public sector compensatory borrowing that has contributed greatly to the ever-growing balance of payments deficit. Estimates for 1985 suggest this borrowing is probably greater than $2 bn. compared with $1½ bn. in 1984 and $¾ bn. in 1980–1 (OECD, 1986: 15).

Part of the reason the public sector has continued to expand is the lack of growth in the private sector and the government's need to provide people, especially its clients, with jobs. Also the people's expectations of benefits from the Greek government have risen over time. One of the main goals of the Minister of the National Economy is to cut public sector borrowing by 4 per cent in 1986 and again in 1987. The public sector also needs significant improvements in productivity and in the quality of its services to the people.

Within the private sector the Greek government is trying to encourage investment through its laws 1262/1982 and 1360/1983 which provide incentives including grants which are exempt from taxes, accelerated depreciation rates, an interest rate subsidy, and untaxable allowances.[6] Early in September 1986 Prime Minister Papandreou indicated that the private sector still depends too much on state subsidies and excessive bank loans, but 706 investment programmes that created more than 7,000 jobs had been completed at a cost of 18.5 bn. drachmas (Embassy of Greece, 1986a: 2). In spite of the various laws that have been formulated, an extremely significant and serious concern plaguing the socialist government is the low private productive investment which fell by over one-quarter between 1980 and 1984. In 1985 private investment declined by 1.3 per cent which was not as great as the declines in 1983 and 1984 (EIU, 1986b: 11). Capital flight appears to be increasing, suggesting an uncertain business climate and more profitable investment possibilities elsewhere (OECD, 1986: 15). In the first half of the 1980s corporate profit deteriorated. In manufacturing industry net profit rates became negative in 1982 compared to positive rates in the mid- and late 1970s. This fall in profit is a major factor in explaining the decline in net private business investment.

Private consumption growth was quite modest in 1984–5, mainly focusing on imported durables and motor cars. Because of the significant change in income distribution since 1980 that has benefited the farmers and low income groups, large sectors of the population are now beginning to buy cars, a purchase which is viewed as an investment in many Greek households. Owing to high taxes, the price of medium-sized cars in Greece is about twice as high as it is in most other OECD countries and for larger cars it is three to four times greater. The real value of cars is much higher in Greece than other OECD nations relative to per capita income, and at times the second hand value of a car is higher in Greece than its price when it was new.

Problematic Firms

In addition to public and private sectors, Andreas Papandreou (1984: 9–11) created the sector of *social experimentation* which consists of certain over-indebted but sound enterprises in the strategic sectors of the economy. One of the major problems facing the Greek government has been rehabilitation of these so-called problematic or over-indebted firms which encountered financial problems and could not pay off their debts. These problematic firms may well number 200 with debts of about 190 bn. drachmas (Tsoris, 1984: 189). Law 1386/83 established the Institution for the Economic Rehabilitation of Firms (IERF), defined 'problematic', and noted relevant procedures for dealing with the firms. More specifically, a firm can either be declared insolvent and closed, or be considered sound and rehabilitated which can involve managerial takeover by the IERF, a restructuring of existing obligations, or self-management by employees. In November 1984 the government restructured thirty-four problematic companies by gaining control of most of the shares in these companies which employed 24,700 workers. A dramatic illustration of the plight of problematic firms is that ninety companies under investigation had 5 bn. drachmas in capital and 130 bn. drachmas in debts (Embassy of Greece, 1984: 3). In 1985 the Hellenic Shipyards, which had been closed for two months, were bought by the state-owned Hellenic Industrial Development Bank.

One may ask why there are so many problematic companies in Greece. Many of the existing big Greek enterprises are family-owned oligopolies that had been protected by subsidies and loans which shielded their inefficiencies until EEC membership. Managers of the companies did not employ up-to-date marketing strategies nor did they innovate their production processes in order to compete with other countries. While the banks realized that the economic status of the firms was deteriorating, they did not push the firms to reorganize or innovate (probably owing to political pressure). Since the banks did not want the companies to go bankrupt, they continued to back them but would not finance projects for their expansion and innovation. In general there was poor administration and a credit system which did not promote development but rather served personal and political interests (Gianaris, 1984; Embassy of Greece, 1984; Tsoris, 1984). Other factors fostering problematic industries include poor investment strategy and the dramatic increase in wages which was much higher than the increase in productivity. In 1975 and after, 35–40 per cent of the industries were in the red and this climbed to 45 per cent in 1982 (Centre of Political Research and Training, 1985).

Multinational Corporations

Multinational corporations (MNCs) represent, in a sense, a two-edged sword for the Greek economy. While Greece needs investments, the major benefits from MNCs may go to a few people at the top of the hierarchy and considerable profits are said to leave Greece. Since MNCs have economic clout, they may also try to obtain political influence. While the MNCs may be helpful in providing technology and managerial skills, at least some elements of the Greek population view them as instruments of foreign domination which could undermine Greek culture and identity.

While MNC investment in the Greek economy became particularly important in the 1950s and 1960s, Yiannitsis (1977) points out that foreign investments also influenced the neo-Hellenic economy from 1830 to 1939. He argues that the investment of foreign capital in Greece has benefited the local capitalists as well as the MNCs. Foreign companies secured favourable conditions from the government and had oligopoly characteristics with high profits; their investments were particularly important in the garment, tobacco, insurance, petroleum, wheat, electro-chemical, and pharmaceutical industries. In spite of a high growth rate after the Civil War, indigenous Greek capital was not invested in the manufacturing sector. For this reason the Greek government enacted a law in 1953 to attract foreign investment and protect foreign capital.

In the early 1960s there was a shift from investment in light consumer-goods industry to capital goods and durables, and foreign capital had an important impact especially on metallurgical, chemical, and metal construction. Monopolistic tendencies accelerated as the share of foreign capital in the GNP steadily increased (2.15 per cent in 1962 to 8.15 per cent in 1972) (Mouzelis, 1978: 122). The military junta especially promoted the investment of foreign capital by offering all kinds of incentives and benefits (Pilisuk, 1972; Kafiris, 1975). Laws passed between 1967 and 1978 provided foreign commercial, industrial, and shipping enterprises in Greece with tax exemptions and other advantages including the right to hire foreign personnel.

In 1975 sixty-five enterprises had more than 50 per cent foreign capital. Twenty-two of the thirty-nine largest industrial firms in Greece are foreign-owned. Direct foreign investment in Greece reached $1.3 bn. by 1978, mainly concentrated in oil-refining and in the manufacture of petroleum products, basic metals, chemicals, and transport equipment. Foreign investment accounts for 60 per cent of industrial exports and 30 per cent of total industrial assets (Gianaris, 1982: 152; Gianaris, 1984: 137). Through Laws 1262/1982 and 1360/1983 the socialist government has provided incentives for both foreign and domestic investment. It expects foreign investors to import modern technology, create new jobs, and promote Greek exports (Hellenic Industrial Development Bank (ETBA), 1983: 65).

In spite of the incentives, Greece is currently encountering serious problems attracting foreign investments. In addition to the problems of insufficient profitability and an uncertain business climate, foreign investors note a shortage of capable Greek partners to set up joint ventures. Foreign manufacturers invested only $11 m. in 1984 (Revzin, 1986). One encouraging sign for potential investment is that in early May 1986 there were discussions between the US and Greece concerning development of commercial relations and possible US investments, including plans submitted from Del Monte, Dow Chemical, Goodyear, and General Electric. Also in August 1986 the Environment Minister signed a £2 m. sterling contract with a consortium of five Greek and seven British companies which are serving as consultants for the construction of a new underground rail system in Athens.

Banking

The most significant characteristic of the Greek banking system is strong government regulation through the central bank, The Bank of Greece. The government oversees Specialized Credit Institutions which serve specific sectors of the economy and holds controlling interest in the largest commercial banks, the National Bank of Greece and the Commercial Bank of Greece which together provide 72 per cent of total commercial bank credit. The Bank of Greece acts as a banker to other banks and implements the monetary policy of the government issuing banknotes and controlling currency circulation and foreign exchange operations. It also announces banking regulations concerning reserve requirements, interest rates on deposits and loans, types of enterprises to which loans may be granted, and purposes of loans. Now its major objectives are to limit excessive borrowing of the public sector and to develop a better policy to finance the public sector deficit.

There are more than twenty-two Greek banks and about nineteen branches of foreign banks operating in Greece with the Greek banks handling about 85 per cent of the total volume of loans and deposits and foreign banks focusing on internationally oriented businesses including multinational corporations, shipping companies, large Greek industries, and public sector corporations. The commercial banks with their extensive branches throughout Greece receive a large part of the private savings and are active in short, medium, and long-term financing. Three investment banks provide long-term loans to Greek manufacturing, tourist, shipping, mining, and exporting concerns.

The OECD (1986) report points out that direct government interference has contributed to the backwardness of commercial banking. In addition, banks, like other institutions in Greece, have developed privileged relationships with a number of enterprises that are based on personal patron-client considerations rather than rational financial criteria. The credit policy of the banking system has been partially responsible for the failure of Greek development and management policies. Halikias (1978) maintains that the very complex system of credit controls has fostered the deterioration of Greek industrial enterprises and the formation of problematic industries. The government had put pressure on banks to continue financing the heavily indebted firms until some means to deal with them could be found, and it is estimated that some one-fifth to one-quarter of total bank credit is going to support enterprises in the red now (OECD, 1986). While some reforms in banking are being implemented to strengthen competition, increase flexibility, and make the financial system open to external influences, what seems to be needed most is the limiting of direct government interference in banking activities and a reduction of loans to the public sector in order to channel resources to the healthy firms with growth potential in the private sector (OECD, 1986: 62).

NATURAL RESOURCES AND SOURCES OF ENERGY

The lack of natural resources and sources of energy strongly affect the Greek economy for Greece is not a particularly rich country. The soil is often poor and owing to inheritance and the dowry system (which existed until recently), the land has been extensively divided into small farms averaging only about 4.6 hectares (12.6 acres). It is estimated that 29.7 per cent of the entire land is agricultural with 25.5 per cent of this being irrigated. Pastureland covers 39.5 per cent and forests about 22.6 per cent (Centre of Planning and Economic Research, 1984: 4). Greece buys basic foodstuffs which currently total about 11 per cent of its imports (EIU, 1984b: 9). The warm, mostly dry climate is excellent for producing olives, vegetables, grapes, and other fruits, and membership in the EEC has tended to stimulate their production. Agricultural products account for about 25 per cent of the total exports including wheat, rice, grain, maize, cotton, and tobacco as well as vegetables, and citrus and other fruits. The most prosperous agricultural regions are Central Greece (including Attica) and Macedonia although agricultural products are also significant in Thessaly, Thrace, coastal Peloponnesos, and Crete. The poorest areas are the Ionian and Aegean Islands, Epirus, and western, central, and eastern Peloponnesos (excluding the plains of Argos and Corinth). As shown in Table 5.2, agriculture is more heavily dependent on crops than livestock.

Mining and quarrying play a relatively small role in the Greek economy, but they may become increasingly significant. Thirty-

TABLE 5.2. *Agricultural Production in Greece 1980/1*

Crop production	%	Livestock production	%
Cereals	15.3	Meat	17.5
Animal Fodder	5.6	Dairy Products	6.5
Industrial Crops	11.4	Other	4.2
Vegetables	10.8		
Vineyard Products	2.7	TOTAL	28.2
Olives and olive oil	10.3		
Fruits	14.3		
Other	0.9		
TOTAL	71.8		

Source: Centre of Planning and Economic Research, 1984: 20

four proven deposits of minerals including lignite and bauxite (alumina), nickel, chromite, magnesite, asbestos, copper, and uranium remain relatively untapped. Greece, one of the leading Western European nations producing bauxite from which aluminum is made (EIU, 1984b; Gianaris, 1984), has reached an agreement with a Soviet company to invest about $450 m. to construct a major alumina factory in Central Greece.

Ever since the oil crises in the 1970s, energy production and consumption have been major concerns throughout the world. There is only limited petroleum production in Greece with the major oil-drilling in the Prinos Field off Thasos, an island near the seaport of Kavalla in eastern Macedonia. By early 1986 this field was operating at full capacity, yielding 1.25 m. tons per year (EIU, 1986a: 21) and additional oil is being produced in offshore drilling at Katakolon in the Western Peloponnesos. Annual production of crude petroleum reserves is estimated at twenty metric tons (Gianaris, 1984: 109).

Per capita energy consumption has increased tremendously from 407 k. in 1960 to about 2,200 k. of coal equivalent recently and is eight times higher in Greater Athens than elsewhere (Gianaris, 1984). In Greece (unlike other OECD countries) total energy requirements have been rising in both absolute terms and in relation to GDP which has led to significant increases in net energy imports. Energy imports in 1983 were estimated at $2.6 bn. or 31 per cent of all imports while energy exports were only $309 m. or 8 per cent of all exports (EIU, 1985a: 15). Following a decline in oil prices and various trading deals, the mean price of oil for Greece dropped from $28.5 per barrel in 1985 to $16.8 in the early months of 1986 (EIU, 1986a: 22). This clearly helps alleviate the balance of payments problem.

The government's Five-Year Plan calls for reducing energy dependence by developing renewable forms of energy and natural resources such as lignite, peat, hydraulic power, and hydrocarbons. The 1985 estimates for supplies of energy are 61 per cent petroleum, 35 per cent solid fuels, and 4 per cent hydropower (EIU, 1985a: 15). Confirmed lignite deposits, some of which are privately owned, may amount to 3 bn. to 4 bn. tons with about 1.6 bn. tons being capable of commercial exploitation. Current production is about 30 m. tons per annum with the output being used by the Public Power Corporation to generate electricity. Greece hopes that by 1990 the percentage of electricity produced by lignite plants will increase from 50 per cent to 80 per cent (EIU, 1985b: 16).

GREECE AND EEC

Greece became an associate member of the EEC in 1959, but during the seven-year military dictatorship its association with the EEC was non-operative. Following the collapse of the military dictatorship in 1974, Greece applied for full membership to the community. The negotiations began in 1976, the Treaty of Accession was signed in Athens on 28 May 1979, and Greece officially became the tenth member of the EEC on 1 January 1981. Full membership in the EEC was a controversial issue opposed by the political forces of the left (PASOK, KKE, and KKE-Interior) and favoured by the conservative and moderate forces (New Democracy and the Centre). Later PASOK and KKE-Interior changed to a more favourable stance provided Greece was treated with special consideration owing to its economic problems *vis-à-vis* the more economically advanced members.

Those who favoured Greece's full membership to the EEC argued that Greece would benefit both economically and politically. From the economic point of view, the Europeanists believed that Greek products would benefit from a larger market of over 200 m. Europeans if Greece joined the EEC. Politically the pro-EEC advocates saw Greece's admission as a guarantee against future military dictatorships and the Turkish threat to Greece's sovereignty. Those who argued against it believed Greece was not in a position to compete with the more technologically advanced EEC members. The question they frequently asked was how can EEC European nations help Greece's economic problems if EEC nations themselves suffer from the same problems as Greece—namely creeping inflation, unemployment, and slow-down of economic growth. Along the same vein, those who opposed Greece's joining the EEC argued that Greece would lose its national identity and independence to more powerful Western nations.

Since the political aspects have already been examined under international relations, only the economic aspects of Greece's entry into the EEC will be briefly discussed. According to Tsoukalis (1981), the Karamanlis government (New Democracy) sought Greece's membership primarily for two main reasons—free access to EEC markets for Greek agricultural exports and the reduction of the balance of payments deficit. The government's fear of Soviet and Eastern Block economic penetration of Greece was another reason for Greece's entry into EEC (Tsakalogiannis, 1980). The decision by the nine EEC members to allow Greece to join the Community was based in part on the fact that Greece is one of the major maritime (commercial) powers in the world. Thus, EEC membership was viewed as beneficial for both Greece and the Community.

The spectacular economic prosperity for the industrialized world in the decades of the 1960s and the 1970s has changed dramatically. The enlargement of the European Community has aggravated the already fragile situation of the EEC which faces high rates of unemployment, inflation, low rates of growth, the energy crisis, international monetary instability and the challenge from the Third World. Greece, Portugal, and Spain traditionally have pursued protectionist policies based on non-tariff measures and have tried to induce the community to freeze many new categories of sensitive items and keep 'excessive' imports at bay. Between 1960 and 1973 Greece, Spain, and Portugal enjoyed higher rates of growth than the community of six *or* nine. While growth rates since 1973 have slowed in all Western European countries, Greece, Ireland, and Spain continued to register the highest rates of economic growth up to the late 1970s (Tsoukalis, 1981), but then growth in Greece declined.

In March 1982 the Greek government submitted a memorandum to the community in which it underlined the problems Greece faces in adjusting its economy to the more advanced and industrialized nations of the West. Greece asked the community to recognize its special problems and give it assistance to bring its economy closer to that of the rest of the community. The community recognized Greece's problems and responded favourably to the memorandum. Prime Minister Papandreou described the resulting agreement on the Mediterranean programmes as 'a diplomatic triumph for Greece' (Blueline Documents, 1985b). Under the agreement, the whole of Greece constitutes a Mediterranean region, and Greece is allowed to absorb 200 bn. drachmas of additional funds from the community for investment and projects in its infrastructure.

In 1975 the European Development Fund was established to help the less favoured regions reach the level and standards enjoyed by the more developed countries in the community. In its first ten years of existence, it has distributed 11.7 bn. dollars to the member nation states for improving infrastructures or launching new economic activities to reduce differences between the nation states. In addition to the regional policy of assistance, the EEC has an agricultural policy and social policy fund to give financial assistance and subsidies to the less developed Mediterranean countries. Agriculture still accounts for a large portion of economic activity in the Mediterranean area: between 20 and 60 per cent of the working population in Greece, Spain, and Portugal are engaged in it. In spite of the radical transformation of the labour force, especially in Greece and Spain, all three countries have a higher percentage of farming population than the other EEC members (Tsoukalis, 1981).

Despite the fact that net transfers from the EEC have averaged $700 m. a year since 1983 (OECD, 1986) the Greek economy has stagnated during the five year period since Greece's accession. According to the Economic Intelligence Unit (EIU, 1986b: 12) Greece's membership in the EEC is not responsible for this economic stagnation but rather it is due to the long-standing economic and structural inadequacies which the European Community has not been able to remedy. If we look at Greece's exports to the community during the five-year period since its accession, they have grown faster than its imports. In 1980 43 per cent of its exports went to the nine EEC European members and 40 per cent of imports came from them; by 1985 the corresponding proportions were 54.1 per cent and 47.0 per cent respectively (EIU, 1986b: 12). In addition, Greece has benefited from grants and subsidies from Community funds, but despite these Greece is considered one of the poorest EEC members. In 1982 Greece's GDP per person was about 56 per cent of the EEC average and in the islands only 44 per cent (EIU, 1986b: 12).

Under the Treaty of Accession, there was a five-year transitional period which ended in December 1985. Greece now has a full customs union with the community under which all customs duties, taxes, and restrictions have been abolished, and tariffs on agricultural imports have also been removed, including common external tariff (EIU, 1986b: 11–12). Greece, however, has been allowed a few more years of grace before implementing all the rules of the EEC concerning free circulation of capital. Greece has not abolished the state monopoly of petroleum products as yet but it will lose its monopoly of matches (EIU, 1986b: 12).

Greece's continuing huge deficit and high inflation have negative effects on its economic relationship with the rest of the EEC. Recently the European Commission, in response to the Greek Government's stabilization measures of 11 October 1985, recommended an overhaul of public utilities and other enterprises in the public sector and urged the government to encourage foreign investment which is declining. It also called on the Greek government to reduce inflation and the public deficit. The root cause of inflation according to the European Council of Finance ministers is the growth of public deficit. The Commission agreed to loan Greece about 1.5 bn. drachmas in instalment payments as long as Greece could bring about significant improvements in its economic situation.

Greece entered the EEC when Europe was facing chronic problems of unemployment, inflation, and slowdown of growth. The Euro-euphoria for being a part of the European Community which existed in the 1960s and 1970s had run its course by the mid-1970s. The 1980s are difficult years not only for Greece but for Europe and the EEC as a whole. Although Greece's entry to the EEC is perhaps politically justified, it is the economic field which will determine the success or failure of Greece's accession. In the meantime, joining the Common Market has made the search for identity problematic for Greece; while Greece desires to be part of the larger European community, at the same time it tries to maintain its national and cultural identity.

TAXATION

Taxation, which is anti-inflationary, is one of the most important ways of financing public expenditures. Like any other country Greece relies on taxation as one of the major sources of national revenue. There are six basic types of taxation: direct taxes on personal income, corporation and real estate, and indirect ones such as stamp duties (imposed on property transfers, incorporation of companies, etc.), turnover tax (on the gross receipts of industrial enterprises, imported goods and the gross receipts of public enterprises), and value added tax (Centre of Planning and Economic Research, 1984).

Personal income tax is imposed on the total income deriving from the operation of production factors and comes from seven sources: buildings, farm land, movable values (chattels), commercial business, farming enterprises, hired services, and professional services (Hellenic Industrial Development Bank, 1983). Interest on bank and savings deposits and the income earned abroad if at least 35 per cent is imported in the form of foreign currency are exempt from any taxes.

In comparison with other Western European countries, Greece has one of the lowest rates of income tax, followed by France (Gianaris, 1982: 174). Personal income taxes as percentages of GDP are less than half (4.4 per cent) of those of the EEC average (11.5 per cent), based on comparisons with France (7.5 per cent), Italy (13.9 per cent), W. Germany (8.4 per cent), and United Kingdom (14.8 per cent). As percentages of total taxation they represent 15.5 per cent or about half of the EEC average which is 30.8 per cent. Taxes on corporate income in Greece, as a percentage of GDP, are again about half or 1.14 per cent compared to the EEC average which is 2.13 per cent (Gianaris, 1984: 171). Greece has moved toward harmonizing its tax system with that of EEC.

Tax evasion in Greece is extremely high, probably the highest in Europe, accounting for about 6 to 8 per cent of the national income, or close to 1.7 bn. dollars in 1981 alone. It cuts across all classes including scientists, artists, writers, and middlemen. The size of the underground and cash economies and the traditional reluctance of the Greek entrepreneurs and individuals to co-operate make the raising of extra revenues a particularly tough task. 'The taxpayers are so smart', says Koulourianos (former Finance Minister) with a smile, 'and whereas I'm running for the public interest, they are running for their own interest, so they run faster'. None the less, the Finance Ministry has been 'spreading its net wider, to catch more fish', (Carson, 1983: 7) and there are some indications that it may be succeeding. The government revenues increased about 40 per cent in 1982 and were projected to rise 35 per cent in 1983.

The Greek Parliament has passed a new property tax law (No. 1364/1982) similar to that of France. Thus, for owners of real estate property worth more than 25 m. drachmas the tax is 0.5 per cent on the first 10 m. drachmas over 25 m. For every additional

10 m. drachmas in property value, the tax rate increases progressively by 0.5 per cent, but to no more than 2 per cent. This property tax is very small compared to those in other Western countries although the average price of land in the Athens area multiplied by more than 1,000 during the last decade. Greece also has a tax on real estate sales or transfers of about 11 per cent or higher depending on the value of the land.

Indirect taxes (sales taxes, excises, stamp duties, and tariffs) account for about 70 per cent of central government's revenue in Greece. The largest proportion of such indirect taxes comes from stamp duties (about 28 per cent of the total indirect taxes), petroleum (14 per cent) and excises on special consumer goods—tobacco, petroleum, beverages (30 per cent). Greece and Italy have the most extensive system of excise taxation in Europe; more than thirty commodity groups are covered. This excise system applies to most luxury items, including radios, tobacco, motor vehicles, television sets, perfumes, and cameras (Gianaris, 1984). Indirect taxes on imports are higher in Greece than in the EEC. The accession of Greece to the EEC means a further decline in indirect taxes collected from imports because the harmonization of taxation between all EEC members includes reduction or elimination of tariffs on EEC products (Gianaris, 1984).

In line with its stabilization measures, the Greek government hopes to reduce its budget deficit in part by a marked increase in tax receipts including a projected increase of 53 per cent in direct tax revenue in 1986. This will partially be accomplished by further curbing tax evasion, widening the tax base, and speeding up the collection of tax arrears. Indirect taxes and stamp duties are projected to increase only somewhat faster than the growth of GDP. Overall it is hoped that the total budget receipts will increase by 32.5 per cent in 1986 (OECD, 1986: 44). Also there is the 'once and for all' surtax on business profits declared during 1984 and taxed during 1985. The taxes range from 3 to 10 per cent of the profits (EIU, 1985b: 9).

INVISIBLES

One major source of foreign exchange is through what is known as invisibles—tourism, shipping, and emigrant remittances. All three sources of invisibles are contingent on the health of the international economy. When the invisibles flourish, the problem with the balance of payments diminishes. Owing to a number of factors including international recession, unemployment, and the energy crisis, all three sources of invisible revenue have declined in the last few years. The depreciation of the drachma discourages Greek emigrant workers from sending remittances to be converted into drachmas. Comparing the first six months of 1984 with 1985, invisible receipts from tourism increased by 2 per cent while emigrant remittances and shipping receipts declined by 14.7 per cent and 10.7 per cent respectively (EIU, 1985b: 14).

Greece is considered a country of tourists for tourism is a major source of foreign exchange and provides employment for over 100,000 seasonal workers in the countryside and the islands, especially during the summer. In 1973 some 3.2 m. foreign visitors came to Greece and spent a total of $514.8 m., while ten years later the number of foreign visitors about doubled (6,613,122) and the gross receipts more than tripled. Most tourists originate from European countries and visit the museums and the archaeological sites of Greece. By 1985 tourist arrivals totalled 7,039,428, up 16.8 per cent from 1984. Increases were quite dramatic for the Dutch, Yugoslavs, Britons, and Swiss (Spotlight, 1986: 8). The depreciation of the drachma may have encouraged tourists to come to Greece, but it has also resulted in a drop in spending per tourist in dollar terms. In fact, spending per person has decreased 24 per cent in dollar terms during the last five years but the first six months of 1985 brought a slight improvement (EIU, 1985b: 14, 1985a: 21).

The National Tourist Organization (EOT) is concentrating less on mass tourism and more on improving existing facilities and spreading tourist flow more widely in terms of seasonal and geographical distribution. None the less, the tourist industry is suffering. Owing to the terrorist hijacking of the TWA plane in June 1985, the American government issued an advisory warning Americans to avoid the Athens airport (but later rescinded it). More recently the US bombing of Libya, the terrorist counter-attack on US citizens, and the Chernobyl radioactive accident have resulted in at least 1,000,000 Americans cancelling their plans to visit Europe and potentially Greece. Despite the massive Greek effort to attract American tourists it is unlikely to be successful in the short run.

The Greek merchant fleet numbering 3,222 ships as of 31 March 1984 is one of the leading fleets in the world and the largest in the

EEC. The remittances from shipping reached their peak in 1980–1 but now have fallen dramatically by almost one half to an estimated annual rate of $1 bn. in the first nine months of 1985 (OECD, 1986: 15). Since 1981 there has been a steady decline of Greek-owned ships; over 1,000 of them are still registered outside Greece.

FOREIGN TRADE AND BALANCE OF PAYMENTS

Since Greece imports more products than it exports, this contributes to the deficit in its foreign trade. There has not been a single year since 1861 in which the value of exports approached the value of imports. The limited domestic market, the lack of natural resources, and the shortages of foodstuffs make it impossible for Greece to be autarkic (Botsas, 1985: 1). In October 1985 the Minister for the Economy, Simitis, stressed that the Greek economy's most serious problem is the balance of payments. In real terms Simitis said that out of every 1,000 drachmas spent by the average Greek, only 920 come from Greece's own production (EIU, 1985b: 13).

The principal category of imported products in recent years has been fuel and lubricants which doubled from 16.4 per cent of the total in 1978 to 32 per cent in 1981, while the importation of most other manufactured consumer goods and raw materials declined. Industrial imports including machinery and private cars accounted for 87.7 per cent of the total. Oil accounted for 23.6 per cent of total imports and cars from Japan for 34.4 (Tsoukalis, 1981).

Traditional exports such as food, beverages, tobacco, and raw materials have declined from 90 per cent of total exports in 1963 to 36 per cent in 1982. Foodstuffs alone accounted for 27 per cent of the total exports in 1982 while in 1963 they accounted for 66 per cent. During the same period exports of manufactured products grew rapidly. An important export item in the 1970s was cement, mainly to the Middle East but Greece exports no heavy machinery or transport equipment. Principal trading partners are the EEC countries, the Middle East and Africa, the rest of OECD countries, Eastern Europe, and the US. Table 5.3 shows that in 1984 8.3 per cent of Greek exports went to the US while 2.9 per cent of Greece's imports were from the United States. Greece's most important trading partner is the European Community, especially West Germany. Trade with EEC is almost symmetrical, with 54.1 per cent of Greece's total exports going to the community and 47 per cent of its total imports coming from the EEC (Centre of Planning and Economic Research, 1984). An important development during the last two decades has been the reorientation of the flow of trade. While in 1963 trade with the Middle East and Africa accounted for only 6 per cent of the imports and 4 per cent of the exports, by 1982 these two areas accounted for 27 per cent of the imports and 24 per cent of the exports (Centre of Planning and Economic Research, 1984).

TABLE 5.3. *Greek Foreign Trade by Country*

	Exports from Greece			Imports to Greece	
	1979	1984		1979	1984
	%	%		%	%
West Germany	19.3	19.7	West Germany	15.9	16.6
Italy	9.8	13.5	Italy	9.3	9.6
France	6.1	8.6	Japan	9.4	7.6
USA	5.6	8.3	France	6.3	6.9
UK	5.2	6.3	Saudi Arabia	6.1	6.8
Saudi Arabia	5.5	5.1	Netherlands	3.3	6.1
Egypt	2.4	3.4	Libya	1.4	5.7
Netherlands	6.3	3.4	UK	5.7	4.0
USSR	1.4	2.5	Iraq	2.4	3.5
EEC	49.0	54.1	USA	4.8	2.9
			EEC	44.2	47.0

Sources: OECD Monthly Statistics of Foreign Trade, Series A, taken from Economist Intelligence Unit, 1985a: 26.

Greece's foreign trade balance deficit increased from $4,432.8 m. in 1978 to $6,696.6 m. in 1981, while in 1982 it went down to $5,927 m. and in 1983 to $5,410 m. This meant that it declined from 6.3 per cent of the GNP in 1981 to 4.8 per cent in 1982 owing especially to the drop in imports (Hellenic Industrial Development Bank, 1983; EIU, 1984c).

The trade deficit used to be covered by a substantial surplus in the balance of invisible payments, but the surplus of invisibles declined from 50 per cent of imports in 1971 to 33 per cent in 1981. Between 1971 and 1981, exports rose from 32 per cent of imports in 1971 to 42 per cent in 1981. During the period 1978–81, the trade deficit worsened because of the rise of petroleum prices. The balance of payments increased from $958.9 m. in 1978 to $2,421 m. in 1981, but in 1982 went down owing to the decline of imports as shown in Table 5.4 (Hellenic Industrial Development Bank, 1983; EIU, 1984c). It increased however to $2,130 m. in 1984 also shown in Table 5.4.

TABLE 5.4. *Balance of Payments (in $m.) 1981–1984*

	1981	1982	1983	1984
Exports	4,771	4,141	4,105	4,394
Imports	(11,468)	(10,068)	(9,491)	(9,745)
TRADE DEFICIT	(6,697)	(5,927	(5,386)	(5,351)
Invisible receipt	6,482	6,098	5,529	5,289
of which:				
tourism	1,881	1,527	1,176	1,313
shipping	1.826	1,657	1,309	1,095
emigrants' remittances	1,080	1,043	935	922
Invisible payments	(2,206)	(2,056)	(2,019)	(2,068)
NET INVISIBLE SURPLUS	4,276	4,042	3,510	3,221
BALANCE ON CURRENT ACCOUNT	-2,421	-1,885	-1,876	-2,130

Source: OECD, 1986: 16

Table 5.5 sheds light on the deterioration of the balance of payments situation between 1983 and 1985 (first ten months of each year). The trade balance grew considerably worse between 1984 and 1985 and was compounded by the continuing decline in invisible surplus.

Given the balance of payments problem and large amounts of public sector debt, Greece has been borrowing at a high rate as illustrated by the fact that since 1980 the government debt has almost doubled every two years. In 1984 Greece's net borrowing

TABLE 5.5. *Balance of payments (in $ m.) for January–October of 1983–1985*

	January–October		
	1983	1984	1985
Trade Balance	−4,430	−4,493	−5,320
Invisible Surplus	2,938	2,795	2,595
Current Balance	−1,492	−1,698	−2,725

Source: OECD, 1986: 16

requirement for financing the public sector was 584 bn. drachmas or 15.5 per cent of the GNP. Foreign borrowing was 29 per cent of the total borrowing with an increasing proportion of the debt being denominated in foreign currency. According to the OECD and the Bank of International Settlements, in June 1983 Greece ranked fifteen out of twenty-three countries in terms of foreign debt. Greece's debt was estimated at $11.9 bn. (EIU, 1984a). The servicing of this debt has created an enormous problem for according to the International Monetary Fund it will cost Greece $2,221 m. in 1986 increasing possibly to $4,151 m. in 1990 (EIU, 1986b: 13).

In conclusion, the Greek economy faces difficult problems. The decline in investments and revenues from invisibles coupled with high public sector borrowing, high inflation, and increasing unemployment contribute to a rather pessimistic outlook for the late 1980s. However, one positive indication that the stabilization measures may be working is that in the first two months of 1986 there was a 33.8 per cent decline in the current account deficit from $737 m. in 1985 to $488 m. (Embassy of Greece, 1986b: 5). The economic picture is further aggravated by the international climate, particularly the tension between Greece and Turkey. Both countries are engaged in an arms race which drains the financial resources of each. In Greece about 13 per cent of the regular budget expenditures for 1985 were allocated to defence. If the economic situation continues to deteriorate and more borrowing is required to meet its obligations, this will have long range impact on Greece's national independence and identity.

Notes

1. The Third Road to Socialism involves 'social control of the means of production' for the broader social interest (Papandreou, 1984). The key elements in the PASOK use of socialism are decentralization and participation rather than nationalization. The socialization of what are already public enterprises and utility companies involves trying to make them more functional by developing better planning, consistent pricing, and an investment policy. They are to be made more accountable to the public and the government rather than give certain advantages to large private interests. In certain strategic sectors of the economy (e.g. mineral resources, defence industry, pharmaceuticals) a system of social control is being achieved either through the outright purchase

(following constitutional provisions) or through the acquisition of majority shareholding.

2. The unit of Greek currency is the drachma. It has fluctuated considerably in relation to the American dollar and other currencies. Since the devaluation, the drachma has been allowed to slide against a group of mainly European currencies in order to maintain competitiveness. From December 1985 to May 1986 the drachma appreciated 9.4 per cent against the dollar but depreciated 3.2 per cent against other OECD currencies (EIU, 1986c: 17). In late October 1986 approximately 135 drachmas equalled $1 (buying rate) and 140 drachmas (selling rate) while £1 sterling approximately equalled 190 drachmas (buying rate) and 198 drachmas (selling rate).
3. For a review of some of the literature concerning world systems theory, see Wallerstein (1974); Chirot (1977); and Chirot and Hall (1982). For information on the semi-periphery and Greece in particular, see Seers *et al.*, 1979; Evangelinides, 1975; and Petras, 1983.
4. The results of the 1984 labour force survey show only 50,000 managerial and administrative workers compared to census reports of 74,000 such workers in 1981. It is difficult to determine how much of this decline is due to the different methods of counting workers in the annual survey and the census reports.
5. This pattern of entrepreneurial ownership especially in the service sector is also characteristic of the Greeks of the diaspora (Kourvetaris, 1987).
6. For an investment to receive Law 1262/1982's benefits, the Ministry of National Economy must first approve it as a 'productive' one (i.e. it is involved perhaps in the construction or extension of factories, the purchasing of new machinery, electronic computers, warehouses, refrigerated ships, new means of transportation, building, extension, or renovation of hotels or spas). In the first eight months of 1985 43.4 bn. drachmas were approved under Law 1262. It takes about 18 months between approval and first disbursements of funds. Proposed investments in manufacturing have been the highest (54 per cent), followed by services (34 per cent), and agricultural, mining, and forestry (12 per cent) (EIU, 1985b: 12). To develop the countryside and promote economic decentralization, Law 1262 divided the country into four regions—developed (A); intermediate (B); backward (C); and frontier (D); with more generous benefits being given for creating employment in backward and frontier/border areas. Usually the companies pay a 40 per cent tax rate rather than a 45 per cent one (Peat, Marwick, Mitchell & Co., 1983; Gianaris, 1984). To provide for greater self-management, Law 1262 also favours the formation of agricultural co-operatives. It provides grants for 10 per cent to 50 per cent of the cost of investment to those who start agricultural, manufacturing, and other productive

enterprises and provides loans with interest subsidization, tax exemptions, and high depreciation allowances. Rural co-operatives are trying to integrate vertically and horizontally to include basic production, processing, and distribution of products like cereals, fruits, cotton, and olive oil.

6

GREEK CULTURE AND SOCIETY*

THIS chapter will highlight some of the salient aspects of Greek culture and society that contribute to the formation of Greek identity. We briefly examine some of the major themes and issues related to language, education, family, religion, and the arts and humanities, all of which have added to the cultural and institutional continuity that has transmitted and maintained Greek identity throughout its long turbulent history. Cultural values and norms are usually channelled through its institutions. Greek identity has been shaped not only by the social institutions of family, religion, and education but also by the rich cultural heritage in literature, music, dance, theatre, and folklore that has long sustained and nourished the Greek people. The arts reflect Greece's customs, traditions, sorrows, and tribulations as well as its elations and triumphs. Greek literature and music, both of Greece and of the Greeks of the diaspora, abound with themes concerning love, yearning, parting, separation, sorrow, death, nostalgia, fate, migration, war, and the like. One cannot understand the Greek identity and the Greek people unless one appreciates Greek culture.

MODERN GREEK LANGUAGE

One of the most dynamic components of modern Greek culture is the language, which is a major aspect of cultural identity and historical continuity. Modern Greek is the spoken language of Greece, Southern Cyprus, and many Greek communities in the diaspora. It has evolved from classical Greek and preserves many of its morphological, syntactic, and lexical elements. Politis (1973) distinguishes three major developments of modern Greek—the Hellenistic *Koine* (AD 300–500), the medieval period (550–1453), and the modern (1453 to the present). Friar (1973) traces modern

* Yorgos A. Kourvetaris wrote the introductory section and those on language, family, religion, and music, and theatre and folklore. Betty A. Dobratz wrote the sections on education and literature.

Greek back to the Hellenistic *Koine* or common Greek which was based primarily on Attic Greek but transformed in morphology, diction, and pronunciation during the period of Alexander the Great. It is in the Hellenistic *Koine* Greek that the New Testament was written, and the modern Greek spoken language *Demotike* evolved from this over the centuries. In other words, it was the Hellenistic *Koine*, the language of the New Testament, that provided the base of medieval and modern Greek. During the time of the birth of Christ an effort was made to revive the classical language of Greece which led to a dichotomy between written and spoken Greek, a bilingual problem or *diglossia* which according to Friar has plagued Greece to the present time.

The *diglossia* of the Hellenistic times led to two basic forms of modern Greek—the *Katharevousa* and the *Demotike*. The *Katharevousa* is a puristic and archaic form with a very complex grammar, syntax, and diction derived from the classical and Hellenistic Greek culture. The *Demotike* on the other hand is a more vernacular form of spoken Greek with easier grammar, syntax, and diction. Greece's development into a nation-state in the mid-nineteenth century was directly connected with the controversy over what form the modern language would take. Two groups of Greek linguistic scholars emerged and persisted until recently. The purists insisted on the adoption of *Katharevousa* and the demoticists advocated the adoption of the vernacular. The linguistic debate was linked to the ideological and political cleavages of the period between the republicans (Venizelists) and the Royalists. The former promoted the adoption of the *Demotike* while the latter advocated the adoption of the *Katharevousa*.

The language issue divided the people between the purists and the demoticists. In 1911 and 1918, the Greek Parliament discussed the language issue. Indeed, the constitutions of 1911 and 1955 established *Katharevousa* as the official language of Greece. However, during their reign in the 1920s, the republicans brought back *Demotike*. Again when the royalists came to power they burned all the books written by the advocates of the *Demotike*. Later, *Demotike* was reinstated by General Pangalos (Psomas, 1974). The form of the language continued to vacillate from the 1920s to the 1960s. During the military dictatorship (1967–74) the colonels brought back *Katharevousa*, but with the restoration of democracy in 1974 *Demotike* was adopted. At present *Demotike* is the accepted language of modern Greece and is used almost universally by newspapers, magazines, and modern writers of poetry and fiction.

Greek is a highly phonetic language, and the sounds of its letters do not change. To facilitate pronunciation, an accent appears on words of more than one syllable. The Greek language has twenty-four letters divided into seven vowels and seventeen consonants. Greek grammar has ten parts of speech. Verbs, nouns, pronouns, adjectives, participles, and articles are the parts that are inflected whereas adverbs, prepositions, exclamations, and conjunctions remain the same. Different letters have the same sound which makes spelling difficult. The modern scientific analysis of Greek linguistics has been influenced by the work of European and American linguistic scholars. Two of the founding fathers of Greek linguistics as a scientific discipline, Jean Psicharis (1854–1929) and George Hatzidakis (1848–1941) were influenced by French and German linguists respectively.

Many Greek and non-Greek linguistic experts have commented on the impressive continuity of the Greek language. Prominent among the Greek scholars was Adamántios Koraés, a classical scholar, a physician, and an *émigré* who spent most of his life in France. Thomson (1966) believes that of all the European languages, Greek has the longest and the fullest recorded history—from the seventh century BC to the present. While Italian, for example, has come to differ radically from classical Latin, modern Greek clearly shows its relationship with classical Greek. In addition, classical Greek has had a marked influence on modern languages, serving as the source for scientific terminology and for innumerable word forms.

EDUCATION

The Greek education system was established in the 1830s, and since then, education has figured as a prominent issue in discussions related to political, cultural, and economic affairs, especially in terms of national development, modernization, and efficient administration. While liberal parties have sponsored a series of generally short-lived reform movements, the educational structure has been remarkably durable and stable owing in part to the extreme centralization of the state bureaucracy and the lack of funding. Two significant reforms that have endured have been the shift from a three-level eleven-year general education programme to a two-level twelve-year system (six years primary school and six years secondary) that passed in 1929, and the extension of free education to the secondary and university levels that became law in 1964. During the last fifty years or so proposed reforms have favoured *Demotike* as the language of instruction, more rationalism and critical thought in programmes, and vocational education (Frangoudakis, 1981: 7).

The late George Papandreou, the former liberal prime minister, made reforms in education in the mid-1960s, but the military dictatorship rejected most of them. However, the New Democracy Party and Karamanlis supported similar reforms in the mid-1970s for it is generally accepted that the military junta's conservative policies left education in a crisis by the time democracy returned in 1974. While new policies were introduced quite rapidly, they were often oriented to a change of method rather than substantive and fundamental reform (Dimaras, 1981; Bombas, 1983).

Three major bills were passed in the mid 1970s. Law 186/75 established a much-needed Centre of Educational Studies and In-Service Training (KEME) to contribute to curriculum development, improve teaching, and generally modernize the educational system. A new law 'On The Organization and Administration of General Education' called for nine years of compulsory education rather than six. *Demotike* language was introduced to all levels of education, and ancient Greek authors were to be read in translation at secondary schools. At the same time Law 576/77 dealt with the organization and administration of secondary and higher vocational and technical schools.

After completion of the ninth grade, students could enter a general lyceum, a technical–vocational lyceum, or a middle technical vocational school with entrance to the former two being based on standardized national examinations. Because many objected to the examination process, believing that a child's chance for university education would be unfairly determined by the time the child was fifteen years old (Kazamias, 1978), the New Democracy government modified its stringent examination and enrolment policy. A 1978 study (Kassotakis, 1981) shows that students continue to reject pre-university technical studies because they feel they will receive a better education and have a greater chance of success in the university if they have had the general secondary programme. As in the US, technical education and employment have low social prestige in Greece.

During the 1970s higher education was divided into two segments: (1) the highest educational institutions—universities and polytechnics—which were self-governing independent institutions and (2) teacher training colleges and higher technical institutions (KATEE) which were not self-governing or independent. Greece follows an admission policy that limits the number of places available in schools (*numerus clausus*) with the number of entrants decided upon each year. While enrolments in higher education have increased to four times the amount they were in the early 1960s, this accommodates only about 20 per cent of those who wish to study (Psacharopoulos and Kazamias, 1980: 139; Dimaras, 1983). At the university level institutions in 1982/3, there were 90,685 students and 3, 352 faculty with doctorates. In 1981/2 in the higher technical and vocational education institutions there were 21,904 students with 5,245 graduating (Ministry of National Education and Cults, 1983: Tables 11 and 15). The number of Greek students abroad has also been increasing (Polydorides, 1978), and in the late 1970s it was estimated that as many as 30,000 students were in universities outside Greece (Bombas, 1983: 70).

Since the early 1900s Greeks could be characterized as having an inflated desire for education (over-education). Even in the countryside the people display a strong passion for education (Lambiri-Dimaki, 1983; Tsoucalas, 1981) and may well expect more benefits from education than is realistic. One study of the structure of earnings in Greece by level of education for 1960, 1964, and 1977 found that the rate of return to school, especially to higher education, decreased dramatically between the early 1960s and the late 1970s probably owing to the increase in the supply of educated students. Thus an anomaly exists with a high social demand for education in the face of relatively low financial remuneration (Psacharopoulos, 1982).

Some characteristics of Greek higher education are atypical in comparison with those of other European societies. For example, the percentage of students in law and the social sciences is the highest while the percentage of technology students is the lowest of any OECD countries (Tsoucalas, 1981: 111–12). Also selection bias according to social class is rare, although children of farmers and workers still suffer some discrimination (Tsoucalas, 1981; Lambiri-Dimaki, 1983). Finally the amount of money spent on education (as a percentage of GNP) is one of the lowest among OECD countries (about 2.1 per cent) although the overall enrolment ratio is one of the highest (Wasser, 1979: 86). Recently, however, the PASOK government is increasing Greece's expenditures on education, so that it now totals 10 per cent of the regular budget expenditures (EIU, 1985a: 23).

There is little major research being done at the universities, and there is often a lack of commitment and involvement on the part of faculty and students. A high number of university students work and thus may not regularly attend lectures and seminars. Also professors may hold several jobs (e.g. as consultants) and thus possibly neglect their university responsibilities (Pesmazoglou, 1981).

In addition to the problems in higher education, there are problems with Greek education in general. Dimaras (1978: 20) maintains that the traditional and authoritarian character of Greek education remains; the emphasis is still on a classical general education with outdated curricula (Kondilis, 1981). The Greek heritage from ancient times that is a part of Greek identity is so rich that educators naturally want students to learn about it in detail. At the same time, however, stressing this means less emphasis on the modern and perhaps more practical subjects. Knowledge is often given rather than discovered, and rote memorization is emphasized. Further, Dimaras (1981: 22) notes that the public used to perceive school as an institution of enlightenment, but now views it as 'an establishment which provides paper qualifications indispensable for the next level of schooling or for employment'. When financially possible, students have resorted to attending crash courses at *frontisteria*, which are private and expensive schools providing tutoring to pass entrance exams and raise students' grades.

Greek education is extremely centralized resulting in government control of almost everything including the relationship between teachers and students, the structure of the classroom, the programmes and timetables, the publication and distribution of all textbooks (Anthogalidou-Vassilakakis, 1981), and the ideological content of the schooling. As in many other societies, the schools in Greece tend to reinforce middle-class values of obedience, piety, hard work, love and respect for family, religious moralism, and nationalism (Persianis, 1978; Dimaras, 1978; Yerou, 1981). Based on a study of about 400 Athenian sixth-graders, Marmarinos (1981) concluded that Greek schools reward convergent or conforming behaviour but not divergent thinking and questioning.

There are also regional, class, and sex discrepancies in education. The primary education offered in one- or two-room schools of mountain towns and on isolated islands as well as the schooling in working-class neighbourhoods in urban areas is probably the worst (Yerou, 1981). Women are much more likely to be illiterate than men and less likely to have completed higher education, secondary, and primary school, although differences are not so great among younger men and women (Dobratz, 1986).

The Reforms under PASOK

Since coming to power in 1981 PASOK has made a number of changes in the educational system in order to modernize and democratize it. The reforms have centred around the abolition of entrance exams for the lycea, changes in university and higher technical and vocational education, and a new selection system for entry to university-level and higher institutions. Those who have completed the ninth grade now have the automatic right to admission (without examination) to either a general or technical lyceum. All students at the general lyceum follow the same courses during the first two years, but in the third year they select one of four streams—emphasizing mathematics, natural science, social science, or the classics—that leads to higher education. A fifth stream stressing liberal arts is available for those who plan to enter the labour force.

The new selection system for higher education is based on the grades received when moving from first to second to third year, the general graduation mark received at the end of the third year, and especially the grades attained in national examinations in the chosen preparatory option stream subjects. As previously, persons who are not accepted may later re-attempt to gain admission by improving their scores, but now the government has set up free state-supported Post-Lyceum Preparatory Centres to help prepare such students and thus neutralize the effect of the private *frontisteria*.

The KATEE (Centres for Higher Technical and Vocational

Education) were abolished in 1983 with Technical Education Institutions (TEI), a self-governed public body, replacing them. The university structure was changed mainly by Law 1268/1982 which tried to decentralize the education system and emphasize the autonomy of individual universities. Instead of professorial chairs, faculties now consist of professors, associate professors, assistant professors, and lecturers. There has been a transfer of authority to the departments which are responsible for formulating teaching and research policy. All segments of the university are to be represented in decision-making including students, who comprise 50 per cent of the number of faculty on a general council which runs a department. Students are also represented on the electoral bodies that choose the administrative heads of the universities. According to Grant (1986), who used interviews and written sources from October 1984 to June 1985, the issue of student participation has been quite controversial. Many faculties question the maturity of the students in dealing with departmental academic issues and dislike the extreme politicization of departmental and administrative concerns. In addition, Grant argues that university administrators and professors, who had previously functioned in a centralized and bureaucratic system, have not totally understood the opportunities available to them for reform.

The Student Movement

While many student movements were gaining attention for their militancy in the late 1960s, Greek students were being repressed by the military dictatorship. The culmination of repression was marked by the November 1973 events at the *Polytechnio* in Athens when students and other dissidents barricaded themselves inside chanting such slogans as 'freedom, bread, and education'. When the students refused to give in, one of the army tanks broke through the iron gates leaving many dead and wounded. Indeed 17 November is still commemorated each year; it symbolizes the struggle for civil liberties and the right to free and participatory education.

The Greek student movement, with its organizations strongly aligned with the various political parties, is now regarded as one of the more radical ones in Western Europe. In the elections held in March 1985 PASP (PASOK aligned) received 27.38 per cent of the vote, PSK (Communist Party) 27.19 per cent, DAP (New Democracy) 27.18 per cent, and Democratic Struggle (Communist Party-Interior) 12.3 per cent. In the 1986 elections, the KKE affiliated PSK was first in both the Higher Education Institutions (AEI) and Technical Schools (TEI) with 29.13 per cent of the vote and 32.73 per cent respectively. New Democracy Party considered itself quite successful because its student group came in second in the AEI with 28.9 per cent (compared to 20.43 per cent for the PASOK affiliated PASP). The PASOK affiliated youth group only narrowly defeated the New Democracy group at the Technical Schools (27.11 per cent to 26.60 per cent). The Communist-Interior student organization (DADE) was fourth with 10.14 per cent of the AEI vote and 6.03 per cent of the TEI vote (Athens News Agency, 19 April 1986d: 7). Thus one sees that university students show much stronger support for the Communist parties than the average Greek voters. On issues related to education, students often have been very critical of increasing the technological and scientific orientation of their curricula, and of the strenuous examination policy. They favour active participation in university decision-making and more open admission policies. On political issues student activists have been critical of the US, the presence of American bases, Greek membership in NATO and the EEC, foreign interference in Cyprus, and exploitation by multinational corporations.

FAMILY

The central role of marriage and the family in the social and cultural life of Greece has been noted by both Greek and non-Greek scholars. Sanders (1967) and McNeill (1978) have singled out the family and religion as Greece's most important social institutions and believe that they sustained Greek identity and culture, particularly through the long Ottoman rule.

Since the 1960s many demographic, economic, political and socio-cultural changes have had a major impact on Greek marriage and the family. The traditional sex roles, male domination, and the institution of the dowry are disappearing, although the changes come unevenly, and more slowly to the rural areas than to the urban. Lambiri-Dimaki (1983) examines a number of shifts that occur as a less permissive society gives way to a more permissive one with egalitarian sex roles. These shifts reflect the rise of egalitarian ideology, the liberalization of social norms, the higher levels of public education, the shifting patterns of population, migration, and occupations.

The urbanization and modernization of Greek society has influenced the already changing social structure of the Greek family. Although the differentiation between urban and rural families persists, it is not as pronounced as it used to be. By and large the family in Greece has become nuclear or conjugal (parents and children only) and married couples are less likely to live close to their parents. Likewise, the patriarchal family has become more egalitarian. Under a recent Family Law both husbands and wives have equal rights and equal obligations, at least in theory if not necessarily in practice. No longer is the husband the sole head of the household.

The most important characteristic of the modern Greek family is the reduction of its size. In fact, the Greek government has offered economic assistance for those who have more than two children. The new low birth rate in Greece is attributed to external migration of the young, the work of women outside the home, urbanization, abortion, and various psycho-social and economic pressures (Safilios, 1967; Presvelou 1976). Although abortion is a controversial issue, like in the US, and it is illegal, it nevertheless takes place especially in big cities.

In the past, the *proxenio* (arranged marriage) was prevalent in the rural Greek family and should be understood in the context of the Greek kinship system, for mate selection was an affair that went beyond the immediate parties concerned. Sanders (1967: 8) distinguished three major types of marital selection in agricultural communities: marriage arranged by parents, marriage with parental consent, and marriage by the future couple themselves. The *proxenio* highlights the importance of marriage and of the family as an enduring, interdependent social institution. Marriage is not to be taken lightly. It is not simply the union of two independent individuals but it was and still is considered a fundamental union of two families. In the past romantic love was not a prerequisite in Greek marriage; today romantic love and physical attraction play a more decisive role, and marriage is less often arranged by parents and relatives in cities where the choice of the marriage partner is usually left to the individual.

An aspect of the arranged type of marriage was the dowry system which called for the bride's family to provide their future son-in-law with a negotiated amount of cash or property in exchange for his acceptance of their daughter's hand in marriage. Although the dowry system has been legally abolished, to some extent it is still practised today, especially in rural Greece. Dowries were considered part of the economic stratification system in general in which marriage became a vehicle of class mobility for the parties concerned and larger dowries were associated with higher socio-economic classes. In the past the dowry system brought tragedy to many poor families in Greece, particularly to those with large numbers of girls. Many early Greek male immigrants sent money back to Greece to provide dowries for their sisters, nieces, or daughters. In the traditional Greek family the first male son had to wait until his sister or sisters were married before he could marry. Today most Greeks are against the institution of the dowry, though it is still favoured by those who are culturally conservative. The development of the institution of the dowry was most prevalent in the southern parts of Greece.

In the rural family, especially during earlier days of the extended family, hierarchy and authority were determined by age and sex with grandfather, father, grandmother, and mother ranked in that order (Campbell, 1964; Viontakis, 1980). However, the rapid urbanization of Greek society, the decline of male authority, and the rapid demise of the extended family even in the rural areas have made the modern Greek family less patriarchal.

On the basis of their research carried out under the Athenian Institute of Anthropos, Spinellis, Vassiliou, and Vassiliou (1970: 311–12) described the traditional male role as follows:

> The man is supposed to have more freedom of movement and to be less restricted than the woman. He has implicit permission to 'trespass' certain social barriers. Moreover, he is expected to be highly competitive and upwardly mobile, asserting himself in any situation. Typically, he has been persuaded to pursue the goals that he shares with his family and mostly with his mother. In this effort he counts on his in-group—those people who show concern for him, who are for the most part members of his family, who are his friends . . . Within this group he is supposed to be loyal, trustworthy, and sincere, responding to the generosity of his friends with even greater generosity.

Spinellis, Vassiliou, and Vassiliou (1970: 312) described the traditional female role in the following way:

From antiquity to the present, the woman has played a rather secluded social role. Early in her life her behavior is restricted and she is required to follow the prevailing moral code much more closely than is the case of the average boy of her age. In fact, Greek women, according to the traditional patterns, are not expected to become involved in socio-economic activities . . . Woman's increased participation in industry has nevertheless failed to elevate her position sufficiently to shape for her a new social role similar to that of the male.

The discrepancy between the 'ideal' and 'real' aspects of husband–wife and mother–father roles is evident if one examines what Friedl (1962) and Campbell (1964) refer to as the 'public' versus 'private' domains of behaviour in the rural family in Greece. In the public/social sphere, both husbands and wives put on a façade and behave according to the prevailing societal cultural norms. These norms depict Greek husbands/fathers as if they were the true masters and dominant figures within the family unit while the wives/mothers are expected to behave in a submissive manner, particularly in public places when their husbands are present. However, in a more private family setting, husbands/fathers and wives/mothers change considerably and behave more naturally. What seems to the outsider to be the unequivocal dominance exercised by the husband over the wife in reality is not so obvious in more informal family settings. Women in Mediterranean societies in general and Greece in particular exercise more power directly and indirectly within the private domain of the home than in the public domain (Friedl, 1962).

Female sexuality is seen as a threat to men and male honour (*timi*) for a woman is expected to guard herself and the reputation of her family by cultivating a sense of shame (*dropi*) (Dubisch, 1983). Safilios (1967) has found that the husband's authority tends to be higher in the absence of children and is lowered when children are born. The presence of children gives a Greek wife a greater authority in child-rearing and decision-making; a wife's employment also lowers the degree of a husband's authority in the Greek family. However, the wife's authority tends to be limited to the 'feminine' decisions and does not threaten the husband's position in the family. Employed wives in Greece tend to be less satisfied than non-employed wives. Those Greek women who tend to be more satisfied are traditional, married to traditional husbands, and accepting of the idea of male dominance. One of the primary functions of the Greek family has been procreation, for the birth of a child is an affair not only of the family but of the Church as well. Motherhood is highly esteemed in the Greek Orthodox church, and those couples who have children are looked upon by the church as fortunate and blessed. Childless couples, especially husbands, are made uncomfortable in the Greek community. Parents tend to over-protect, overfeed, and over-support their children. Vermuelen (1970) found that the same sex parent tends to be more controlling and nurturant, while the cross-sex parent tends to be more protective. He also believes that parents who are dominating in their conjugal roles tend to be dominant in their parental roles. The power of the father is lower in the higher social classes especially in so far as boys are concerned.

Amicability has not been a significant concern in Greek marital relationships: 'The relationship between husbands and wives is strongly oriented around their roles as parents rather than around their roles as spouses' (Vermeulen, 1970). The focus of the Greek family is the children's welfare, and boys have more privileges than girls. Around adolescence children become more detached from their father (Viontakis, 1980), although a mother-and-daughter relationship continues even beyond the latter's marriage. For many daughters the adjustment after marriage is never completed because they remain emotionally dependent on their mothers.

Most of the literature on sex roles reflects research and findings of the 1960s and 1970s, but there have been some recent changes in sex roles especially in the last few years which reflect greater equality of the sexes. More specifically Lambiri-Dimaki (1983) notes the following indications that values are shifting: (1) more and more women are playing a public role rather than being limited to the home; (2) males are no longer defined as superior nor females as inferior; (3) women are actively promoting their own interests by joining women's organizations etc.; (4) there is a wider realization that women need not be fulfilled solely by marriage and motherhood; (5) the younger generation considers companionship, understanding, independence of the couple from family interference, and mutual attraction to be more important factors in sustaining marriage than financial interests and raising children.

The PASOK government has established councils on equality of the sexes which operate in every prefecture in Greece. The wife of the Prime Minister, Margaret Papandreou, has spearheaded the women's movement in Greece along with a number of upper-middle-class Greek women, particularly from the Athens area. Since 1975 the Greek constitution has specified (article 4 paragraph 2) that 'Greek men and women have the same obligations and rights.' The new family law of 1983 provides that (1) both parents, not just the man, decide about family matters; (2) the institution of dowry is abolished but the wife has the obligation to contribute to the family income according to her economic resources; and (3) the surname does not have to change with marriage. The rise of PASOK contributed to the acceptance of these liberalized laws which are in accordance with the articles of the 1975 Constitution.

RELIGION

Religion has been a dominant and conservative force in all facets of modern Greek history. The Orthodox church has spread to Eastern Europe, Russia, the eastern Mediterranean, Australia, North and South America, and parts of Africa and Asia. While the primary cultural influence on Orthodoxy is Greek, this does not mean that the Greek Orthodox Church is exclusively Greek, just as the Roman Catholic Church is not purely Italian.

Eastern Orthodoxy can be considered a third branch of Christianity. Like Protestantism, Eastern Orthodoxy is a multi-denominational Christian grouping that includes Greek, Russian, Serbian, Romanian, Albanian, Syrian, and other ethno-religious groups. But unlike Catholicism and Protestantism, Eastern Orthodoxy derives its cultural traditions from Christian Byzantium rather than from the West. Furthermore, each Eastern Orthodox denomination is a distinct ethnic denomination. Each one is autocephalous (self-governing) and only symbolically, dogmatically, and historically identifies itself as a member of the Eastern Orthodox Church.

The first Greek Christian church was founded in about AD 50 by St Paul who visited Athens and spoke to the Athenians about the unknown god. The Athenians of this period still believed in polytheism, but St Paul's preaching converted many of them to Christianity. The famous epistles that Paul wrote to various Christian communities in Greece and Asia Minor continue to be read in biblical Greek in all Greek Orthodox churches to this day. For 1,000 years, Eastern Orthodox Christianity was very influential in the Eastern Roman Empire known also as Byzantium. Constantine the Great, the Christian emperor of the Eastern Roman empire, officially legitimized Christianity in the East as the state religion in about AD 330.

The Greek Orthodox religion is an integral part of the Greek nation. Greek Orthodoxy is the national religion of Greece, and for the majority of Greeks, Orthodoxy and Greekness are inseparable. Since the Greek language was once spoken everywhere in the East, Hellenistic culture and civilization influenced Christianity and were accepted everywhere in the Eastern Roman world. Although in 146 BC the Romans subjugated Hellas (Greece), the Greeks continued to influence the Romans through their culture, religion, art, science, philosophy, and literature. Greeks later became partners with the Romans in what is known as Greco-Roman Civilization.

In 1054 Christianity bifurcated into what is known as the Western and Eastern churches. The reasons for the split were political, historical, administrative, and dogmatic. The Crusades, the influence of the Venetians, the neighbouring Arabs, Persians, and Slavs, and the rise of Islam weakened the Byzantine empire, and subsequently the Ottomans (the ancestors of modern Turks) sacked Constantinople (1453) and conquered the eastern Mediterranean including Greece. The Eastern Orthodox Christians in the Balkans became subjects of Ottoman Muslim rule.

The major Fathers of the Greek Orthodox Church, John the *Chrysostomos* (the golden-mouthed), St Basil the Great, and St Gregory the Theologian, established the social, intellectual, and theological foundations of Eastern Orthodox tradition. The first two wrote liturgies of the Greek Orthodox church which are still used today. They were exposed to Greek philosophy and tried to blend theology and philosophy as did the Western patristic and scholastic thinkers. During their lifetimes Eastern Orthodox Christianity reached its golden age. All three were prolific writers and had a profound influence on the Eastern Greek Orthodox church not only in the spiritual realm but also in social, moral, and charitable areas.

World Orthodoxy is composed of self-governing churches and consists of four ancient patriarchates, those of Constantinople (Istanbul, Turkey), Alexandria (Egypt), Antioch (Syria), and Jerusalem (Israel). Historically, the patriarchate of Constantinople occupies a special position and ranks first among the four. The heads of these churches bear the title of Patriarch. There are eleven other autocephalous churches—those of Russia, Romania, Serbia (Yugoslavia), Greece, Bulgaria, Georgia (USSR), Cyprus, Poland, Albania, Czechoslovakia, and Sinai. Except in the cases of Czechoslovakia, Poland, and Albania, all these churches are in countries where the Christian population is predominantly Orthodox. The churches of Greece, Cyprus, and Sinai are Greek, while the churches of Russia, Serbia, Bulgaria, Czechoslovakia, and Poland are Slavonic. The heads of the Russian, Romanian, Serbian, and Bulgarian churches also bear the title of patriarch, but the head of the Georgian church is called *Catholicos* and the heads of the other churches are called archbishops or metropolitans. The Greek Orthodox Church of North and South America is under the jurisdiction of the patriarchate of Constantinople.

Historically the Orthodox church of Greece is associated with the Ecumenical patriarchate and every other Orthodox church. According to the 1977/590 law the church and the state collaborate in the areas of religion, marriage, divorce, and the education of the young. The Greek Orthodox church in Greece includes the archdiocese of Athens and 77 other metropolises. The highest ecclesiastical authority of the Greek church is vested with the Holy Synod of the ecclesiastical hierarchy and includes the archbishop of Athens and all of Greece as the president along with the metropolitans (bishops) of the various districts of Greece.

Many Orthodox scholars agree that one of the most distinctive characteristics of Orthodox faith is its changelessness—its sense of living continuity with the past. This continuity manifests itself in the Orthodox tradition which is not only viewed as 'a protective conservative force but a principle of growth and regeneration' (Ware, 1963: 5, 203–7). That tradition includes the entire system of church doctrine, governance, worship, and art within Orthodoxy. The manifestations of Orthodox belief include the Bible, the Creed, the decrees of the Ecumenical Councils, the writings of the Eastern Orthodox fathers, the customs, the service books and the holy icons.

There are some basic dogmatic differences between the Orthodox and western churches. Unlike the Roman Catholics and the Protestants, the Orthodox believe that the Holy Spirit proceeds from the Father only and not from the Son. This dispute refers to the interpretation of the Holy Spirit in the Nicene-Constantinopolitan

Creed. Originally, the Creed read 'I believe . . . in the Holy Spirit, the Lord, the Giver of Life, who proceeds from the Father, who with the Father and the Son together is worshipped and together glorified.' This original form is recited unchanged by the East but the West inserted an extra phrase 'and from the Son' (in Latin *filioque*) after 'who proceeds from the Father'. The Orthodox argued that the Ecumenical Councils forbade any changes in the Creed which is the common possession of the whole church, but the West arbitrarily changed it without consulting the East. According to Greek Orthodox doctrine the trinity (father, son and holy spirit) are 'one in essence'—(*homoousios*) yet each is distinguished from each other. The father is the source of Godhead and is the principle (*arche*) of unity among the three. The Son is born of the Father and the Spirit proceeds from the Father.

The issue of infallibility of the Roman Catholic Pope which the Eastern church does not accept marks another major difference between Roman Catholics and Eastern Orthodox. While the Pope views infallibility as his own prerogative, the Greek Orthodox and all Orthodox Christians in general believe that in matters of faith the final decision rests not with the Pope alone but with a council representing all the bishops of the church (Ware, 1963: 57).

Other distinctions of lesser importance include clerical marriage, which the Orthodox Church allows although the Catholics practice celibacy, and different days of fasting. Additionally, Greeks use leavened bread in the Eucharist while the Catholics use unleavened bread or uzymes. In most other matters the Orthodox resemble the Catholics, holding in common, for example belief in the seven sacraments.

Owing to secularization, industrialization, urbanization, and political change the influence of the Orthodox church is declining in Greece. This is evident not only from the problems of recruiting clergy but also from church attendance which is higher in small towns and villages than in large cities. A further indication of deterioration in relations between church and state is the decision by the socialist government of PASOK in April 1987 to nationalize the monastic land owned by the church. This legislation has upset the church which threatened to join the Orthodox Church of Constantinople. Since the assumption of PASOK in 1981, the issue of separation of state and church has been raised.

The country church is the major institution in the life cycle of

Greeks, performing marriages, baptisms, and funerals, and is a communal-traditional organization. Festivities and holidays mean more in the countryside than in polluted and noisy Athens. This country church life was transplanted to America and other communities of the Greek diaspora and has become the focal point of community life for ethnic Greeks.

The most important religious holidays in the Greek Orthodox calendar are Easter, Christmas, and the Assumption of the Virgin Mary. Easter, rather than Christmas, is the major holiday for the Orthodox. Recently in annual meetings of Greek theologians there has been an effort to steer Orthodoxy back to its historical roots and its own eastern Byzantine tradition, which stress family, community life, other-worldliness, mysticism, ritual, and the like.

The religious element in the Greek identity is derived more from the East and Byzantine tradition than from the West. This problem of the dual identity—one religious and another secular—is not as pronounced among the Catholics and Protestants. It seems to us the Catholics and Protestants derive their identity from the same Western tradition while in both its secular and religious aspects, the Greek Orthodox faith has its own version of fundamentalism; it tries to resist modernizing and secularizing influences by adhering to an earlier code of religious discipline and dogma.

ARTS AND HUMANITIES

Greece is a country rich in the arts and humanities. Wherever one goes or looks there is a statue, a museum, a legend, a custom, a dance, a folk-tale, or folk art. Greece is full of poets and schools of poetry, and it is one of the few countries which has received two Nobel and two Lenin prizes in poetry during the last thirty years. Since we cannot cover all aspects of the arts and humanities, we must be selective in our discussion. We briefly examine music, theatre and dance, folklore, and literature as major contributing factors of Greek identity.

Music

Greece has a rich repertoire of music which reflects the different aspects and periods of Greek culture and society. The five most important types of music are ballads (*demotika*), popular folk-songs (*laika*), death laments (*miroloyia*), songs of the underclass (*rebetika*) and the Byzantine hymns or hymnology of the Greek Orthodox Church. During the long Ottoman rule Greeks developed *demotika* songs which are anonymous, heroic in character, and reflect the Greek people's struggles for freedom and independence from foreign rule. The *demotika* songs nourished the Greek national consciousness and maintained Greek ethnic identity, kept the flame of patriotism burning, and prepared the Greeks for the national awakening in 1821 against the Ottoman rule. Themes of freedom, death, motherland, parting, mountains, rulers, love, pain, persecution, justice, and the heroic deeds of Greek fighters are replete in *demotika* songs and *demotike* poetry. There are *demotika* songs for different occasions, i.e. for dinner, weddings, dancing, death, and mourning. The French scholar Claude Fauriel collected the first *demotika* songs.

The popular or *laika* folk-songs are the most universal form of music for Greeks everywhere. There is a proliferation of folk-singers and song-writers in Greece and even in the most remote villages you can hear most popular tunes. The themes of these songs are love, hate, parting, youth, death, mother, lovers, justice, village life, migration, and the sea. Many of the popular musicians and singers used to tour the Greek communities overseas in the past, but since external migration has steadily declined, musical groups less frequently go abroad.

Another type of music is the so-called *miroloyia* or the death laments. These death songs vary from area to area where women mourn outwardly, crying and wearing black during funerals of beloved ones; even after burial there is a long mourning period. Black, associated with death rituals and reinforced by the Eastern Orthodox faith, is common among the peoples of the Middle Eastern societies. There are laments about Greeks in foreign lands, themes of parting—*xenetia* (immigration to foreign lands), *patrida* (fatherland), yearning, and nostalgia. Parting or separation from family and friends is considered a form of death (Danforth, 1982). The southernmost part of Peloponnesos, known as Mani, is well known for its *miroloyia*.

Rebetica, the songs and music of the underclass or all those who are marginal or outlaws, emerged during the end of the nineteenth and the beginning of the twentieth century. The major theme of *rebetica* is love. Other themes tangentially related to love are hashish-smoking, drinking, being broke, and homesickness. The *rebetica* are songs of transition from tradition to modernity and are in decline as a modern form of music. *Rebetica* flourished alongside industrial development and the creation of the proletariat class. Damianakos (1976) found that *rebetica* express the ideology, the psycho-sentimental attitudes, the way of life, the idiosyncrasy, morality, and the philosophy of life of *rebetes* or the people who have rejected the conventions of society. He distinguished three major periods of the *rebetica*: the primary period (–1922), the classical period (1922–40), and the working class period (1940–53). The first period is characterized by songs about those who commit illegal and deviant acts i.e. alcoholics, inmates of prisons, people of the underclass, and the non-conventional. The second period includes songs of love and women, sadness, despair, protest, hedonism, amoralism, and the like. The working-class period overlaps with the second period and includes songs of love, women, protest, working-class life, emigration, dreams, and working-class consciousness.

The Greek Orthodox hymnology which has a Byzantine influence and tradition is also an important type of Greek music. Chanting is an essential aspect of Greek Orthodoxy. There are Greek Orthodox hymns for different occasions, i.e. for weddings, baptisms, funerals, feasts of saints, name days, and religious holidays.

The most popular performer and composer both inside and outside of Greece is Theodorakis whose popularity lies in his ability to write melodies. According to him, the three types of melody that the Greeks respond to are the music of the Orthodox church, the folk music of various regions of Greece, and the *rebetica*, Greece's urban 'blues' music (Holst, 1980). Theodorakis was among the first of modern Greek composers to organize large public concerts of his work and the work of his Greek colleagues, and to set to music the poetry of world-renowned writers.

In opera, the late Maria Callas was a celebrated diva and the late Nikos Moscona was an acclaimed baritone of the New York Metropolitan Opera. Some other prominent names in the world of music have been Mitropoulos, Xenakis, Skarlotas, Kalomiris, Hatzidakis, and Markopoulos. Greece is also a country of popular singers and musicians including such singers as Gounaris, Sophia Vebo, Tsitsanis, Xylouris (all deceased), Parios, Rousos, Dalaras, and others.

Theatre and Folklore

For the last ten years or so, there has been a cultural and artistic renaissance in Greece. Melina Mercouri, the internationally known actress who became famous from her role in the film 'Never on Sunday', is the Minister of Culture and Sciences. The most important classical outdoor theatre is the National Theatre of Epidaurus which every summer presents Greek classical dramas written by Aeschylus, Euripides, and Sophocles and comedies written by Aristophanes. At the Theatre of Dionysus of the Atticus by the foot of the Acropolis, plays are also presented as they are in other national and regional theatres such the lyrical opera of Athens, the national theatre of Northern Greece in Salonica and many more theatres in provinces.

The shadow theatre, known as 'Karaghiozis' is a *marionette* theatre which has an artistic, cultural, and folkloric element and is as much a *didactic* device as an amusement. Many scholars trace its origins and techniques to the religious and mystic theatre of the Far East, particularly of India and China. The appearance of 'Karaghiozis' shadow theatre in Greece is first mentioned during King Otho's time in the 1830s. During the mid-nineteenth century various newspaper accounts indicated that the shadow theatre was introduced by a Greek 'Karaghiozis player' from Constantinople. Originally, its main characters were Turkish and the content of the plays was so vulgar that it provoked feelings of indignation on the part of the Greek bourgeois audience. At the turn of the nineteenth century 'Karaghiozis' was Hellenized. The Greek 'Karaghiozis' portraying the intricacies of everyday life thrived as a popular spectacle which amused all social classes and had political, nationalist, and social class overtones. The early decades of the twentieth century were considered the golden period of the Greek 'Karaghiozis', but now it has declined as a form of entertainment.

Greece has a rich folkloric tradition that is an integral part of its neo-Hellenic civilization. The Greek term for folklore is *laographia*. Nicholas Politis (1852–1921) is the founder of Greek folkloric studies and the Greek folklore society which published the *Journal of Laographia* that now includes many volumes of legends and folk-tales. One of Politis's disciples, Stelpon Kyriakides (1887–1964), and the more modern folklorist George Megas are considered the leading folkloric scholars in Greece. All three stress the continuity between ancient and modern folklore. Many Greek folkloric scholars look at language, religion (the worship of saints, feasts), customs, myths, traditions, folk-tales, and superstitions for clues to the continuity between the past and present Greek culture and ethnic identity. For example, in modern Greek Orthodox Christianity the Archangel St Michael is closely linked to *charos*, the god of death. In fact many saints of the Orthodox religion closely correspond to ancient Olympian anthropomorphic gods, i.e. St George or St Demetrios can be compared to *Ares* (Mars), the god of War, or St Nicholas, the patron saint of the seamen, can be compared to Poseidon (Neptune), the god of the sea.

Austrian Johann George Van Hahn first collected Greek folk-tales and much later George Megas (1970) compiled a large number of them. The folk-lore archives in the Academy of Athens founded in 1927 has over 20,000 folk-tales. There are different types of folk-tales on fate (*moira*), mermaids (*gorgones*), fairies (*neraides*), dragons, the mother-in-law (an evil image in Greek folklore), animal tales, wonder tales, religious tales, tales of kindness and the like. After they left their village communities, the Greek immigrants vividly recollected these folk-tales and traditions and passed them on from generation to generation. Every Greek, for example, knows about the evil eye (the power superstitiously attributed to a person who inflicts injury or bad luck by a look). Many of these traditions were preserved through the Greek Orthodox church, families, and folk societies and organizations. Through the various religious feasts and celebrations the Greeks managed to maintain the social bonds of ethnic and cultural identity.

The folkloric tradition is alive in every corner of the country. One thousand or more cultural groups and folkloric dancing troupes rich in tradition operate in Greece. There are 300 or more folk museums and organizations which reflect the sustained interest of their creators and the people of Greece and thousands of objects of folkloric interest which represent the special customs of the agrarian, pastoral, and fishing life of the Greeks from 1453 to the present. Some of the most important centres of Greek folklore are the museum of popular/folk art in Athens, the educational and ethnological Museum of Macedonia in Thessaloniki, and the folkloric museum of history of the Peloponnesos (Nafplio) (Interview with Mr Provatakis, Ministry of Culture and Sciences, Summer 1984).

Every part of Greece has its links with nature, art, and history, and folk art remains one of the most important parts of the Greek culture. It tells of sorrows, passions, hopes, despair, elation, pride, persecution, homelessness, uprootedness, love, and parting. In most Greek cities and towns one finds some museum or workshop of popular or folk art that might include embroidery, weaving, tapestries, wood carving, and bronze, silver, and gold artifacts. Historically, during the eighteenth and early nineteenth centuries, folk art allowed Greeks to express their love for freedom and desire for national independence from Ottoman rule. The traditional art of silvercraft, for example, in Ioannina, the capital of Epirus, goes back two centuries. At present there are many silver workshops and even a school of silversmiths operating in Ioannina; 80 per cent of their products are hand-made. Local customs, nature, and modern and Byzantine art inspire themes and designs in folk art. It is a living history which is flourishing throughout Greece even in isolated mountain villages.

Greek Literature[1]

Greek literature has done much to capture and preserve the essence of Greek culture and identity. While poetry is by far the most significant form of literature in Greece, there was a limited tradition of novel writing even before the Greek War of Independence. These early novels focused on traditional village life and ethnographic studies; by the start of the 1900s authors were writing about city life especially in Athens. Writers like Theotokas, Kazantzakis, and Vassilikos used the novel as a medium to illustrate how people tried to answer questions about man's destiny in the world and the meaning of freedom, love, sacrifice, life, and death. Vassilikos, whose work reflects the conflicts and contradictions of Greek life and the struggle of people to maintain their culture and identity, has written more than fifty books including *Z*, based on the political assassination of Greek leftist deputy Lambrakis, *Photographs*, *The Monarch*, and *My Whole Life*.

Kazantzakis (1883–1957) wrote travel books, essays, poetry, and such novels as *Zorba the Greek*, which proclaims a dionysian thirst for life and vitality. Kazantzakis, whose work reflects existentialist ideas, believed that man's first duty was to the mind which imposes order on disorder and establishes rational boundaries, his second duty was to his heart which rejects rational boundaries, and his third duty was to free himself from the hope that either the mind or the heart could provide a deep understanding of the essence of phenomena. To show his vision of life, Kazantzakis wrote the long narrative poem *The Odyssey: A Modern Sequel* asking what is freedom and what is God? For him the fundamental nature of God is embodied in man's ceaseless search for freedom and salvation. God is created out of tragedy and strife rather than out of happiness. The dualities expressed in Kazantzakis's work are exemplified in the statement by his Odysseus: 'Death is the salt that gives to life its tasty sting' (Friar, 1973: 37). While one may have expected *The Odyssey* to be written in the classical tradition, it was basically anti-classical and anti-Hellenic. Kazantzakis also wrote invocations for such diverse characters as Dante, Greco, Saint Theresa, Don Quixote, Nietzsche, Buddha, and Mohammed.

In 1956 Kazantzakis was awarded the State Prize for drama and in 1957 the International Peace Prize, but he never received the Nobel Prize although nominated by Albert Schweitzer and Thomas Mann. His works have been translated into more than twenty languages. The Greek Orthodox church expressed its extreme dissatisfaction with parts of Kazantzakis's *Freedom or Death* and all of *The Last Temptation of Christ*. Therefore when he died in 1957 the Archbishop of Athens refused to allow his body to lie in state in Athens or be buried in a church cemetery. Thus he is buried on the Martinego Bastion, the old Venetian Wall that still surrounds part of his home town of Irakleion, Crete. On his grave is inscribed: 'I fear nothing, I hope for nothing, I am free.'

The major contribution of modern Greece to world literature is its poetry which has the 'longest and perhaps noblest tradition in the Western world' and has 'achieved universal validity' (Trypanis, quoted in Friar, 1973: 3). The written roots of Greek poetry go back to the *Iliad* and the *Odyssey*, although a long oral tradition existed even before them. The first didactic poet was Hesiod (*c.* 750 BC) who portrayed pastoral life in epic verse. With great emotion, Alcaeus, Sappho, and Anacreon (sixth century BC) wrote of love, war, and death.

Another significant period of Greek poetry before nationhood was the golden age of Cretan poetry (1590–1669) which began with the pastoral poem *The Shepherdess* (author unknown), a simple love story of a shepherd and shepherdess. The most renown works of the Cretan golden age are dramatic, and are regarded as the apex of Greek renaissance literature. Georgios Chortatsis, a versatile dramatic poet and contemporary of Shakespeare, introduced the theatre to Crete. His famous tragedy *Erophile* deals with the power of love between the daughter of a king and the prince of the court. Vitsenzos Kornaros (1553–1617) is probably not only the greatest of all Cretan poets but one of the most influential in the entire course of Greek poetry. His *Erotokritos*, a heroic verse romance, is regarded as a milestone in Greek literature (Trypanis, 1981).

The quality of modern Greek poetry is well known, but the quantity is also great,[2] representing possibly more published living Greek poets than American poets. It has been suggested that Greek writers, living in the face of wars, occupations, conflict, and political domination by stronger foreign countries, created an ideal imaginary world to help them escape reality and to counter the fact that Greece was no longer conquering other lands (Mackridge, 1983).

Greek poets draw on the ideal of 'know thyself', generally keep close to the popular tradition, and use the *Demotike* language. The poetry often uses Homeric and classical myths and motifs, especially the myth of Odysseus, the hero/wanderer with whom most Greeks identify owing to his complex and contradictory character. There is also a pervasive use of Eastern ritual, image, and ceremony associated with the Byzantine Church and Empire. Some of the favourite images in Greek poetry are the personification and glorification of the light and sun, the description of the azure sky as a dazzling dome of blue enclosing beautiful objects of nature, and the sea, sometimes fierce and stormy, other times peaceful, bringing people to the Greek shores or more often carrying them away from their homeland.

One of the predominant themes of the Greek poets is the search for national identity or what Nobel prize winning poet Elytis calls trying 'to find the true face of Greece'. The Greek poet has to accommodate his rich—sometimes too rich—past while developing his own style and voice (Keeley, 1983: xv). Friar (1973: 129) describes this search as follows: 'All modern Greek poets, whether consciously or subconsciously in the formulation of their aesthetics, their views of self and the world, must sooner or later come to terms with their glorious but burdensome heritage in their struggle to create an identity in their own epoch without betraying their past.'

Another significant theme is the search for freedom which is part of what Ikaris (1978) refers to as the Greek passion for liberty, love of justice, and thirst for truth. Kazantzakis stressed the relentless struggle for freedom even though he believed one could not attain the ideal. In *Romiosini* (1945–7) Ritsos brought forth the image of a freedomfighter who is a miniature of the Greek landscape, blending in with its tradition. In *Axion Esti* (1959) Elytis strives for liberation from suffering and pain through a meditation on the sea and landscape of the Aegean.

A third significant theme is the preoccupation with the sense of 'absence' and 'presence', or the relationship between the living and the dead. In Greek poetry the dead tend to be the famous ancestors of the Greek race who are talked to in periods of crisis. Encountering death forces one to evaluate the meaning of life. While it is useful to generalize about Greek poetry, one should be aware that as with Odysseus, the essence of the Greek national character and identity is found in its contradictions, its complexity, and its struggling opposites. The ancient contends with the modern, the East with the West, and the Dionysian—wild, uninhibited, frenzied—with the Apollonian—rational, ordered, disciplined, moderate.

In order to develop an appreciation of modern Greek poetry, we will briefly note some of its developments by looking at some of the major schools of poetry and poets. Following Greece's liberation, a literary group now known as the Old School of Athens emerged and flourished from 1830 to 1880. The poets who belonged to this school drew from the romantic themes of such poets as Byron, Shiller, and Hugo, and expressed their patriotism and nostalgia for the classical motifs. The School of the Ionian Islands developed at the same time but under Venetian influence since these islands had not been under Turkish rule and were not part of independent Greece until 1864. The poetry in this school was also patriotic and displayed nostalgia for union with the Greek nation. The greatest Ionian poets were probably Andreas Kalvos (1792–1869) and Dionysios Solomos (1789–1857) who may be considered the father of Greek demotic poetry. Early in 1823 Solomos write *Hymn to*

Liberty, part of which became the Greek national anthem, and in 1824 he wrote *On the Death of Lord Byron* in 166 quatrains.

Later, a group of young poets founded the New School of Athens which laid the groundwork for the influence of symbolism. One of its prominent figures, Kostis Palamas (1859–1943), had a profound effect on modern Greek poetry. To him all elements of Greece's long history and literature were significant, and he strove to blend the traditions and thought of both East and West to develop a sense of Greek consciousness.

The late nineteenth and early twentieth century was a time of turmoil and transition in Greek literature as well as for the Greek nation. After two humiliating defeats by the Turks in 1897 and 1922, frustrated Greeks had to face the end of the Great Idea. Symbolism, imported from France, became the dominant medium in poetry which was to be understood intuitively, symbolically, through the senses and not through the mind. It became modern in tone and suggestive, dreaming, drawing on symbols of one thing to represent another. Sikelianos, Varnalis, and Cavafy each adopted symbolism to enrich their own orientations. Both Sikelianos and Varnalis adhered to their generation's traditional techniques of writing, but Cavafy is often considered a forerunner of modern Greek poetry.

Angelos Sikelianos (1884–1951), born on the Ionian island of Lefkada, wrote *Prologue to Life* (1915–16) which focused on Greek landscape, the Greek race, woman, faith, and personal creativity, and later during the German–Italian occupation wrote poems of resistance and rebellion entitled the *Akritic Songs* (named after a border guard of the Byzantine Empire). The images of Eros and Hades were used in his work to help achieve a mystical communion with God. Sikelianos was a visionary and prophet who tried to assimilate the cultural heritage of Greece and the modern world and established the Delphic Ideal of brotherhood and peace including the idea of a centre in Delphi where the nations of the world might meet to discuss international issues.

Varnalis was born in Bulgaria in 1884 and died in 1974. As a youngster he idealized the Greece of his dreams, but when he came to Athens to study he became torn between the ideal image of ancient Greece and the real troubled world of modern Greece. He is credited with writing the first thoroughly leftist poem in Greece, *The Burning Light* (1922), which portrays man's fight for freedom based on the figures of Prometheus, Christ, and a modern proletarian leader. Most likely for political reasons Varnalis was fired from teaching literature in a secondary school in 1925. He wrote *Slaves Besieged*, a long epico-lyrical poem based on his feeling of despair over Greece's defeat in Asia Minor, and other poems expressing concern for social justice and hatred of war and of the oppression of the masses. In 1958 he was awarded the Lenin Peace Prize.

Cavafy (1863–1933), born in Alexandria, Egypt, is known as a cynical realist and an ironical commentator on human weakness who probably experienced guilt feelings concerning his own homosexuality. In his poetry he expressed two worlds: one had semi-historical and semi-fictional Hellenistic, Greco-Roman, or Byzantine settings, while the other displayed idealized and timeless love reflected in nostalgia, reminiscence, and the erotic poems of homosexual youths. Cavafy's characters often displayed human frailty, worldliness, opportunism, and egoism, which he depicted with tolerance and understanding. His famous 'Waiting for the Barbarians' reveals mankind's suppressed desire to be forced to yield to someone else's rule and to get rid of the responsibilities of making decisions.

The emergence of modern Greek poetry with free verse and restrained tones may best be marked by George Seferis's work, *The Turning-Point* (1931) and *Mythistorima* (*Myth of Our History*) (1935). Mackridge (1983) claims that Seferis (1900–1971), a Greek born in Asia Minor, lost his sense of home and thus the ideals and optimistic beliefs of his youth. Seferis agonizingly contrasts past glory with modern cultural and ethical deterioration in *Mythistorima* where various characters express despair as they wander among the statues, 'broken marbles', and 'tragic columns' symbolizing in part the drying up of the human imagination in the modern world. The landscape with dry cisterns and empty wells symbolizes the wasteland of the spirit and only in death can one find true serenity. Seferis's themes include the sense of separation, exiled wandering, nostalgia to return home, and the desire to communicate with the dead, to learn from them, and to compare past glory with the wasteland of modern life. In 1963 he was awarded the Nobel Prize for Literature.

Yannis Ritsos, who was born in the Peloponnesos in 1909 and experienced a tragic childhood, is generally regarded as an heir of

Varnalis because of his poetry of social protest and his humanitarian concern for suffering people. *Epitaphios*, his revolutionary lament of a mother for her son killed in a demonstration during strike-breaking activities of the police and military, was confiscated and burned during the Metaxas dictatorship. Under various governments including the recent military regime, he was imprisoned for his left wing activities and participation in the resistance movement. *Eighteen Short Songs of the Bitter Motherland* was written during the military junta as was *Scripture of the Blind* (1979). Some of Ritsos's images of the dictatorship were night arrests, handcuffs, betrayals, exile, surgeons, the rubber hose, identity cards, confessions, the pall hanging over family gatherings, and red eggs of Easter next to bread riddled with bullets.

The concept of freedom is especially significant in Ritsos's work as seen in *Romiosini* (1966), an untranslatable term that becomes inseparable from freedom and embraces the entire modern Greek experience, the very essence of neo-Hellenism and Greek identity. For Ritsos, nothing is completely good or completely bad: loneliness can lead to self-knowledge, serenity can be found in agony, goodness in bitterness, and death can be positive because it strengthens the sense and value of life. Ritsos has developed a humanistic, mature, and dual view of the world from which he can condemn its wrongs and yet understand and express compassion for the weaknesses of humankind. He has published more than eighty books of poetry and two plays, with his work being translated into more than forty languages. He received the Lenin Prize in 1977 and has been nominated several times for the Nobel Prize.

Odysseus Elytis, born in Irakleion, Crete in 1911, was a surrealist stressing man's spiritual powers. He challenged the Western model of rationalism and was more sympathetic to the Eastern. Known as the poet of the Aegean, he saw this region as a special repository of Greek identity. The sun and light of the Aegean have played a major role in his poetry as shown in his *Sun the First*, which suggests that in Greece the sun is the absolute monarch. The sun is used as a magical sign to conjure away evil; its light creates justice. Elytis's vision of the ideal world seems to be the Aegean landscape in the midday heat filled with innocent, beautiful, and uninhibited youth.

Elytis experienced very real pain and suffering when he served during the Albanian campaign (1940–1); this led him to compose the *Heroic and Elegiac Song for the Fallen Second Lieutenant in Albania* (1945) which describes the dreadful events of war. *Axion Esti (Worthy It Is)* is the spiritual autobiography of the poet and a synthesis of his visions and experience. This long poem has three parts: (1) 'Genesis'—birth and early innocence; (2) 'The Passions' portraying the experiences of World War II by bringing innocence face to face with evil and suffering; and (3) 'Gloria'—a more cultivated innocence based on experience and a reaffirmation of the values of goodness and beauty expressed at the beginning of the poem.

In 1979 Elytis won the Nobel Prize for his poetry 'which against the background of Greek tradition, depicts with sensuous strength and intellectual clearsightedness modern man's struggle for freedom and creativeness' (Greek Embassy, 1979a: 1). Elytis clearly describes the nature and purpose of his poetry:

> My ambition is simply that young people should be able to turn to my books when they feel lonely. This sort of indirect contact, provided it is lasting, is what I consider all-important. For me poetry is a war against time and decay. I wage this war alone in my flat, and that's how I find satisfaction, whether or not I win. In a materialist age which values quantity above quality, I regard poetry as the only thing that can preserve man's spiritual integrity (Greek Embassy, 1979b: 5).

The writers of Greek poetry most clearly embody the search for identity and the struggle to reconcile the past with the present. While they are painfully aware of the differences between their ancient and modern history and between the East and West, their poetry becomes the means to synthesize these varied antitheses and dualities.

In conclusion, we can see that Greece's cultural norms, values, traditions, and social institutions are interdependent although at the same time possibly in conflict with each other. There is a strong stream of Eastern cultural influence reflected in the language, religion, poetry, customs, and folklore, but the educational, political and economic structures are more rational reflecting Western influences. Without the knowledge of both, one cannot understand the struggles and agonies of Greeks searching for identity and community through their turbulent modern history.

Notes

1. A few of the numerous sources available on Greek literature include *A History of Modern Greek Literature* by C. Th. Dimaras (1972) (tr. M. Gianos), *History of Modern Greek Literature* by L. Politis (1973), *Modern Poetry in Translation: Greece* by P. Merchant (1968), *Greek Poetry From Homer to Seferis* by C. A. Trypanis (1981), *Modern Greek Poetry* by Kimon Friar (1973), *Voices of Modern Greece* tr. and ed. E. Keeley and P. Sherrard (1981), *Modern Greek Poetry* by Keeley (1983), and *Modern Greece* (ch. 7, 'Modern Greek Literature') by J. Campbell and P. Sherrard (1968). The Politis (1973) source has a sixteen-page chronological table comparing modern Greek literature, Greek historical events, and history and literature outside Greece. The Trypanis (1981) book illustrates how voluminous Greek poetry is since it devotes almost 900 pages to Greek poetry from the time of Homer to the 1940s. This section draws considerably upon the work of Friar (1973).
2. According to Friar poets may comprise the largest category of people next to peasants in Greece. Many of these poets are self-published.

7

CONCLUDING REMARKS

THROUGHOUT its modern history Greece has struggled first to establish and then to maintain its national identity and independence from external domination. In its long history of wars, internal conflicts, invasions, and occupations, the institutions of the family and religion along with the linguistic tradition have contributed to its cultural identity, especially during the Ottoman rule. Greek literature, particularly poetry, folklore, and music have also nourished the development and continuity of Greek cultural identity. According to Ikaris (1978: 6), 'Modern Greece was reborn after centuries of foreign oppression because the Greek consciousness learned from bitter experience to retain its cultural heritage when barbaric masters were about to snatch it away and destroy it utterly.' Further testimony of this struggle is illustrated in the words of Friar (1973: 5–6): 'I know of no other country, at least in the Western Hemisphere, which has retained such identity and integrity under such crushing odds.'

Greek identity has a historical dimension which is related to the issue of continuity vs. discontinuity and impinges on the notion of Greekness or who is a Greek. Within Greek identity, a major duality exists, one along the Western rational model, and the other rooted in Eastern culture. In the former, the identity of Greece can be seen through the eyes of Western writers and scholars who stress its Hellenic roots as the mother of Western civilization. Such an identity can also be seen in the political and educational institutions —as exemplified by Western constitutions, bureaucratic organization, and rationalism. The Eastern stresses the emotional, spiritual, and ethnic sensibilities and draws upon the Byzantine and Oriental traditions and local culture as seen by the poets, folklorists, and writers. An additional dimension is the geographical environment with its natural setting of the sea, sun, valleys, islands, and rough terrain molding the Greek identity and character.

During the periods of classical Greece, the rule of Alexander the Great, and the Greco-Roman and Byzantine Empires, Greek culture played a significant role in the region, but this pattern of influence was disrupted by 400 years of Ottoman rule. Once Greece was liberated, a new nation state was born giving impetus to a political identity as well as strengthening the previously existing ethno-cultural identity. The development of the political identity was long, arduous, and incomplete and a large number of 'cultural' Greeks with shared religion, family, and traditions remained outside the limited boundaries of the newly created nation-state. By the early 1900s Greece had redeemed a large segment of its Greek population that had not been included in its original borders. In the 1920s the dreams of further territorial gains were destroyed by the Asia Minor débâcle, but the population transfer resulted in a more ethnically homogeneous Greek nation state.

There is a wide discrepancy between the Greece 'that was' and the Greece 'that is'. For many Westerners the image of Greece is that of classical Greece, the birthplace of democracy. Often foreigners have little understanding of the turbulent events in the modern political history of Greece. Rather modern Greece has been overshadowed by ancient Greece and is viewed as a tourist haven of historic ruins and relics, beautiful Greek isles, and sun-drenched beaches.

On the one hand Greeks strive to maintain their cultural identity, uniqueness, and historical continuity with the glorious past, but at the same time they are attempting to develop their social, political, and economic institutions. The Greek identity is problematic because of its dependent economy and poor natural resources. Greece is not industrially developed and while the occupational structure is changing, small owners and farmers still play important roles in the economy. Greece has developed its service sector at the expense of the industrial and its public sector at the expense of the private. The changes in the world economy affect the invisibles of tourism, shipping, and remittances of immigrants, and as long as Greece has not developed a strong independent economic foundation it will be difficult to maintain its independence in international affairs.

In the political realm the New Democracy Party promoted a Western European identity as typified by the phrase 'Greece belongs to the West' while PASOK capitalized on the search for a new Greek identity independent of Western and American domination as illustrated in the slogan 'Greece belongs to the Greeks'. The demise of the political centre has meant that PASOK and New Democracy are the two major contending forces for the support of the middle of the road and moderate Greek voters. PASOK thus far has successfully captured a large segment of the middle ground through its 'catch-all' strategy and its nationalistic appeal attracting less privileged segments of Greek society and those who are upwardly mobile and desire change. New Democracy, representing the democractic right, has made an effort to rejuvenate itself by bringing young and dynamic politicians into its ranks, but still it has not been able to rid itself of its past image as a party of the 'old establishment' and of the more privileged favouring stability over social change. At the political party extremes we also see the conflict over the issue of Greek identity. The extreme right (EPEN) is the most pro-Western, pro-NATO, and pro-American while the Communist Party (KKE) is allied with the Soviet Union.

The inability of both Greece and Turkey to resolve the long standing conflicts over Cyprus and the Aegean has created an atmosphere of tension, which has contributed to the escalation of an arms race draining the national budgets of both countries. In most respects all parties of Greece since 1974 recognize the seriousness of the Turkish threat and are frustrated by the lack of a solution to the Cyprus problem. There is a strong national unity among political parties and between the armed forces and society when it comes to the issue of territorial integrity and national sovereignty. Greeks believe that they have been loyal to the West as evidenced by their participation in World War I, World War II, and the Korean War, and thus feel betrayed by the West, especially in terms of the perceived US tilt toward Turkey in recent years. The feeling of betrayal also exists among a dynamic segment of Greek communities abroad, especially in the US, Australia, and Canada.

Ancient Greeks have left their legacy to the West especially through the lofty ideals of democracy and freedom, and touched nearly every aspect of intellectual endeavour including philosophy, the arts, sciences, history, religion, medicine, and mathematics. Despite its small size, modern Greece, like ancient Greece, has made its mark on the world. Its people are highly enterprising, entrepreneurial, vibrant, and dynamic, whether in their own country or abroad. Greece belongs to two major alliances, NATO and EEC, which make it a participant in many important political and economic events. Under Prime Minister Papandreou Greeks have been especially active in the anti-nuclear and peace movements and are speaking out for the rights of smaller nations. That Greece is in the process of defining its identity and Greekness internally is manifested in many spheres of political and social endeavour including the development of a multi-faceted, independent, foreign policy which is often critical of the Western World.

There is an ambivalence surrounding Greek identity or the desire to avoid either/or distinctions which makes Greek identity problematic. This ambivalence is reflected in its geographical position, politics, international relations, and economy. Geographically Greece can simultaneously be considered in the Balkans, the Mediterranean, and in Western Europe; each of these regions has differing implications for Greekness. East of Greece is Turkey, a country hostile to Greece throughout much of its history, and to Greece's north nations currently with different political systems but with whom Greece shares the experience of Ottoman domination. Politically various parties align with the East, the West, or pursue more independent postures. In international relations Greece has been regarded as part of the Western alliance, but now it questions the value of the alliance particularly in view of the Cyprus issue and the Aegean dispute with Turkey. In the economic system, the ambivalence of Greece's position is further illustrated because it has broadly been labelled as semi-developed or in the semi-periphery. Even if Greece wishes to avoid defining its identity in absolute terms and being classified as either East or West, it will be extremely difficult to maintain such a position because other nations will still define Greece's identity.

Despite this ambivalence in identity, Greeks have a strong sense of community, national identity, family, religion, and tradition in general. Greek poets, renowned throughout the world, stress this search for national identity and for freedom. Modern Greeks want recognition and respect in their own right not for 'what was' but for what modern Greece 'is' in the family of nations.

ANNOTATED BIBLIOGRAPHY

ANASTAPLO, GEORGE. 'Retreat from Politics'. *The Massachusetts Review*, 9 (1968): 83–113. The author discusses the end to parliamentary politics in Greece.

ANTHOGALIDOU-VASSILAKAKIS, THEOPOULA (trans. E. Pahus). 'The Greek Educational System as it has Developed Since the 1976 Reforms'. *Journal of the Hellenic Diaspora*, 8 (1981): 25–35. This article contains information on the Greek school reforms during the 1970s.

ATHENS NEWS AGENCY. 'ND Ready, Mitsotakis Tells Party Congress'. *Athens News Agency Daily Bulletin*, 17 Feb. (1986a): 1–2. This article reports on the second ND party Congress. It notes Mitsotakis's criticisms of PASOK and his claim that ND is ready to lead the country to recovery.

—— 'Spokesman: Government Determined to Complete Its Four-Year Term'. *Athens News Agency Daily Bulletin*, 21 Oct. (1986b): 1–3. Final election tallies are reported as well as New Democracy's challenge to the official results. Papaioannou maintains that the government is determined to complete its four-year term.

—— 'PASOK Candidates Win Most Municipalities, Lose Three Biggest Cities'. *Athens News Agency Daily Bulletin*, 20 Oct. (1986c): 1–4. Municipal election results and statements from various party leaders and candidates are included in this discussion.

—— 'KKE Affiliate Heads Student Elections'. *Athens News Agency Daily Bulletin*, 19 Apr. (1986d): 7. This article outlines the results for the April 1986 student elections in both the Higher Education Institutions and Technical Schools.

AXT, HEINZ-JÜRGEN. 'On the Way to Self-Reliance? PASOK's Government Policy in Greece'. *Journal of Modern Greek Studies*, 2 (1984): 189--208. Axt considers various options of PASOK's policy and how its policy has changed related to the development of self-reliance. The first two years of PASOK in power are considered.

BARDIS, PANOS. 'The Changing Family in Modern Greece'. *Sociology and Social Research*, 40 (1955): 19–23. This describes the changes in the traditional Greek rural family.

BARNET, RICHARD. *Intervention and Revolution*. New York: The New American Library, 1972. This book includes a description of the Greek military intervention in politics.

BERMAN, BRUCE. 'Clientelism and Neo-colonization: Centre-periphery Relations and Political Development in African States'. *Studies in*

Comparative International Development, 9 (1974): 3–25. This article provides a general framework on clientelism as well as applying it to African nations.

BIALOR, PERRY A. 'Greek Ethnic Survival Under Ottoman Domination'. In *The Limits of Integration: Ethnicity and Nationalism in Modern Europe*, ed. Oriol Pi-Sunger. Research Reports, no. 9. Amherst: University of Massachusetts, 1971. Some of the structural factors that militated against ethnic assimilation of Greeks and other groups in the Ottoman empire are discussed.

BLUELINE: GREEK AND MEDITERRANEAN INTELLIGENCE, vol. 1 no. 4 (Oct. 1984). This is a monthly newsletter on Greek affairs published with the co-operation of the Institute of European Studies and Research.

BLUELINE: GREEK AND MEDITERRANEAN REPORT. 'Papandreou calls for "National Effort" For Economy'. *Monthly Newsletter*, vol. 2, no. 8, Aug.–Sept. (1985a): 1–2. This article presents material from A. Papandreou's speeches on the economic crisis in Greece.

—— 'IMPs: An Answer to the Greek Memorandum'. Blueline Documents, vol. 2, no. 5, May–June (1985b): 1–4. This is devoted to Greek–EEC relations, based on views expressed by high echelon officials of the Greek Ministry of Foreign Affairs.

BOMBAS, LEONIDAS C. 'Towards A Socialist Reform in the Greek Educational System?' *Hellenic Studies*, 1 (1983): 63–83. Bombas provides a brief historical review of educational reform in Greece and discusses more fully the current and possible reforms under the new socialist government.

BOTSAS, ELEFTHERIOS. 'Greece and the East: The Trade Connection, 1851–1984.' A paper presented at the International Symposium of the Modern Greek Studies Association Ohio State University, 7–10 Nov. 1985. A historical analysis of the Greek trade with the East (Turkey, Egypt, Russia) between 1851 and 1984.

BOULAY, JULIET DU. *Portrait of a Greek Mountain Village*. Oxford: Clarendon Press, 1974. This book describes the traditions and beliefs of a mountain village in central Greece.

BUCK, CARL DARLING. *The Greek Dialects*. Chicago and London: University of Chicago Press, 1968. Buck provides an extensive discussion of the grammar of the Greek dialects including a brief section on the classification and interrelation of these dialects.

BURY, J. B. and MEIGGS, RUSSELL. *A History of Greece: To the Death of Alexander the Great*. London: Macmillan and Russell Meiggs, 1975. This work begins with origins of the Greeks and ends with the death of Alexander the Great. It includes a chronological table of the period and a select bibliography.

CAMPBELL, J. K. *Honor, Family, and Patronage*. Oxford, 1964. This is a study of the Sarakatsanoi family in central Greece.

—— 'Regionalism and Local Community'. In *Regional Variation in Modern Greece and Cyprus: Toward a Perspective on the Ethnography of Greece*, ed. Muriel Dimen and Ernestine Friedl. New York: Annals of the New York Academy of Sciences, vol. 268, 1976. This is an analysis of regionalism and localism as barriers to modernity.

—— 'Traditional Values and Continuities in Greek Society'. In *Greece in the 1980s*, ed. Richard Clogg. London: Macmillan, 1983. Author surveys traditional rural Greek values and changes taking place in modern Greece.

CAMPBELL, JOHN, and SHERRARD, PHILIP. *Modern Greece: Nations of the Modern World*. London: Ernest Benn Limited, 1968. The authors examine the origins of modern Greece, the historical development of the state, the church, literature, countryside, city and state, economic dilemmas, and political events since the Civil War.

CARMOCOLIAS, DEMETRIOS. 'Image of NATO and the U.S. in the Athens Daily Press, 1974–1980'. *Journal of Political and Military Sociology*, 9 (Spring, 1981): 229–40. Carmocolias uses content analysis of Athenian daily newspapers to assess attitudes toward NATO.

CARSON, J. GRAHAM. *Greece: New Policies, a New Confidence*. No city listed: Institutional Investor (sponsored by Bank of Greece), 16 pp., 1983. This is an interesting booklet on the Greek economy sponsored by the Bank of Greece but written independently by the author. It is based in part on interviews with Greek officials.

CENTRE OF PLANNING AND ECONOMIC RESEARCH. *The Greek Economy Today*. Athens: Centre of Planning and Economic Research, 1984. The booklet provides statistics on the country, people, economic structure, public sector, foreign trade, energy supplies, income and prices, and labour market.

CENTRE OF POLITICAL RESEARCH AND TRAINING. Special Issue on Problems and Prospects of the Greek Economy. *Epicentra*, 47, Dec. 1985, This issue is devoted to problems of various facets of the economy.

CHIROT, DANIEL. *Social Change in the Twentieth Century*. NY: Harcourt, Brace Jovanovich, 1977. Chirot discusses the capitalist world system including international stratification, struggle in the core and semi-periphery, and revolutions in the periphery.

—— and HALL, THOMAS D. 'World-System Theory'. *Annual Review of Sociology*, 8 (1982): 81–106. The authors review world system theory including how it differs from modernization theory and note some criticisms of it.

CHRISTIAN SCIENCE MONITOR, 25 Jan. 1985, p. 9.

CLOGG, RICHARD. 'Aspects of the Movement for Greek Independence'. In *The Struggle for Greek Independence*, ed. Richard Clogg. London: Macmillan, 1973. The author describes the nature of Greek society before independence and notes selected features of the movement for independence.

—— *A Short History of Modern Greece*. Cambridge: Cambridge University Press, 1979. Clogg provides an insightful concise history of Greece from the downfall of Byzantium to the return of democracy.

—— 'Notes on Recent Elections: The Greek Elections of 1981'. *Electoral Studies*, 1 (1982): 95–106. Clogg discusses the results of the national and European Parliament elections in 1981. Characteristics of the voting procedure and of the Greek voter are noted.

—— 'Troubled Alliance: Greece and Turkey'. London: Macmillan, In *Greece in the 1980s*, ed. R. Clogg. London: Macmillan 1983. This article provides a historical perspective of Greek–Turkish relations.

COMMITTEE ON FOREIGN AFFAIRS (Subcommittee on Europe and the Middle East), US House of Representatives. *Developments in Europe, August 1983*. Washington, DC, US Government Printing Office, 1983. This report updates Greek–Turkish–NATO relations as well as others in Europe.

COMMUNIST PARTY OF GREECE (KKE). 'The Platform of the Communist Party of Greece (KKE) for the June 2 Parliamentary Elections'. Athens News Agency Feature Stories, 36, 1985. This provides the text of the Platform of the Communist Party on major issues including foreign policy, economy, tax and income policy, agricultural policy, and trade unions.

COMPARATIVE EDUCATION REVIEW, 'Symposium on Educational Reform in Greece', vol. 22, no. 1, Feb. (1978). This contains ninety-five pages of articles on the Greek educational reforms of the 1970s.

CONSTANTELOS, DEMETRIOS J. 'Byzantine Religiosity and Ancient Greek Religiosity'. In *The 'Past' in Medieval and Modern Greek Culture*, ed. Speros Vryonis, jun. Malibu: Undena Publications, 1978. The importance of religion and the influence of ancient Greek religion on Christianity is treated in this article.

COUFOUDAKIS, VAN. 'Greco-Turkish Relations and the Greek Socialists: Ideology, Nationalism and Pragmatism', *Journal of Modern Greek Studies* (Oct. 1983): 373–92. This is a perceptive analysis of Greek–Turkish relations and issues between 1973–1983.

—— 'Cyprus: From Independence to Partition'. Paper presented at the AHEPA Conference on Cyprus. Washington, DC, 1985. It is a review of the Cyprus issue in view of the political developments of partition.

COULOUMBIS, THEODORE A. 'Defining Greek Foreign Policy Objectives'. In *Greek American Relations*, ed. Theodore Couloumbis and John

Iatrides. New York: Pella Publishing, 1980. Couloumbis discusses the various political parties in Greece and their foreign policy positions.

—— 'The Structures of Greek Foreign Policy'. In *Greece in the 1980s*, ed. Richard Clogg. London: Macmillan, 1983a. This article presents a cogent analysis of Greece's attempt for a multidimensional foreign policy.

—— *The United States, Greece, and Turkey: The Troubled Triangle*. New York: Praeger, 1983b. It surveys issues in the foreign relations field since late 1940s among three major actors US, Greece and Turkey. It is useful in placing this troubled triangle in a perspective.

—— and IATRIDES, JOHN O. (eds). *Greek-American Relations: A Critical Review*. New York: Pella, 1980. This is a historical critical review of Greek–American relations with emphasis on the 1967 coup and the Turkish invasion of Cyprus (1974).

—— PETROPULOS, JOHN A.; and PSOMIADES, HARRY J. *Foreign Interference in Greek Politics: A Historical Perspective*. New York: Pella Publishing Co., 1976. The authors examine the primacy of foreign policy over domestic, the irredentist state, Greece between the world wars, and Greek–American relations.

CRAIG, PHYLLIS R. 'The United States and the Greek Dictatorship'. *Journal of the Hellenic Diaspora*, 3 (1976): 5–15. The article presents information on the US support of the military regime.

DAMIANAKOS, STATHIS. 'Sociology of the Rebetica' (Greek). Athens: Hermeas, 1976. A Ph.D. sociological study of an important phenomenon of the rebetica (rascals) songs of the urban underclass, marginal, and proletariat subculture.

DANFORTH, LORING. *The Death Rituals of Rural Greece*. Princeton, NJ: Princeton University Press, 1982. A study of death laments in Greece.

DANOPOULOS, C. 'From Balconies to Tanks: Post Junta Civil-Military Relations in Greece', *Journal of Political and Military Sociology*, 13 (1985a): 83–98. This is an analysis of civil–military relations since 1974. The author concludes that both the military and civilian élites learned their lesson, and it is unlikely that praetorianism will be repeated in Greece as long as the corporate interests of the military are not encroached and the threat of Turkey is real.

—— *Warriors and Politicians in Modern Greece*. Chapel Hill, NC: Documentary Publications, 1985b. The author examines the role of the Greek military in politics including a discussion of civil–military relations since 1974.

DIAMANDOUROS, N. 'Political Modernization, Social Conflict and Cultural Cleavage in the Formation of the Modern Greek State, 1821–1828'. Ph.D. thesis. New York: Columbia University, 1972. This dissertation focuses on the divisions between the modernizers and traditionalists on the creation and shape of the Greek nation-state.

—— 'Bibliographical Essay'. In *Hellenism and the First Greek War of Liberation* (1821–1830), ed. N. Diamandouros, J. Petropulos, and P. Topping. Thessaloniki: Institute for Balkan Studies, 1976. The author provides a thorough examination of the primary and secondary sources on the struggle for liberation.

—— 'Greek Political Culture in Transition: Historical Origins, Evolution, Current Trends'. In *Greece in the 1980s* ed. Richard Clogg. London: Macmillan, 1983. The author traces modern Greek political culture from its source in Ottoman times and examines major institutions in Greek society.

DIEM, AUBREY. *Western Europe: A Geographical Analysis*. NY: John Wiley and Sons, 1979. One of the chapters presents a geographical profile of modern Greece.

DIMARAS, ALEXIS. 'The Movement for Reform: A Historical Perspective'. *Comparative Education Review*, 20 (1978): 11–20. Dimaras gives a historical survey of the educational system stressing stability over change.

—— 'Greek Education: A Story of Frustrated Reform'. *Journal of the Hellenic Diaspora*, 8 (1981): 19–24. This article presents a brief view of the history of relatively unsuccessful reform in Greek education.

—— 'Europe and the 1980s: A Double Challenge for Greek Education'. In *Greece in the 1980s*, ed. Richard Clogg. London: Macmillan, 1983. This contains an evaluation of the Greek educational system noting that stability rather than change characterizes it.

DIMARAS, C. TH. (trans. Mary P. Gianos). *A History of Modern Greek Literature*. Albany, New York: State University of New York Press, 1972. This book begins by considering the roots of modern Greek literature before Turkish domination and brings the discussion up to 1922. There is a fifteen page supplement updating the book.

DIMITRAS, ELIE, and VLACHOS, EVAN. *Sociological Surveys on Greek Emigrants*, No. 3. Athens: National Centre of Social Research, 1971. This is an analysis of the life and work of Greek migrant workers in West Germany.

DIMITRAS, PANAYOTE E. 'Elections for the European Parliament in Greece, 1981–84'. Paper presented at the International Symposium on European Elections 1979/81 and 1984. Mannheim, FRG, Nov. 1983. The author discusses the recent national elections results and the European Parliament result in 1981 as well as implications for the 1984 European Parliament election.

—— 'Greece'. *Electoral Studies*, 3 (1984a): 285–9. Dimitras analyses the results of the 1984 European Parliament elections in Greece.

—— (ed). *Greek Opinion: A Bimonthly Survey of Greek Public Opinion Trends*, 6, 1984b. This issue provides information on Greek public opinion at the third anniversary of PASOK's electoral victory.

—— (ed.) *Greek Opinion: A Bimonthly Survey of Greek Public Opinion Trends*, 3, 1984c. This issue focuses on foreign policy questions.

—— 'Special Report on Greek Politics: The New Electoral Law'. *Greek Opinion: A Bimonthly Survey of Greek Public Opinion Trends*, Special Report no. 1 (13), 2 (1985a): 1–9. This special report discusses the implications of the new electoral law for the 1985 elections.

—— (ed). *Greek Opinion: A Bimonthly Survey of Greek Public Opinion Trends*, 1, 1985b. This issue examines public opinion in the beginning of 1985 on the electoral law, presidential elections, Greek–Turkish relations, and the Cyprus problem.

—— (ed.). *Greek Opinion: A Bimonthly Survey of Greek Public Opinion Trends*, 3, 1985c. This issue provides information on the electoral geography of the various political parties after the June 1985 elections.

—— (ed.). *Greek Opinion: A Bimonthly Survey of Greek Public Opinion Trends*, 5, 1985d. The focus of this issue is on Greeks and their history, including public opinion concerning the prime ministers, the monarchy, KKE's historical leaders, the Civil War, national schism, and alliances with the west.

—— (ed.). *Greek Opinion: A Bimonthly Survey of Greek Public Opinion Trends*, 6, 1985e. This issue examines public opinion after the October 1985 economic austerity measures were announced.

DOBRATZ, BETTY A. 'Greece and Its Relations with the West: A Case Study of International Conflict'. *The International Journal of Sociology and Social Policy*, 5 (1985): 1–18. This article contains information on the influence of foreign policy variables on voting according to surveys conducted in 1977 and 1980.

—— 'Socio-Political Participation of Women in Greece'. In *Women and Politics*, vol. 2 of *Research in Politics and Society*, ed. Gwen Moore and Glenna Spitze. Greenwich, Ct.: JAI Press, 1986. This paper looks at the political participation of Greek men and women in light of women's place in the other major institutions of society (family, religion, and economy).

—— and KOURVETARIS, YORGOS A. 'Electoral Voting Preferences and Political Orientations of Athenians in Greece: A Three-Perspective Model'. *European Journal of Political Research*, 9 (1981): 287–307. Based on interviews with Athenians in 1977, the authors found issue orientations and primary group relations more important than socio-economic characteristics in influencing voting patterns.

DOUKAS, MICHAEL. *Decline and Fall of Byzantium to the Ottoman Turks* (an Annotated Translation of 'Historia Turco-Byzantina' by

Harry J. Magoulias). Detroit: Wayne University, 1975. This book is written in a vivid journalistic style by Michael Doukas, a historian of the fifteenth century who is descended from the famous ancient Doukas family.

DUBISCH, JILL. 'Greek Women: Sacred or Profane'. *Journal of Modern Greek Studies*, 1 (1983): 185–202. She argues against the prevailing dichotomy in the anthropological literature which associates women with nature and the profane and men with culture and the sacred.

ECONOMIST INTELLIGENCE UNIT (EIU). *Quarterly Economic Review of Greece*, 3, 1984a. This issue of the quarterly report provides figures on the economic structure of Greece, reviews of the politics and economy, and prospects for the future.

—— *Quarterly Economic Review of Greece*. Annual Supplement 1984b. Each year the Economist Intelligence Unit provides a yearly summary of the economic developments in various countries including Greece.

—— *Quarterly Economic Review of Greece*, 2, 1984c. This issue discusses the economic outlook for Greece including wages and prices, agriculture, foreign trade and payments, and reviews the political scene.

—— *Quarterly Economic Review of Greece*. Annual Supplement 1985a. This is a yearly summary of Greek society and economy for 1985.

—— *Quarterly Economic Review of Greece*, 4, 1985b. This issue includes a discussion of the October 1985 austerity measures introduced by the government.

—— *Country Profile Greece 1986–1987*. 1986a. This new annual review provides basic economic, political, and social information on Greece.

—— *Quarterly Economic Review of Greece*. 1, 1986b. This issue discusses the target of the stabilization programme, the state budget, outlooks for exports and imports, and servicing the debt.

—— *Country Report Greece*. 3, 1986c. This issue includes discussion of the stabilization measures and changes in the cabinet of the government.

ELEPHANTIS, ANGELOS. 'PASOK and the Elections of 1977: The Rise of the Populist Movement'. In *Greece at the Polls: The National Elections of 1974 and 1977*, ed. Howard Penniman. Washington, DC: American Enterprise Institute, 1981. Elephantis, who is critical of PASOK, analyses the ideology of populism, the organizational structure of PASOK, and the leadership of A. Papandreou.

EMBASSY OF GREECE, WASHINGTON, DC. *The Week in Review*, Embassy of Greece, 26 Nov. 1984. A weekly summary of the political, economic, and social events occurring in Greece. This one deals with the week ending 26 Nov. 1984.

—— *Greece: The Week in Review*, Embassy of Greece, 10 June 1985. This weekly review contains information on PASOK's electoral victory in 1985.

—— *The Week in Review*, Embassy of Greece, 8 Sept. 1986a. This weekly review highlights Prime Minister Papandreou's review of the Greek economy in his speech opening the 51st Thessaloniki International Fair.

—— *The Week in Review*, Embassy of Greece, 28 Apr. 1986b. This weekly review includes discussions of the foreign policy debate, Papandreou's cabinet reshuffling and economic policy.

EVANGELINIDES, MARY. 'Regional Development—Core–periphery relations: The Greek Case'. *The Greek Review of Social Research*, 24 (1975): 320–55. The author examines the theoretical background of the core–periphery framework, provides historical background on the Greek case, and then discusses Greek regional economic development.

FEATHERSTONE, KEVIN. 'Elections and Parties in Greece'. *Government and Opposition*, 17 (1982): 180–94. In this article Featherstone analyses the party platforms and the 1981 national election results.

—— 'The Greek Socialists in Power'. *West European Politics*, 6 (1983): 237–50. This article considers the performance of PASOK since its election victory in 1981. It contrasts PASOK with other European socialist parties.

—— and KATSOUDAS, DIMITRIS K. 'Change and Continuity in Greek Voting Behaviour'. *European Journal of Political Research*, 13 (1985): 27–40. The authors analyse the geography of the election results from 1963 to 1981 and discuss a pre-election opinion survey in 1981. While there are important parallels between support for the old Centre Union and PASOK, the exceptional uniformity in support for PASOK is highlighted.

FINLAY, GEORGE. *A History of Greece From Its Conquest by the Romans to the Present Time B.C. 146 to A.D. 1864* (In Seven Volumes). New York: AMS Press, 1970. The seven volume work is edited by H. F. Tozer. Each volume contains a chronology of the historical period it deals with.

FLORAKIS, HARILAOS. 'Full Text of a speech by Communist Party of Greece (KKE) Secretary General Harilaos Florakis in Thessaloniki Tuesday 14 May, 1985'. Athens News Agency Feature Stories, 33, 1985. This speech illustrates the Communist point of view on Greek politics.

FRANGOUDAKIS, ANNA. 'The Impasse of Educational Reform in Greece: An Introduction'. *Journal of the Hellenic Diaspora*, 8 (1981): 7–18. Her article introduces a special issue on education in Greece through the late 1970s.

FRIAR, KIMON. *Modern Greek Poetry*. New York: Simon and Schuster, 1973. This book of more than 700 pages provides excellent commentary as well as hundreds of pages of translations of modern Greek poetry.

—— and MYRSIADES, KOSTAS. 'Introduction' to *Scripture of the Blind* by Yannis Ritsos. Columbus: Ohio State University Press, 1979. The authors discuss the life and work of Greek poet Yannis Ritsos including the major themes in *Scripture of the Blind*.

FRIEDL, ERNESTINE. *Vasilika: A Village in Modern Greece*. New York: Holt, 1962. This is one of the original social-anthropological studies of a Greek village.

GENERAL SECRETARIAT OF PRESS AND INFORMATION. *Greece Today*. Athens: Printing Unit of the Ministry of Finance, no. 2, Feb. 1983. This issue provides information on a variety of changes brought about by PASOK.

GIANARIS, NICHOLAS V. *The Economies of Balkan Countries*. New York: Praeger, 1982. The author examines the socio-economic background, organizational and developmental aspects, and foreign trade and economic co-operation of six Balkan countries including Greece.

—— *Greece and Yugoslavia: An Economic Comparison*. New York: Praeger, 1984. Gianaris analyses the socio-economic background, domestic factors of development, and international trade and economic co-operation of two countries at the crossroads of Europe, Africa, and Asia.

GRANT, GLENN H. 'University Reform in Greece: 1982 and After'. *Journal of Modern Greek Studies*, 4 (1986): 17–31. Based on sixty interviews with professors, students, union leaders, and government officials, the author evaluates Law 1262/82 on higher education.

GREEK EMBASSY OF WASHINGTON, DC. 'Nobel Prize to Odysseus Elytis'. *Greece: A Monthly Record*, vol. 5, no. 7 (1979a): 1, 3. This is a brief article on the award of the Nobel Prize to Odysseus Elytis, the poet of the Aegean.

—— 'World Critics' Praise for Nobel Laureate Odysseus Elytis'. *Greece Information*, 7 Dec. (1979b): 1–5. This article presents the comments of various critics on the poetry of Elytis.

GREEK ORTHODOX ARCHDIOCESE OF NORTH AND SOUTH AMERICA. *1984 Yearbook*. New York: Greek Orthodox Archdiocese of North and South America, 1984. A compendium of the major church institutions and holidays of the Greek Orthodox Church in the Americas.

GREEK PRESS AND INFORMATION OFFICE, LONDON 'Local Elections: Messages for All'. *Greece: Background, News, Information*, 14, 13 Nov. 1986. This is a serial publication providing information on Greece.

HALIKIAS, D. J. *Money & Credit in a Developing Economy: The Greek Case*. New York: New York University Press, 1978. Halikias examines the Greek credit system including the evolution of credit policies. The author evaluates the effectiveness and effects of the credit policies.

HELLENIC INDUSTRIAL DEVELOPMENT BANK SA (ETBA). *Invest-*

ment Guide in Greece. Athens: Mihalas SA, 1983. This book provides information on Greece particularly related to economic development (e.g. bank financing, taxation, membership in the European Economic Community, labour legislation).

HERZFIELD, MICHAEL. *Ours Once More—Folklore, Ideology, and the Making of Modern Greece.* Austin: University of Texas Press, 1982. A book on Greek folklore.

HIRSCHON, RENÉE B. 'The Social Institution of an Urban Locality of Refugee Origin in Piraeus'. Ph.D. Thesis, Oxford Univeristy, 1976. An analysis of refugee social institutions in Piraeus, Greece (from Asia Minor).

HITCHENS, CHRISTOPHER. *Cyprus.* New York: Quartet Books, 1984. An in-depth analysis of the international intrigue and external power manipulation of the Greek and Turkish inter-ethnic conflict.

HOLDEN, DAVID. *Greece Without Columns.* Philadelphia: Lippincott, 1972. The author, a journalist, discusses the questions of Greek identity and character including an examination of the military junta.

HOLST, GAIL. *Theodorakis: Myth and Politics in Modern Greek Music.* Amsterdam: Adolf M. Hakkert, 1980. An analysis of the music and the politics of Mikis Theodorakis.

HOUSE OF PARLIAMENT. *Constitution of Greece.* Athens: House of Parliament. 1979. This presents the Constitution of Greece accepted by Parliament on 9 June 1975 and effective 11 June 1975.

IATRIDES, JOHN O. 'Greece and the United States: The Strained Partnership'. In *Greece in the 1980s* ed. Richard Clogg. London: Macmillan, 1983. The author outlines Greek–American relations since World War II and identifies key events and issues that need to be re-examined.

IKARIS, DESPINA SPANOS. 'Editorial (to the New Poets)'. *Charioteer,* 20 (1978): 4–10. The author briefly assesses modern Greek poetry and its influence in America.

INSTITUTE FOR POLITICAL STUDIES. 'Student Elections Towards a Better System of Education'. Spotlight, 21, 21 Apr. 1985, p. 6.

JOURNAL OF THE HELLENIC DIASPORA, 'Education in Greece Today: A Symposium', vol. 8, nos. 1 and 2, spring–summer (1981). This is a special double issue with sixteen articles on Greek education.

JECCHINIS, CHRISTOS. *Trade Unionism in Greece: A Study in Political Paternalism.* Chicago: Roosevelt University, 1967. The author discusses the role of trade unions in Greek society over a period of time. The state has always played a strong role in the unions.

JOURNALISTS' UNION OF THE ATHENS DAILY NEWSPAPERS. *Threat in the Aegean.* Athens: The Journalists' Union, 1984. An illustrated and well-documented analysis of the Aegean dispute.

KAFIRIS, VASILIS. 'The Greek Economy under the Dictatorship (1967–1974): An Overview'. *Journal of the Hellenic Diaspora*, 2 (1975): 37–41. Kafiris describes the junta's economic policies including its attempt to attract multinational investment at almost any cost.

KALKAS, BARBARA, 'Aborted Economic and Social Development in Egypt: New Leaders in an Old System', A Ph.D. dissertation. Evanston: Northwestern University, 1979. This is a study of nineteenth-century Egyptian capitalism.

KASSOTAKIS, MICHAEL. 'Technical and Vocational Education in Greece and the Attitudes of Greek Youngsters Toward It'. *Journal of the Hellenic Diaspora*, 8 (1981): 81–93. Based on survey results, the author found the majority of students studied rejected pre-university technical studies. Reasons are given for this rejection.

KATRIS, JOHN. *Eyewitness in Greece: The Colonels Come to Power*. St Louis: New Critics Press, 1971. The author examines the decade of the 1960s with particular emphasis on the takeover of the military junta in 1967. The role of the CIA, the Pentagon, and NATO are critically examined.

KATSANEVAS, THEODORE K. *Trade Unions in Greece*. Athens: National Centre of Social Research, 1984. Katsanevas analyses the factors determining the growth and recent structure of trade unions.

KAUFMAN, ROBERT. 'The Patron–Client Concept and Macro-Politics'. *Comparative Studies in Society and History*, 16 (1974): 284–308. This article provides information on clientelism at the national and international levels.

KAYSER, BERNARD, and THOMPSON, KENNETH, *Economic and Social Atlas of Greece*. Athens: National Centre of Social Research, 1964. (In English, French, Greek.) This is an excellent diagrammatic reference book on the economic, social, and geographical aspects of Greece.

KAZAMIAS, ANDREAS M. 'The Politics of Educational Reform in Greece: Law 309/1976'. *Comparative Education Review*, 22 (1978): 21–45. This article focuses on the Education Act of 1976 by examining the process of educational reform in Greece.

KAZAMIAS, ANDREAS M., and PSACHAROPOULOS, GEORGE. 'Student Activism in Greece: A Historical and Empirical Analysis'. *Higher Education*, 9 (1980): 127–38. The article discusses the historical origins of student activism in Greece and presents data from a survey of 1500 students.

KEELEY, EDMUND. *Modern Greek Poetry: Voice and Myth*. Princeton: Princeton University Press, 1983. Keeley considers 'voice' and 'myth' in the poetry of Cavafy, Sikelianos, Seferis, Elytis, and Ritsos.

KEELEY, EDMUND, and SHERRARD, PHILIP, eds. *Voices of Modern*

Greece: Selected Poems. Princeton: Princeton University Press, 1981. This book provides translations of many poems by Cavafy, Sikelianos, Seferis, and Elytis.

KITROMILIDES, PASCHALIS. 'The Dialectic of Intolerance: Ideological Dimensions of Ethnic Conflict'. *Journal of the Hellenic Diaspora*, 6 (1979): 5–30. An analysis of the politics of extremism and unreason in Cyprus is provided.

—— 'The Last Battle of the Ancients and Moderns'. In *Modern Greek Studies Yearbook 1985*, ed. Theofanis Stavrou. University of Minnesota Press, Minneapolis, 1985. Author examines the Neo-Hellenic Revival which involved a struggle between ancient Greek ideas and modern European ones.

KOHLER, BEATE. *Political Forces in Spain, Greece and Portugal*. London: Butterworth Scientific, 1982. This book includes analyses of the return to democracy, the political forces, and the implications of EEC membership for all three countries.

KONDILIS, MARIANNA. 'The New Educational Policy of the 1976 Reform'. *Journal of the Hellenic Diaspora*, 8 (1981): 41–7. Kondilis considers the changes in the elementary and secondary education systems due to the 1976 legislation.

KOTY, JOHN. 'National Traits and Basic Sociological Characteristics of the Greek Culture'. In *The Institutions of Advanced Societies* edited by Arnold M. Rose. Minneapolis: University of Minnesota Press, 1958. This article deals with the institutions of Greece including the dichotomies of Greek character.

KOURVETARIS, YORGOS A. 'The Greek Army Officer Corps: Its Professionalism and Political Interventionism'. In *On Military Intervention* edited by Morris Janowitz and Jacques Van Doorn. Rotterdam: Rotterdam University Press, 1971a. A study of military intervention in the 1967 coup. The reasons the officers gave were communist threat, political incompetence, moral decay, and extreme forms of social inequality.

—— 'Professional Self-Images and Political Perspectives in the Greek Military'. American Sociological Review, 36 (Dec. 1971b): 1043–57. This is part of the author's Ph.D. dissertation on the analysis of military professionalism and military interventionism in national politics.

—— *First and Second Generation Greeks in Chicago*. Athens: National Centre of Social Research, 1971c. This is a comparative analysis of stratification and mobility patterns between first and second generation Greeks in Chicago.

—— 'Brain Drain and International Migration of Scientists'. *The Greek Review of Social Research*, 15–16 (1973): 2–13. This is a survey of

Greek professionals and students who left Greece in the 1950s and 1960s mainly for the US.

—— 'Greek Service Academies: Patterns of Recruitment and Organizational Change'. In *The Military and the Problem of Legitimacy*, ed. Gwyn Harries-Jenkins and Jacques Van Doorn. Beverly Hills, California and London: Sage Publications, 1976a. An analysis of recruitment patterns of Greek service academies and organizational change up to the 1970s.

—— 'Survey Essay on the Cyprus Question'. *Journal of Political and Military Sociology*, 4 (1976b): 151–64. This article reviews five books on the Cyprus crisis.

—— 'Attilas 1974: Human, Economic, and Political Consequences of the Turkish Invasion of Cyprus'. *Journal of the Hellenic Diaspora*, 4 (1977a): 24–7. This assesses the human, economic, and political consequences of the 1974 Turkish invasion of Cyprus.

—— 'Civil–Military Relations in Greece: 1909–1974'. In *World Perspectives in the Sociology of the Military*, ed. G. A. Kourvetaris and Betty A. Dobratz. New Brunswick, NJ: Transaction, 1977b. Using Moskos's convergent, divergent, and pluralistic models, an effort is made to examine civil–military relations in Greece between 1909 and 1974.

—— 'The Greek American Family'. In *Ethnic Families in America: Patterns and Variations*, ed. Charles H. Mindel and Robert W. Habenstein (2nd edn.). New York: Elsevier, 1981. An analysis of first, second, and third-generation Greek–American families.

—— 'Greek Armed Forces and Society in the 19th Century, with Special Emphasis on the Greek Revolution of 1821'. In *War and Society in East Central Europe*, ed. Bela Kiraly. vol. iv. New York: Social Science Monographs Brooklyn College Press. 1984. Using a sociological framework the role of the Greek guerrilla bands is assessed during the Greek Revolution against the Turks.

—— 'Greek and Turkish Interethnic Conflict and Polarization in Cyprus'. Paper presented at Midwest Sociological Society Meeting, Des Moines, IA, 26–9 Mar. 1986. It is argued that the rise of nationalism and the growth of separate ethnic identities manipulated by outside powers created the present situation.

—— 'The Greeks of Asia Minor and Egypt as Middleman Economic Minorities During the late 19th and 20th Centuries'. *Ethnic Groups*, 7 (1987): 1–27. The author analyses the middle-man economic hypothesis of Greeks of Asia Minor and Egypt.

—— 'The Southern Flank of NATO: Conflict and Change in Greek–Turkish Civil–Military Relations'. Forthcoming in *East European Quarterly* in December 1987. It deals with the major issues of contention between Greece and Turkey including the Cyprus and Aegean issues.

—— and DOBRATZ, BETTY A. 'Public Opinion and Civil–Military Relations in Greece Since 1974'. *The Journal of Strategic Studies*, 4 (1981): 71–84. Based on interviews of Athenians in 1977, the authors examine perceptions concerning civil–military relations since the restoration of democracy.

—— 'Political Clientelism in Athens, Greece: A Three Paradigm Approach to Political Clientelism'. *East European Quarterly*, 18 (1984): 35–59. The authors analyse political clientelism by examining the appropriateness of three theoretical frameworks. Empirical findings about clientelism are presented based on interviews with Athenians.

KOZYRIS, P. J. 'The Legal Status of the Aegean'. Paper presented at the 1985 Modern Greek Studies Association, Ohio State University, 7–10 Nov. Professor Kozyris, an international legal scholar, examines the legal aspects of the Aegean dispute.

KRIMPAS, GEORGE. 'The Greek Economy in Crisis'. In *Europe's Economy in Crisis*, ed. Ralf Dahrendorf. New York: Holmes & Meier Publishers, 1982. The author examines the Greek economy during the crisis period of the 1970s and comments on the interplay between politics and economics and the prospects for the future.

LAMBIRI-DIMAKI, JANE. 'Regional, Sex, and Class Distribution among Greek Students: Some Aspects of Inequality of Educational Opportunities'. In *Regional Variation in Modern Greece and Cyprus: Toward a Perspective on the Ethnography of Greece*, ed. Muriel Dimen and Ernestine Friedl. New York: The New York Academy of Sciences, 1976. This is an analysis of educational opportunity among urban and rural youth.

—— *Social Stratification in Greece: 1962–1982*. Athens: Ant. N. Sakkoulas, 1983. This is a collection of previously-published essays on various aspects of stratification in Greece.

LEE, DOROTHY. 'Greece'. In *Cultural Patterns and Technical Change*, ed. Margaret Mead. Paris: UNESCO, 1953. It is an analysis of the concept of Greek *philotimo* (honour, self-esteem).

LEGG, KEITH R. *Politics in Modern Greece*. Stanford, California: Stanford University Press, 1969. Legg analyses the background of Greek politics, the political system (interest groups, political parties, parliamentary and extra-parliamentary politics, the military oligarchy), and political recruitment.

—— 'Political Change in a Clientelistic Polity: The Failure of Democracy in Greece'. *Journal of Political and Military Sociology*, 1 (1973): 231–46. Legg suggests that attempts to modernize the Centre Union Party and disrupt the system of clientelism may have provoked the military intervention in 1967.

LIVAS, HARIS. 'A New Wind Blowing: Reformation in the School System'. Feature Stories, Athens: Athens News Agency, 22 Nov. 1983. This article discusses the reform going on in Greek education in the 1980s.

LOULIS, J. C. 'New Democracy: The New Face of Conservatism'. In *Greece At the Polls: The National Elections of 1974 and 1977* ed. Howard Penniman. Washington, DC: American Enterprise Institute, 1981. Loulis examines the success and the problems of Greece's major conservative party New Democracy.

LYRINTZIS, CHRISTOS. 'The Rise of PASOK: The Greek Election of 1981'. *West European Politics*, 5 (1982): 308–13. Lyrintzis compares the results of the 1981 national elections and European Parliament elections and explains the growth of PASOK.

—— 'Political Parties in Post-Junta Greece: A Case of "Bureaucratic Clientelism"?' *West European Politics*, 7 (1984): 99–118. The phenomenon of clientelism in various Greek political parties is analysed since the return to democracy in 1974.

MACKRIDGE, PETER. 'Brussels and the Greek Poetry Mountain: Some Thoughts on Greek Culture'. In *Greece in the 1980s*, ed. Richard Clogg. London: Macmillan, 1983. Mackridge discusses various aspects of Greek culture, particularly modern poetry and music.

MACRIDES, ROY C. 'Greek Political Freedom and United States Foreign Policy'. *The Massachusetts Review*, 9 (1968): 147–54. Macrides examines the relationship between the US and Greece including the military takeover in 1967.

MAKRIAS, PANAYOTE (ed.). 'Editorial'. *NEA YORKH* (a bi-monthly Greek American publication) Oct. (1980): 27.

MARKIDES KYRIACOS C. *The Rise and Fall of the Cyprus Republic.* New Haven and London: Yale University Press, 1977. Using a politico-sociological approach, the author examines the politics of unreason and nationalism which contributed to the demise of the Cyprus Republic.

MARMARINOS, JOHN. 'Relationships of Creativity to Socioeconomic Status and Grade-Point Average in Eleven-Year-Old Children'. *Journal of the Hellenic Diaspora*, 8 (1981): 71–4. Marmarinos examines the relationship between socio-economic status of parents, originality of ideas, and grade-point average. Sixth-graders from twenty-seven randomly selected elementary schools in Athens were sampled.

MCNALL, SCOTT G. *The Greek Peasant.* The Arnold and Caroline Rose Monograph Series of the American Sociological Association, Washington, DC: The American Sociological Association, 1974. This is a qualitative, short, and descriptive study of the values and social structure of two villages near the Gulf of Euboea.

—— 'Barriers to Development and Modernization in Greece'. In *Regional*

Variation in Modern Greece and Cyprus: Toward a Perspective on the Ethnography of Greece, ed. Muriel Dimen and Ernestine Friedl. New York: Annals of the New York Academy of Sciences, vol. 268, 1976. Author argues regionalism is an impediment to development and modernization.

McNeill, William H. *The Metamorphosis of Greece Since WWII*. Chicago: University of Chicago Press and Oxford: Blackwell, 1978. This is a short qualitative analysis of social change in postwar Greece.

Megas, Georgios A. *Folktales of Greece* (Trans. from the Greek by Helen Colaclides). Chicago: University of Chicago Press, 1970. A collection of Greek folktales.

Merchant, Paul. *Modern Poetry in Translation: Greece*. London, New York: Grossman Publishers in Association with Cape Goliard, 1968. This book contains the work of six Greek poets including Seferis, Ritsos, and Elytis.

Ministry of National Education and Cults. *The Education System in Greece*. Athens: Ministry of National Education and Cults, 1983. This booklet presents information on the structure and operation of the Greek educational system since PASOK came to power.

Moskos, Charles. 'The Breakdown of Parliamentary Democracy in Greece, 1965–67'. *Greek Review of Social Research*, 7–8 (1971): 3–15. Moskos discusses the reasons for the instability of this period that led to military rule. In particular he considers clientelism and the factions in the political parties.

Mouzelis, Nicos. *Modern Greece: Facets of Underdevelopment*. New York: Holmes & Meier Publishers, 1978. The author examines various theories of development relating them to Greece. Overall the author supports a neo-Marxist view.

National Statistical Service of Greece. *Statistical Yearbooks of Greece 1964, 1970, 1981, 1983, 1984*. Athens: National Statistical Service of Greece, 1965, 1971, 1982, 1984, 1985. These yearbooks provide information on population, banking, trading, occupational characteristics, etc. of Greece.

—— *Research on Labor Force, 1984*. Athens, Greece: National Statistical Service of Greece, 1985. This presents statistics based on annual surveys of the Greek labour force.

Nea Demokratia. *Nea Demokratia: A Profile*. Athens: Nea Demokratia, 1984. This is a brief description of the beliefs and accomplishments of New Democracy.

Nikolaidou, Magda. 'The Working Woman in Greece'. *Greek Review of Social Research*, 25 (1975): 470–506. A survey of the role of the working woman in Greece.

Organization for Economic Co-operation and Develop-

MENT [OECD]. *Greece: Economic Surveys 1983–1984*. Paris: OECD, 1983. A survey of major economic trends and policies during 1983 and 1984 in Greece.

—— *Greece: Economic Surveys 1985/1986*. Paris: OECD, 1986. This is the current OECD survey of the Greek economy including a discussion of the stabilization programme and prospects for the future.

PANHELLENIC SOCIALIST MOVEMENT (PASOK). *National Independence, Popular Hegemony, Social Liberation and Democratic Processes*. Athens: PASOK, 1976. This booklet provides the PASOK programme and ideology in 1976.

—— 'Panhellenic Socialist Government Programme (Part 1).' Athens News Agency Feature Stories, 31, 1985. This provides a survey of part of the 1985 PASOK programme.

—— *Andreas Papandreou: The Man, His Beliefs, His Goals. Five Interviews*. Athens: PASOK, no date. This provides information on Andreas Papandreou's political attitudes based on five interviews with the Greek press.

PAPACOSMA, S. VICTOR. 'The Historical Context'. In *Greece in the 1980s*, ed. Richard Clogg. London: Macmillan, 1983. Papacosma examines the historical forces influencing Greek national development since 1821.

PAPANDREOU, ANDREAS. *Democracy at Gunpoint: The Greek Front*. New York: Doubleday, 1970. The Prime Minister provides his political memoirs of the period from the Metaxas dictatorship to the early years of the military dictatorship. It includes discussions of the Aspida affair and his relationship with his father George Papandreou.

—— *Greek Government Programme*. Athens: General Secretariat For Press and Information, 1981. This gives the platform of PASOK, presented by Andreas Papandreou to the Greek Parliament in November, 1981.

—— 'Prime Minister Andreas Papandreou's Address to the PASOK Congress Organizing Committee at the Park Hotel, on 8 Feb. 1984.' Part II, Athens News Agency Feature Stories, 134, 1984. This provides the latter half of A. Papandreou's speech concerning the transition to socialism, PASOK's accomplishments, and programme.

PAPAYANNAKIS, MICHALIS. 'The Crisis in the Greek Left'. In *Greece at the Polls: The National Elections of 1974 and 1977*, ed. Howard Penniman. Washington, DC: American Enterprise Institute, 1981. The author discusses the history of the Left in Greek politics and the divisions that now exist.

PAZARZI-NINA, HELEN. 'The Contemporary Greek Family and its Trend Toward Urbanization' (in Greek). *Review of Social Sciences*, 2–3 (1979–80): 14–16. A brief report on the modern Greek family.

PEAT, MARWICK, MITCHELL, & CO. *Investment in Greece.* Athens: Peat, Marwick, Mitchell & Co., 1983. This booklet on Greece is one of a series of handbooks on investments and doing business in a foreign country.

PENNIMAN, HOWARD (ed.). *Greece at the Polls: The National Elections of 1974 and 1977.* Washington, DC: American Enterprise Institute, 1981. This book analyses the results of the 1974 and 1977 Greek elections. Various articles consider the major Greek parties, electoral law, political modernization, and foreign policy.

PERSIANIS, P. K. 'Values Underlying the 1976–1977 Educational Reform in Greece'. *Comparative Education Review*, 22 (1978): 51–9. Persianis discusses democratization, modernization, cultural, social, economic, and educational values that influenced the educational reforms of the mid-1970s.

PESMAZOGLOU, STEFANOS. 'Some Economic Aspects of Education'. *Journal of the Hellenic Diaspora*, 8 (1981): 131–60. Pesmazoglou provides data on the gap existing between Greece and the other EEC countries concerning public financing of education.

PETRAS, JAMES. 'Greece: Democrcy and the Tanks'. *Journal of the Hellenic Diaspora*, 4 (1977): 3–30. Petras analyses the positions and objectives of the Greek political parties that emerged after the military regime.

—— 'Class Formation and Politics in Greece'. *Journal of Political and Military Sociology*, 11 (1983): 241–50. Petras points out the movement of males from proletarian to petty bourgeoisie with age. There is also widespread landownership coupled with unpaid household labour. Existing world-system and modernization frameworks are viewed as inadequate to analyse Greek development.

PETROPULOS, JOHN. *Politics and Statecraft in the Kingdom of Greece 1833–1843.* Princeton: Princeton University Press, 1968. Petropulos studies the political groups during the first decade of the Kingdom of Greece. The political parties helped shape the structure of the modern Greek state.

—— 'Introduction'. In *Hellenism and the First Greek War of Liberation* (1821–1830), ed. N. Diamandouros, J. Anton, J. Petropulos, and P. Topping. Thessaloniki: Institute for Balkan Studies, 1976. The author points out why the term 'the Greek war of liberation' is more appropriate than war of independence or revolution. He provides excellent background information on this major period in Greek history.

PILISUK, MARC. *International Conflict and Social Policy.* Englewood Cliffs: Prentice-Hall, 1972. Part of this book contains information on Greece particularly related to the military junta.

POLITIS, LINOS. *History of Modern Greek Literature.* London, Oxford:

Clarendon Press, 1973. This book presents information on the first songs, legends, and poems of Greece as well as the consideration of the various schools of poetry after Greek independence through the 1930s.

POLYDORIDES, GEORGIA K. 'Equality of Opportunity in the Greek Higher Education System: The Impact of Reform Policies'. *Comparative Education Review*, 22 (1978): 80–93. The author argues that specific educational reforms have not been able to bring about equality of opportunity in education.

PRESVELOU, CLIO and TEPEROGLOU, AFRODITE. 'Sociological Analysis of Abortion in the Greek Space'. *Greek Review of Social Research*, 28 (1976): 275–85. A statistical analysis of birth rate and abortion rates in Greece.

PSACHAROPOULOS, GEORGE. 'Earnings and Education in Greece, 1960–1977'. *European Economic Review*, 17 (1982): 333–47. This article provides data showing the rate of return to schooling has declined in Greece between the early 1960s and the late 1970s. The author finds a very strong demand for higher education in Greece, but in the mid-1970s the economic rate of return for the years of education is not very high.

—— and KAZAMIAS, ANDREAS. 'Student Activism in Greece: A Historical and Empirical Analysis'. *Higher Education*, 9 (1980): 127–38. The article considers the origins of the student movement in Greece and present activism based in part on a sample of 1,500 students.

PSOMAS, ANDREAS I. 'The Nation, The State, and The International System: The Case of Greece'. Ph.D. dissertation. Stanford: Stanford University, 1974. An historical analysis of the Greek nation state within the international system in the mid-nineteenth century is given.

REVZIN, PHILIP. 'Greek Drama: Athens' Fortunes Rest On Ability of Socialists to Woo the Capitalists'. *The Wall Street Journal*, 28 Mar. 1986, pp. 1, 8. The author discusses the dissensions between the socialist government and the business community.

SAFILIOS-ROTHSCHILD, CONSTANTINA. 'A Comparison of Power Structure and Marital Satisfaction in Urban Greek and French Families'. *Journal of Marriage and the Family*, 29 (1967): 345–52. An analysis of Greek and French urban families.

SAKELLARIOU, MICHAEL B. 'Hellenism and 1848'. In the *Opening of an Era 1848: An Historical Symposium*, ed. Francois Fejto. New York: Howard Fertig, 1966. This article considers the importance of 1848 in the historical development of Greece.

SANDERS, IRWIN, *Rainbow in the Rock: The People of Rural Greece*. Cambridge: Harvard University Press, 1962. It is a socio-ethnographic descriptive analysis of rural Greece.

—— 'Greek Society in Transition'. *Balkan Studies*, 8 (1967): 317–32. An analysis of value changes in rural Greece since World War II is provided.

SANDIS, EVA. *Refugees and Economic Migrants in Greater Athens.* Athens: National Centre of Social Research, 1973. This is a study of Asia Minor refugees and internal migrants in Greater Athens.

SEERS, DUDLEY; SCHAFFER, BERNARD; AND KILJUNEN, MARJA-LIISA, (eds.). *Underdeveloped Europe: Studies in Core–Periphery Relations.* Atlantic Highlands, NJ: Humanities Press, 1979. This book contains articles on the core–periphery system in Europe including transnational corporations, tourism, and the case of Greece.

SKIOTIS, DENNIS. 'The Nature of the Modern Greek Nation: The Romaic Strand'. In *The 'Past' in Medieval and Modern Greek Culture*, ed. Speros Vryonis, jun. Malibu: Undena Publications, 1978. The author considers the gradual change from a millenarian movement for liberation to a modern revolutionary one in which nationalism was substituted for religion.

SPINELLIS, C. D.; VASSILIOU, VASSO; and VASSILIOU, GEORGE. 'Milieu Development and Male-Female Roles in Contemporary Greece'. In *Sex Roles in Changing Society* ed. Georgene H. Seward and Robert C. Williamson. New York: Random House, 1970. The article explores persistent patterns and changing sex roles in modern Greece.

SPOTLIGHT (a bi-monthly publication of current Greek affairs), 1 Dec. 1984.

—— 'EEC to Support Greece'. 1 Dec. 1985, no. 32, p. 1.

—— '1985 Figures of Tourism'. 1 Feb. 1986, no. 36, p. 8.

STAVRIANOS, L. S. *Greece: American Dilemmas and Opportunity.* Chicago: Henry Regnery Co., 1952. This book considers the relationship between Greece and the US particularly related to the post-World War II period.

—— *The Balkans since 1453.* New York: Holt, Rinehart and Winston, 1958. Stavrianos provides a detailed and interesting history of the Balkans including Greece.

STAVROU, THEOFANIS G. 'Introduction' to *Eighteen Short Songs of the Bitter Motherland* by Yannis Ritsos. Minneapolis: North Central Publishing Company, 1974. Stavrou provides an interesting introduction to Ritsos's work stressing the theme of freedom.

STOCKTON, BAYARD. *Phoenix With a Bayonet.* Ann Arbor: Georgetown Publications, 1971. This is a rather sympathetic account of the Greek coup of 1967. It is a journalist's interim report based primarily on interviews and quotations from many individuals directly or indirectly responsible for the 1967 coup.

STOIANOVICH, T. 'The conquering Balkan Orthodox Merchant'. *Journal of Economic History*, 20 (1960): 269–73. This article considers the importance of merchants in the Balkan countries during the Ottoman Empire.

THOMSON, GEORGE. *The Greek Language*. Cambridge: W. Heffner Ltd., 1966. This is a historical analysis of the evolution of Modern Greek.

TRIANDIS, HARRY C.; VASSILIOU, VASSO; and NASSIAKOU, MARIA. 'Three Cross-Cultural Studies of Subjective Culture'. *Journal of Personality and Social Psychology*, Monograph Supplement 8 (1968): 1–42. A socio-psychological analysis of Greek personality traits is presented.

TRYPANIS, CONSTANTINE A. *Greek Poetry: From Homer to Seferis*. London and Boston: Faber and Faber, 1981. In five parts and almost 900 pages Trypanis analyses Greek poetry. The major parts focus on ancient Greece, the Hellenistic age, the Byzantine world, the Greeks under the Franks and the Turks, and modern Greece. (1829–1940).

TSAKALOGIANNIS, PANOS. 'The European Community and the Greek–Turkish Dispute'. *Journal of Common Market Studies*, 19 (1980): 35–54. Author assesses the role of the EEC in the Greek-Turkish dispute in Cyprus and the Aegean.

TSAOUSIS, D. G. 'Hellenismos Kai Hellenikotita'. In *Hellenism and Greekness* (in Greek) ed. D. G. Tsaousis. Athens: Kollaros and Co., 1983. A historical and socio-political analysis on the making of modern Greekness and Greek national identity are discussed.

TSOKOU, STAVROULA; SHELLEY, MACK C., II; and DOBRATZ, BETTY A., 'Some Correlates of Partisan Preference in Greece, 1980: A Discriminant Analysis'. *European Journal of Political Research*, 14 (1986): 441–63. The authors examine a number of demographic, foreign policy, and domestic issues that form the basis of partisan preference in Greece. Although foreign and domestic attitudinal variables are more important than demographic characteristics, the authors argue that each of the three perspectives are important for understanding the complex process by which a Greek decides what party to support.

TSORIS, NICHOLAS D. *The Financing of Greek Manufacture*. Athens: Centre of Planning and Economic Research, 1984. The author studies the financing of Greek manufacturing from 1959 to 1981 by examining balance sheets and results accounts. He also discusses the development of problematic industries.

TSOUCALAS, CONSTANTINE. 'On the Problem of Political Clientelism in Greece in the Nineteenth Century'. *Journal of the Hellenic Diaspora*, 5 (1978): 5–15. Tsoucalas considers the reasons for the development of clientelism in Greece during the 1800s.

—— 'Some Aspects of "Over Education" in Modern Greece'. *Journal of the Hellenic Diaspora*, 8 (1981): 109–21. This article contains information on the inflated Greek university student body and makes some comparisons with other nations.

TSOUKALIS, LOUKAS (ed.). *The European Community and its Mediterranean Enlargement*. London: George Allen and Unwin, 1981. Articles in this book discuss various aspects of the possible full EEC membership of Spain and Portugal in addition to Greece. Included are discussions of its effects on Greek manufacturing, agriculture, balance of payments, politics, and foreign policy.

VEGLERIS, PHAEDO. 'Greek Electoral Law'. In *Greece at the Polls: The National Elections of 1974 and 1977*, ed. Howard Penniman. Washington, DC: American Enterprise Institute, 1981. Vegleris explains the Greek electoral system including the right to vote and the reinforced proportional system.

VEREMIS, THANOS. *Greek Security Considerations: A Historical Perspective*. Athens: Papazissis Publishers, 1980. A historical survey of national security and civil–military relations of Greece.

—— 'The Union of the Democratic Centre'. In *Greece at the Polls: The National Elections of 1974 and 1977*, ed. Howard Penniman. Washington, DC: American Enterprise Institute, 1981. Veremis discusses the decline of the Union of the Democratic Centre during the 1970s.

—— 'An Overview of Greek Security Concerns in the Eastern Mediterranean and the Balkans'. *Lo Spettatore Internationale*, 17 (Oct.–Dec. 1982): 339–45. This article analyses the national security concerns of Greece and civil–military relations within the context of the alliance.

—— 'Security Considerations and Civil–Military Relations in Post-war Greece'. In *Greece in the 1980s*, ed. Richard Clogg. London: Macmillan, 1983. A commentary on some post-war security issues and civil–military relations within the context of the western alliance.

VERGOPOULOS, KOSTAS. *Kratos Kai Oikonomiki Politiki ston Dekato Enato Aiona (State and Economic Policy in the 19th Century)* Athens: Exandas, 1975. It is a historical and socio-political, economic analysis of the making of the Greek state.

VERMEULEN, CORNELIS J. *Families in Urban Greece*. Ithaca, NY: Cornell University Press, 1970 (Ph.D. dissertation). This book is based on an empirical survey of boys and girls in public and private schools along with parents on conjugal and parental relations.

VIONTAKIS, POPE. 'Family and Adolescence in Greece and the U.S.' *Greek Review of Social Research*, 39–40 (1980): 267–82. A comparative analysis of agrarian and urban families both in Greece and the US.

VLAVIANOS, BASIL J. 'An Interview with former U.S. Admiral Jene R. LaRocque'. *Spotlight* (1 July 1984) (originally published in *Proini*, Greek–American daily).

VOROS, F. K. 'Current Educational Reforms: An Overview'. *Comparative Education Review*, 22 (1978): 7–10. This article briefly examines the educational changes of the mid-1970s.

VRYONIS, SPEROS, JUN. *Byzantium and Europe*. London: Harcourt, Brace and World, 1967. The author considers the transition from antiquity and the emergence of Byzantium through its decline and collapse.

—— 'The Greeks Under Turkish Rule'. In *Hellenism and the First Greek War of Liberation (1821–1930)*, ed. N. Diamandouros, J. Anton, J. Petropulos, and P. Topping. Thessaloniki: Institute for Balkan Studies, 1976. Vryonis identifies and analyses eight major changes in Greek life with the advent of Turkish rule.

—— 'Recent Scholarship on Continuity and Discontinuity of Culture: Classical Greeks, Byzantines, Modern Greeks'. In *The 'Past' in Medieval and Modern Greek Culture*, ed. Speros Vryonis, jun. Malibu: Undena Publications, 1978. The major schools of thought concerned with the question of continuity or discontinuity of the ancient Greeks, Byzantines, and modern Greeks are examined.

—— *Studies on Byzantium, Seljuks, and Ottomans*. Malibu: Undena Publications, 1981. This reprinted set of articles concerns the relations of Turks and Greeks from the eleventh century to the Greek Revolution (1821).

WALLERSTEIN, I. *The Modern World System: Capitalist Agriculture and the Origins of the European World-Economy in the Sixteenth Century*. NY: Academic, 1974. Wallerstein develops his ideas related to world system theory in this book.

WARE, TIMOTHY. *The Orthodox Church*. England: Penguin Books, 1963. A useful and concise introduction on the doctrine, history, faith, and worship of the Orthodox church.

WASSER, HENRY. 'A Survey of Recent Trends in Greek Higher Education'. *Journal of the Hellenic Diaspora*, 6 (1979): 85–95. The article considers problems and changes in the universities and causes of student dissatisfaction.

WOODHOUSE, C. M. *Modern Greece: A Short History*. London: Faber and Faber Limited, 1984. Woodhouse provides a brief history of Greece from the foundations of Constantine (324–641) to the late 1970s.

XYDIS, STEPHEN. *Greece and the Great Powers, 1944–47*. Thessaloniki: Institute for Balkan Studies, 1963. Xydis examines the interaction between Greece and the major powers at the end of World War II and the early stages of the civil war.

—— '*Modern Greek Nationalism*'. In *Nationalism in Eastern Europe*, ed. Peter F. Sugar and Ivo J. Ledger. Seattle: University of Washington Press, 1969. The development of the phenomenon of nationalism is traced from its origins through the military coup in 1967.

YEARBOOK, *Yearbook, 1982*. Athens: Praktoreio Ellinikou Typou (in Greek). 1982. This yearbook contains information on a variety of aspects of Greek society including election results.

YEARBOOK OF THE GREEK CHURCH, 1984. Athens: The Apostoliki Diakonia of the Church of Greece (in Greek), 1984. A useful compendium of the calendar and organization of the Greek Orthodox and other Eastern Orthodox churches.

YEROU, THEOPHRASTOS. 'Basic Education Today'. *Journal of the Hellenic Diaspora*, 8 (1981): 37–40. This article contains information on the inequality of basic education, the expansion of compulsory education, and the ideological content of basic education.

YIANNITSIS, A. K. 'Foreign Direct Investments and the Creation/Morphology of the New Hellenic Economy (1830–1939)' (in Greek). *Greek Review of Social Research*, 30–1 (1977): 234–53. This article discusses the role of multinational capital in the growth of the Greek economy from 1830 to 1939. While multinational investments were important, they did not dominate.

Zakythinos, D. A. *The Making of Modern Greece: From Byzantium to Independence*. Oxford: Basil Blackwell, 1976. The author examines factors related to the formation of the Greek nation state beginning with the establishment of Turkish rule and concluding with a chapter on some general principles in the national life of Greece. Helpful chronological tables from 1451 to 1839 are presented in the appendices.

JOURNALS AND PERIODICALS ON GREECE[1]

Athena Magazine: Review of Current Events
24 Dimitriou Soutsou, 115 21 Athens.

Balkan Studies: A Biannual Publication of the Institute for Balkan Studies
Institute of Balkan Studies, Thessaloniki, Greece; U.S. Subscription Agent: F. W. Faxon Co., 515 Hyde Park Ave., Boston, MA 02131.

Bulletin of the Modern Greek Studies Association
185 Nassau Street, Princeton, NJ 08540.

Byzantine and Modern Greek Studies
Basil Blackwell and Mott Ltd., 108 Cowley Road, Oxford OX4 1JF.

The Charioteer: An Annual Review of Modern Greek Culture
Pella Publishing Company, Inc., 337 West 36th St., New York, NY 10018.

Country Reports: Greece (formerly *Quarterly Economic Review of Greece*)
Economist Intelligence Unit, 40 Duke Street, London W1A 1DW.

Greece: The Week in Review
Embassy of Greece, Press and Information Office, 2211 Massachusetts Avenue, NW, Washington, DC 20008.

Greek Opinion: A Monthly Survey of Greek Public Opinion Trends
EURODIM, 82, Constantinople Ave., GR-104 35 Athens.

The Greek Review of Social Research
National Centre of Social Research, Sophocleous 1, Athens, Greece 10559.

Hellenic Studies (both in French and English)
5582 Waverly Street, Montreal, Quebec, H2T 2V1.

Journal of the Hellenic Diaspora: A Quarterly Review
Pella Publishing Co., Inc., 337 West 36th Street, New York, NY 10018.

Journal of Modern Greek Studies: A Semi-annual Publication
The Johns Hopkins University Press, 34th & Charles Streets, Baltimore, MD 21218.

[1] This is a very selective list of journals and periodicals on Greece in the English language (except for *The Greek Review of Social Research*).

Journal of Modern Hellenism (Quarterly)
CUNY, Queens College, Flushing, NY 11367.

Mandatoforos
Byzantijns-Nieuwgrieks Seminarium, Nieuwe Doelenstraat 16, 1012 CP Amsterdam.

Modern Greek Society: A Social Science Newsletter
PO Box 9411, Providence, RI 02940.

Modern Greek Studies Yearbook
Modern Greek Studies, 646 Social Sciences Building, University of Minnesota, 267–19th Avenue South, Minneapolis, MN 55455.

New York, Greek-American
Semi-monthly, 130 W. 42nd Street-Suite 704, New York, NY 10036.

The Patristic and Byzantine Review
Box 353–A, Kingston, NY 12401.

Spotlight: *A Bi-Monthly Publication of Current Greek Affairs*
46, Sevastis Kallisperi, Halandri, Athens, Greece.

SELECTED BIBLIOGRAPHIES, GENERAL REFERENCE BOOKS ON GREECE, AND RESEARCH INSTITUTES

Bibliographies

CLOGG, J. and CLOGG, R. *Greece.* World Bibliographical Series, Vol. 17, Oxford: Clio, 1980. This is an excellent annotated bibliography of 830 entries of various studies and publications on modern Greece.

INSTITUTE FOR BALKAN STUDIES. *Balkan Bibliography*, Vol. VI-1977. Institute for Balkan Studies, Thessaloniki, 1981 (A supplement volume). This is part of a series of volumes on annotated studies and articles, translations, and commentaries by Greek and non-Greek scholars interested in the Balkans.

INSTITUTE FOR BALKAN STUDIES. Index to volumes 1–20 (1960–79). Indexed and ed. Mersini Morelli-Cacouris and Thomy Verrou-Karakostas. This is an excellent multilingual source of studies and reviews published between 1960 and 1979 in the *Balkan Studies* biannual publication.

KITROMILIDES, PASCHALIS M. and EURIVIADES, MARIOS L. *Cyprus.* World Bibliographical Series, Vol. 8. Oxford: Clio, 1982; This excellent volume includes an annotated bibliography about the most important works and writings on Cyprus, a total of 689 entries.

MODERN GREEK SOCIETY: A SOCIAL SCIENCE NEWSLETTER. This biannual publication sponsored by the Modern Greek Studies Association of the United States and Canada is an excellent source of past and current social science publications and research on Greece.

RICHTER, HEINZ. *Greece and Cyprus Since 1920: Bibliography of Contemporary History.* Heidelburg: *Wissenschaftlicher Verlag Nea Hellas*, 1984. This is a comprehensive multilingual bibliography of more than 11,000 sources on Greek contemporary history, Greek communism, socialism, and trade unionism, and contemporary history of Cyprus.

General Reference Books on Greece

CAMPBELL, JOHN and SHERRARD, PHILIP. *Modern Greece.* London: Praeger, 1968. A comprehensive introduction on modern Greek society and culture including modern political history, church, literature, the countryside, and the city.

CLOGG, RICHARD (ed.). *Greece in the 1980s.* London: Macmillan,

1983. This volume contains thirteen articles on a variety of topics (politics, geography, foreign policy, church, education, etc.) of importance as Greece enters the 1980s.

CLOGG RICHARD. *A Short History of Modern Greece.* Cambridge: CUP, 1979. This book sketches the troubled modern history of Greece from the downfall of Byzantium (1204–1453) through the return to democracy in Greece in the 1970s.

CONSTANTELOS, DR J., and EFTHYMIOU, C. J. (eds.). *Greece: Today and Tomorrow.* N. Y. Krikos, 1979. A useful collection of essays and research papers on a variety of socio-cultural, economic, educational, technological, and communication issues and problems of Greece.

COULOUMBIS, THEODORE A. and IATRIDES, JOHN O. (eds.). *Greek American Relations: A Critical Review.* New York: Pella, 1980. This volume contains articles that focus on the policies of the US toward Greece and Cyprus since World War II and on the causes of the deterioration in Greek–American relations. In addition to the ten chapters, there is a bibliography on the topic.

COULOUMBIS, THEODORE A., PETROPULOS, JOHN A. and PSOMIADES, HARRY J. *Foreign Interference in Greek Politics: A Historical Perspective.* New York: Pella, 1976. The authors examine the importance of foreign policy in Greek politics, the irredentist state, Greece between the world wars, and Greek–American relations.

DIEM, AUBREY. *Western Europe: A Geographical Analysis.* N.Y.: John Wiley and Sons, 1979. This book includes a geographical profile of modern Greece.

DIMEN, MURIEL and FRIEDL, ERNESTINE (eds.). *Regional Variation in Modern Greece and Cyprus: Toward a Perspective of the Ethnography of Greece.* New York: New York Academy of Sciences, 1976. This is a useful collection of conference papers on a variety of ethnographical and anthropological regional studies.

THE EUROPA YEARBOOK. *Greece.* London: Europa Publications, 1986. It provides a brief survey of Greece's major social, economic, and political developments.

GREEK PRESS AGENCY (PET). *Yearbook.* (Amerikis 4, Athens) 1982. A useful compendium of general information on many social, political, economic, educational, cultural, artistic, sport, and international organizations, and current events of Greece.

KAYSER, BERNARD and THOMPSON, KENNETH. *Economic and Social Atlas of Greece.* Athens: National Center of Social Research, 1964 (in English, French, Greek). An excellent diagramatic reference book on the economic, social, and geographical aspects of Greece. It is not however updated.

KOHLER, BEATE. *Political Forces in Spain, Greece and Portugal.* London, Butterworth Scientific, 1982. This book focuses on the breakup of authoritarian regimes in Spain, Greece, and Portugal in the 1970s. Chapters on Greece consider the transition to democracy, the alignment of political forces, the constitutional framework, and the political implications of Greek entry into the European Community.

KOTY, JOHN. 'National Traits and Basic Sociological Characteristics of the Greek Culture'. In *The Institutions of Advanced Societies* edited by Arnold M. Rose. Minneapolis: University of Minnesota Press, 1958. An anthology of social institutions of western societies.

LAMBIRI-DIMAKI, JANE. *Social Stratification in Greece 1962–1982: Eleven Essays.* Athens: Ant. N. Sakkoulas, 1983. This book contains ten studies on aspects of social stratification in Greece, tradition and change. Various topics include the generation gap and sex, class, regional, and residential stratification patterns.

MCNEILL, WM. H. *The Metamorphosis of Greece Since WWII.* Chicago: The University of Chicago Press, 1978. This is a historical analysis of Greece since World War II.

PENNIMAN, HOWARD R. (ed.). *Greece at the Polls: The National Elections of 1974 and 1977.* Washington DC: The American Enterprise for Public Policy Research, 1981. This volume contains articles on the Greek elections and electoral law of the 1970s, the various political parties, and foreign policy objectives.

STAVRIANOS, L. S. *The Balkans Since 1453.* New York: Holt, Rinehart and Winston, 1958. Although now quite dated, this book provides a detailed history of the Balkans to the 1950s.

TSOUKALIS, LOUKAS (ed.). *Greece and the European Community.* Oxford: Saxon House, 1979. This is a collection of essays on Greek entry into the EEC and its effects on the industrial and agricultural sectors of the economy.

TZANNATOS, ZAFIRIS (ed.). *Socialism in Greece: The First Four Years.* Aldershot, England: Gower, 1986. This book contains general articles on socialism in Greece and more specific ones on political economy, state and civil society, and social services.

WOODHOUSE, C. M. *Karamanlis: The Restorer of Greek Democracy.* London: OUP, 1982. This book details the life of Constantine Karamanlis whose political career lasted forty-five years.

—— *Modern Greece: A Short History.* London: Faber and Faber, 1984. This is a compact yet scholarly volume on modern Greek history from Constantine the Great (324–641) all the way to the fall of the junta in 1974 and the restoration of democracy in Greece.

Research Institutes

Centre of Planning and Economic Research (KEPE).
22, Hippokratous Street, 106–80 Athens, Greece.
This is a research centre specializing in economic issues and publishing various monographs.

Centre of Political Research and Education
Mauvromation 12, Athens, Greece.
This is a conservative research centre specializing in political and economic issues. It publishes a bi-monthly political and economic review in Greek.

Foundation For Mediterranean Studies
Lykavetou 2, Athens, Greece.
This is a more liberal-oriented research organization conducting socio-political research.

Institute for Balkan Studies
Tsimiski 45, Thessaloniki, Greece.
This research institute specializes in Balkan studies and publishes a biannual publication.

National Centre of Social Research (EKKE)
Sophocleous 1, Athens, Greece 10559.
This social science research centre conducts empirical social science research on the more applied aspects of Greek society. It publishes a journal in Greek.

National Statistical Service of Greece (ESYE)
14–16 Lycourgos Street, Athens 112, Greece.
This is the equivalent of US Census Bureau of Greece.

INDEX